Photoshop
Pro Photography
Handbook

CHRIS WESTON
& ADAM JUNIPER

ILEX

Photoshop Pro Photography Handbook

First published in the UK in 2007 by
ILEX
The Old Candlemakers
West Street
Lewes
East Sussex BN7 2NZ
www.ilex-press.com

Copyright © 2007 The Ilex Press Limited

Publisher: Alastair Campbell
Creative Director: Peter Bridgewater
Associate Publisher: Robin Pearson
Editorial Director: Tom Mugridge
Art Director: Julie Weir
Designer: Ginny Zeal
Design Assistant: Kate Haynes
Publishing Assistant: Martha Evatt

British Library Cataloguing-in-Publication Data
A catalogue record for this book is available from
the British Library

ISBN 10: 1-905814-06-2
ISBN 13: 978-1-905814-06-0

For more information on this title, and some
useful links, navigate to:
www.web-linked.com/pspruk

Printed and bound in China

Contents

Pro Photography
Handbook

introduction

Photoshop is probably the most powerful software tool you'll ever use, yet it comes on a silver disc smaller than your hand-span. That's digital technology for you, and it has long since come of age. There is no longer any serious debate over the best way to capture images, especially for the working professional, so this book won't concentrate on making a gradual switch to digital, nor will it lament the demise of film. This is a book for anyone serious about photography, because Photoshop will be center-stage in everything you do.

Introduction

Digital photography is still photography. The methods might be different and there might be more that you can achieve, but the fundamentals have changed a lot less than many people imagine.

The widely celebrated photographer Ansel Adams once wrote, "The negative is the score, the print is the performance." What did he mean by that? In modern terminology, simply that the photographic image produced by the camera is merely a conglomeration of data that requires interpretation (in the form of a print) for it to truly reveal its creator's vision—in much the same way that musical notes are nothing more than ink marks until they are brought to life by skilled musicians.

And, just as a musical score can be performed in different ways, so too can many variations of a photographic image be created from the original base data. It is down to the photographer to take that data and turn it into a visual performance (a print) that announces his intent and manifests his meaning.

In Ansel Adams' day, that work was done in a darkroom, using chemicals and light. Today, invariably, photographers use what we term the digital darkroom, using numbers to achieve the same goal. But whatever the methods, the process and the results are largely the same. Certainly, digital technology has made image processing easier, quicker and, let's face it, far more convenient. It has opened new opportunities for photographers who have never ventured into a blacked-out bathroom (to the frustration of many long-suffering family members), bringing the complete photographic experience to the masses in a way barely contemplated just a few years ago.

What digital hasn't done is alter the purpose of image processing, which has remained fairly constant throughout photographic history. Contrary to the claims of its detractors, digital image processing is no more "cheating" than is its wet-process predecessor. In fact, many of the tools found in image-processing software are drawn directly from the traditional darkroom of yesteryear. In this respect, digital photography is still photography. The fact that digital processing is more conveniently achieved is to be celebrated rather than decried.

Which brings us to this book. *Photoshop Pro Photography Handbook* is written for photographers by photographers and, as such, concentrates on those aspects of Photoshop that mimic traditional processes with the aim of producing the best possible image output, whether that be in the form of a print or via electronic media.

In totality Photoshop is a complex software package with many facets. But like many things in life, some elements are more important than others, and some you may never need to use at all. What we have attempted here is to define those aspects of the software that will prove most useful in a pure photographic context and expand on how to make the most of the relevant tools.

In so doing we have taken our own experiences of Photoshop and married it with that of other photographers who use the package in different but equally important ways. Some of that knowledge is openly visible, included in the workthroughs that appear throughout the book. Otherwise, its inclusion is more subtle and to be found within the main text. Either way, the aim has been to provide a broad spectrum of ideas, experience, and knowledge that identifies the common tools and offers guidance on how to use them to your best advantage.

It is also important to note that the ideas and processes put forward in these pages aren't necessarily the only ways to achieve a particular goal, simply ways that are proven to work for me and for other professionals. And, just as experimenting with new and varied techniques was part of the fun of image processing in the darkroom, so trying new things and different ideas is the best way to learn Photoshop and to understand how it best fits into your own workflow. To that end, my advice is, once you have read this book, turn on your computer, practice the techniques described, and then experiment with your own ideas. In that way, not only will you get Photoshop working, you'll get Photoshop working for you.

The images opposite demonstrate how much—and how little— photography has changed since Ansel Adams' day. They're not all black and white, but each image is still a different performance of the same piece.

Getting the most from this book

Photoshop is a huge program. We've made this book as easy to follow as possible, whether you're dipping in or reading straight through. Here are some hints on where to find the information you need.

While it might be considered patronizing to lecture you on something as personal as how best to absorb the words in this book, this seems a timely moment to suggest some alternative strategies for using these pages to best effect. After all, very few images will require you to use every single tool in Photoshop, so you may well be able to save time by avoiding information that you simply don't need right now. That said, in the long run you will almost certainly find that you do need to know about every tool in this vast program, if only to help you make an informed decision about workflow.

Many of Photoshop's image corrections can be made directly to the image, to the image as an overlaid "adjustment layer," or—if you're working with RAW files—achieved as you import your image with Adobe Camera Raw. Which method you use is your choice, and this book concentrates on making those changes at the best possible point. Since this is often at the initial importing stage, the functionality of Camera Raw is also replicated in a separate program called Adobe Lightroom—and, possibly, any Raw software that was supplied with your camera. If you use your camera's own software then you might want to review these sections to see whether the tools discussed here are more appealing, but generally speaking you will not need both. They are all specifically designed to be part of the photographer's workflow.

On the subject of workflow, streamlining the way you process images is vital for any photographer, since digital technology can quickly produce streams of pictures and data that, while perhaps easier to catalog than transparencies, can easily spiral out of control. For that reason we have devoted much of Chapters 1 and 2 to discussing workflow and the equipment that it might involve. If you already have a well-established workflow that's suited to your needs I'd recommend skimming through this section, but don't ignore the notes

Keyboard shortcuts

Macs and PCs differ slightly in their keyboard arrangement since both Apple and Microsoft have chosen to emblazon their logo on one of the modifier keys. In this book we've given the most common symbols for both keys, so for example the command to bring up the keyboard shortcuts menu is written Ctrl/⌘ + Alt/⌥ + Shift + K. On a PC you would press and hold the Control (Ctrl) key, Alt key, and the Shift key and tap the K key. On a Mac you would do the same with ⌘ + ⌥ + Shift (sometimes marked ⇧) + K. Here is a list of some other symbols you might see on your keyboard.

Symbol	Equivalent
⌘	⌘, Command
⌥	Alt, Option
⎋	Escape
⇧	Shift
⇪	Caps Lock
⌫	Backspace
⌦	Delete
⌤	Enter

TIP

If you have an older Mac without a right button on the mouse, pressing Ctrl as you click will have the same effect. The "context-sensitive" menus—those which only offer options based on the place the mouse is clicked—are increasingly part of the operating system and other programs, so it's well worth investing in a mouse with a right button.

Where to go?

Chapter 1—Getting set up

Covers all things technical, including computer technology, the Mac versus PC debate (and why you don't need to be involved), color theory, and the roots of a good color workflow.

Chapter 4—Enhancement

Go here for the first changes you'd make to an image after importing, including cropping, rotating, lens corrections, and improving color and tone.

Chapter 2—Your way around

This chapter concentrates on workflow, handling your files as efficiently as possible using Photoshop's in-the-box browser utility, Bridge, as well as other tools.

Chapter 5—Manipulation

Here you'll find tricks to transform the image, moving and even eliminating subjects for more dramatic alterations than those covered in the previous chapter.

Chapter 3—The first steps

With a heavy emphasis on the differences between Raw, JPEG, and TIFF file formats, this chapter introduces the Camera Raw importer and helps you get to work.

Chapter 6—Print and beyond

Hints and tips on producing the best-quality output, whether you're sending your image to a printer or displaying it on the Internet.

---

on Bridge, which has developed rapidly since it was first introduced and might well offer more than you expect. If it isn't already a tool you use regularly it's well worth a look.

One other point is that there is no truly logical way to order a book covering as much of the program as this one does, so you will sometimes find features covered some way away from others that fit next to each other in your workflow. While we've tried to minimize this, everyone is different. For that reason there is a comprehensive index on pages 220-223 where you should have no problem locating the details you need.

Anyway, it's time to introduce no more and to get started. Above all else the important thing is to enjoy using Photoshop—it is a tool of your trade as much as your camera, lenses, or anything else in your kit bag. In fact, thanks to relentless miniaturization, it can even travel with you in that bag without being the most cumbersome thing in it (depending on the size of your telephoto, of course). So go on, learn what you need (and perhaps a little more besides), and you'll soon be creating professionally and artistically rewarding work, whatever your photographic specialty.

Latest Photoshop features

If you're upgrading from an older version of Photoshop, you'll be particularly interested in coverage of the newer tools. Some of the most exciting are:

The new interface—see pages 44-47

All new Camera Raw features discussed from page 80, including Parametric curves on 84 and Healing within Raw on page 87

The main Curves tool itself has been updated (don't worry, it's only getting better)—see page 112-115

Brightness/Contrast tool has been dragged into the 21st century—see page 118

The Black and White conversion tool—see page 190

The Refine Edges dialog to help tidy up selections—see page 158

Auto-align layers, see page 188, and associated improvements to the Photomerge tool, page 186

Clone Source palette—see page 176

The Print dialog has been updated—see page 202

1 getting set up

Your experience with Photoshop can only be as good as the equipment you use, and how you set that equipment up. Because perfect results are essential—not a mere aspiration—it's vital that you consider your workflow right from the start. What can be loosely described as your "hardware," and by that I mean everything both inside—and connected to—your computer that isn't Photoshop, has control of everything from the importing of images to how the colors actually appear on screen, so it's worthwhile reading this chapter carefully to make sure things are right.

Attaching a backup hard disk drive or tweaking system settings for faster performance are not, perhaps, the most exciting things you'll ever do, but their importance cannot be measured, especially when your main hard drive gives up the ghost. Similarly, understanding the complexity of color management is the only way you can safely sit back and relax, safe in the knowledge that the computer is making the right decisions for you. Get things right the first time and you'll be able to work more effectively and, in so far as is possible, make yourself disaster-proof.

The physical space

Setting up your workspace correctly is important for a number of reasons—not just for your own comfort, but also to ensure optimum performance from sensitive devices like monitors and mice.

Although your digital darkroom is less fussy about its environment than its light-loathing film equivalent, there are certain adaptations you can make to the physical space around your computer equipment that will enhance the accuracy of your image processing and make the whole job more comfortable.

First of all, make sure that you have enough space in which to work comfortably. Your desk should be at a comfortable height when sitting, and must be stable. If you plan on spending any length of time at the computer I would advise investing in an ergonomically designed chair that supports the body in a healthy position. And, although I offer no views on the existence or otherwise of the medical condition R.S.I. (repetitive strain injury), I would at least also advise making your own comfort a priority when it comes to operating the keyboard and mouse.

To minimize the occurrence of flare and reduce the strain placed on your eyes, position your monitor centrally, at eye level and away from any direct light source, such as a lamp or window. Peripherals that you access regularly should be kept close to hand, and other devices, such as external hard disk drives (HDD) can be positioned away from the main workspace.

While lack of light was the essential consideration for a wet darkroom, the right kind of light is important in a digital darkroom. Any walls or ceilings that reflect light onto the computer monitor should be of a neutral color. Ideally this would be medium gray, but that might be taking things a bit too far—and, assuming you don't want gray walls, white will do! The main light source in the room should also be at a color temperature equivalent to daylight. Special daylight bulbs can be purchased from many major retail electrical stores.

Make sure that light falls evenly onto your computer system from a neutral source.

Electricity

You will be amazed at the number of electrical plugs that sprout from the equipment used in a digital darkroom. These should always be connected properly, in accordance with the manufacturer's guidelines, and you should use a purpose-designed extension/adaptor when connecting multiple appliances to a single electrical wall outlet. To avoid damage to your computer equipment, a surge protector is a worthwhile investment. An uninterruptible power supply (UPS) is another useful item to protect against losing unsaved work in the event of a power cut.

WARNING

Health considerations

Spending many unbroken hours sitting in front of a computer monitor is unhealthy. Take regular breaks away from the screen to rest your eyes and stretch your muscles. If you begin to suffer frequent headaches, consider visiting your doctor or an optician.

A daylight lightbulb. Daylight adjustment is especially important with low-energy bulbs like this as traditional fluorescent tubes do not perform evenly across all the hues in the spectrum.

A scanner is essential if your photo collection isn't wholly digital. Just as with the other devices, make sure you are able to open the lid the whole way. Many scanners also allow the scanning of slides via an adaptor, so you'll need somewhere safe to store this where it won't be broken or lost.

Your printer should be readily accessible so it can easily be reloaded. Be warned, this is far from convenient in many so-called computer desks, even if they do have space for a wide format printer like this.

TIP

You can continue the theme of a correctly lit working environment by altering the background color when working in full screen mode. Just Right/Control+click and choose a neutral grey or perhaps a black depending on the image you are working on.

Computers and operating systems

The long-running Mac versus PC debate is one for the school playground, but there are still serious factors to consider when it comes to choosing equipment.

A sometimes heated still debate rages about whether PCs are better than Macs. In reality, today, it really makes no difference. Historically, Macs were the machine of choice for the design and publishing professions, and a lack of cross-platform compatibility made Mac the sensible choice for digital photographers. Those compatibility issues are now largely non-existent and processing speed is the defining factor. On that front, there's little to choose between the two formats.

The computer's speed is determined by two main factors: the speed of the internal computer processor, shown in gigahertz (GHz), and the capacity of the RAM (random access memory). The faster the processor and the greater the RAM capacity (see page 17), the quicker Photoshop will be to process actions. However, before you rush out and buy the latest and greatest computer, the processor in almost any computer purchased in the last three years will be sufficient to operate Adobe Creative Suite 3. CS2 is another matter; versions of Photoshop prior to CS3 may actually perform better on the older PowerPC processors, because CS3 is the first version to be optimized for the new Intel-based Apple computers. PowerPC processors, also known as G3, G4, and G5, have now been phased out by Apple, but are still supported by Photoshop CS3 too.

It's also worth noting that more GHz does not necessarily mean a faster computer. Many modern processors employ a number of "cores." Each core is a separate processor chip, so a computer with two cores can—theoretically—do twice as much in the same time. Photoshop will gladly take advantage of the extra power (but not all programs will).

One aspect of your workstation that is critical is the version of your operating system (OS). Photoshop CS3 requires a minimum of Mac OS X 10.4 ("Tiger") or Windows 2000, XP, or Vista.

Computers come in all shapes and sizes.

Windows PC

Apple Macintosh

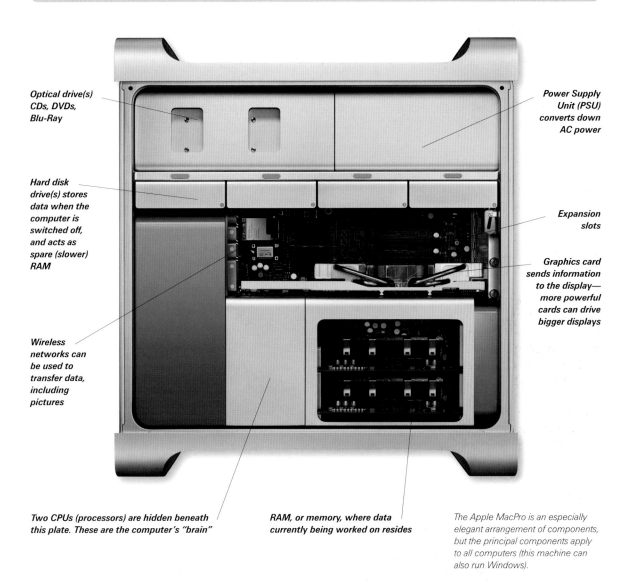

Optical drive(s) CDs, DVDs, Blu-Ray

Power Supply Unit (PSU) converts down AC power

Hard disk drive(s) stores data when the computer is switched off, and acts as spare (slower) RAM

Expansion slots

Graphics card sends information to the display—more powerful cards can drive bigger displays

Wireless networks can be used to transfer data, including pictures

Two CPUs (processors) are hidden beneath this plate. These are the computer's "brain"

RAM, or memory, where data currently being worked on resides

The Apple MacPro is an especially elegant arrangement of components, but the principal components apply to all computers (this machine can also run Windows).

Memory (RAM)

For Photoshop to operate at an optimum level, it requires five times more RAM than the size of the file you're working on. For example, an image file of around 17MB (a typical RAW file from a 6MP camera) would require a minimum 85MB of available RAM, bearing in mind that some RAM will be taken up by the OS and any other programs that are open simultaneously. CS3 requires a minimum of 384MB of RAM to open the program and at its maximum can utilize around 3.3GB. As a practical minimum your workstation should have 1GB of RAM capacity. Ideally, you would aim for 6GB, which allows for Photoshop's maximum and the rest for OS overheads.

> **TIP**
>
> **Freeing RAM capacity**
> *If you find Photoshop processing slow, check which other programs on the computer are open and close those that aren't immediately necessary. This will free RAM capacity for Photoshop to address.*

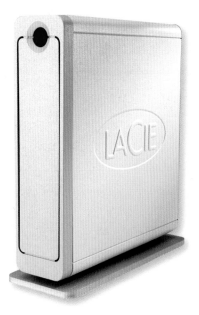

A typical external hard disk drive.

Scanners

Film requires scanning to convert the analog information (the film) into digital data. This can be done either at an external lab or using your own scanner device. If relying on an external lab, use one that has a drum scanner, which will provide the best possible quality. A slightly less expensive but good quality alternative is a virtual drum scanner (e.g. the Imacom Flextight scanner). In either event, the scan should be provided in RGB or LAB color mode (as opposed to CMYK).

Scanning tips

Always make sure that film is clean of dust and dirt prior to scanning. Scan in Adobe RGB or LAB color modes and at the highest possible resolution. Save the file in TIFF or native Photoshop (.psd) format (never JPEG).

Hard disk drive (HDD)

The hard drive is where you will store your images and so should have sufficient capacity for both current and future needs. Drive capacity is relatively cheap these days and most current workstations come with a minimum of 80GB, even at entry level. However, an 80GB HDD will hold around only 9,000 8-bit TIFF images from a 6MP camera and less than half that for some high-specification D-SLRs (the work from a single assignment for me), so my advice is to use an external device for image storage (see Storage—page 20) leaving the internal drive to hold the software programs and unrelated files.

Input devices

How you get a digital image "into" the computer will depend on the format of the original photograph. A digital camera produces a digital file and so can be transferred directly with no additional processing. A film image, however, will need to be scanned first to turn it into a digital file.

Downloading digital photographs

Digital photographs can be downloaded directly from the camera using a USB connection, or via a third-party device such as a card reader or portable hard disk drive. The latter two are my preferred solutions and I advise using a USB2 or Firewire compatible device to speed up the process.

Two scanners: a large drum scanner (top) and a desk-sized film scanner.

If you want to purchase your own scanner, the choice is between a film scanner and flatbed. As their name suggests, flatbed scanners are designed primarily for scanning flat media, such as paper. This doesn't exclude them from scanning film but makes them less than ideal. The alternative is a film scanner, which is designed specifically for scanning transparencies and negatives.

There are many competing models. The best quality will come from a virtual drum film scanner, as mentioned above (e.g. the Imacom Flextight), but you will pay a high purchase price for the quality. Otherwise the models available from manufacturers such as Nikon, Minolta, and Canon all produce reasonable results. If your budget allows, opt for a model that has 12- or 14-bit depth, a density in excess of 3.5 and optical scanning resolution of 2,900 PPI (pixels per inch) or better.

As important as the quality of the scanner is the type of software it uses. Only consider a scanner that enables alterations and adjustments to be made pre-scan, otherwise any changes you make will be to actual data and may degrade image quality. This is less important if your scan is at a 14-bit depth, but good software will always produce better results. Some users swear by separate scanning software, rather than that supplied by the manufacturer. VueScan is perhaps the most common, and well worth looking up (http://www.hamrick.com).

Monitors

The most critical part of the digital darkroom is the monitor. This is the tool you will use to assess the accuracy of exposure, color reproduction, and sharpness, among other factors. If the digital process is wrong here, it will remain so throughout the workflow.

Just as an enthusiastic debate persists over the question of Mac versus PC, so passions run high when it comes to a choice between CRT and LCD monitors. Historically, the preferred choice of professionals was the CRT (cathode-ray tube) type, despite its bulk and desk-print. However, as technology has developed there are some equally strong contenders among LCD monitors, and their slight design is appealing.

What is important is the number of colors the monitor is capable of displaying (it should be in the millions), and the screen resolution, which should be a minimum of 1,024 × 768 or, better still, 1,600 × 1,200 or higher. The monitor should also have manually adjustable controls for brightness and contrast, as well as convergence (which reduces the occurrence of color fringing).

For Photoshop work the minimum practical screen size is 17 inches, but again, bigger is better. Photoshop provides many palettes, which can obscure the image if

LCD and CRT monitors both have their advantages.

there is too little screen space. The ideal monitor size is 21 or 23 inches, although 19 inches is practical.

Another option is to run two monitors simultaneously—one for displaying the image and a second to display the Photoshop tools and palettes—thereby extending your on-screen workspace. The second monitor need not be of such a high quality so long as it isn't used for displaying an image. Your workstation will need a suitable video card that enables the use of multiple monitors.

Once up and running you will need to regularly calibrate the monitor (see Calibration, page 28).

Storage and disaster planning

Though it sounds tedious, storage is critically important for any photographer. Losing your family photos is bad enough, but if your back catalog is also your livelihood, the loss could have far-reaching consequences.

Storage is a massively important aspect of digital photography that includes not just where to store your image files, but also how to back them up and guard against permanent loss or damage. As a professional photographer, one thing I have found is that the so-called savings on film and processing that shooting digitally provides are quickly eaten away by the additional expenditure on hard drives. At the professional level it's a complex and critical area.

I prefer to use external hard drives for image storage. There are several reasons, the main ones being that I can easily add and daisy-chain additional drives as and when required, and that I can easily unplug the drive(s) from one machine and plug them into another, if necessary. It also allows me to separate my image files from other computer files.

When choosing an external hard drive, plan ahead. Choose a drive that has spare capacity for the foreseeable future. When I first began shooting digitally I spent more money than I needed to by buying low-capacity drives, thinking they would last. In the end, I dumped the lot and now buy drives in capacities of 1TB. Also, the connection should be USB2 or Firewire. Avoid USB1 devices, as they are slow—very slow! Otherwise, reliability is the most important factor when choosing a drive.

Using external hard drives

Hard disks are mechanical devices that have the potential to wear out over time. Only switch on a drive when it is needed and be sure to disconnect the drive(s) as per the manufacturer's instructions.

A small RAID system can be little bigger than an external hard drive, but has all the advantages of secure data.

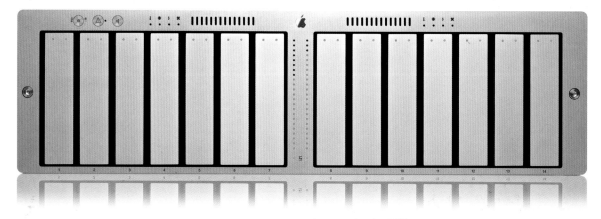

An enterprise-class RAID system, capable of storing over 10TB (one Terabyte is 1024 Gigabytes). This is necessary only for the busiest of photographic studios.

Backup solutions

Unless you want to end up crying a river you must back up your image files to a separate media or one having built-in redundancy (for example, a RAID drive that automatically backs itself up). The cheapest backup solution is to copy files from your hard drive to CD, DVD, or Blu-Ray media. These disks should then be stored in a safe place. However, there is a question mark over the longevity of these types of disk and they are certainly not foolproof. And, although a cheap backup solution in terms of cost, they provide a far from efficient solution.

A second, more convenient (but more expensive) option is to acquire two external hard drives and copy the data from one to the other. The second drive acts as the backup drive and can similarly be stored away from the workstation in a safe place and only used as and when required. In effect, this is a manual form of mirroring.

A third option, one used extensively in businesses of all sizes, is to use a RAID-based system of storage. This involves multiple disks within a system being managed by a RAID controller, which will, depending on the level of RAID applied, write data to the disks in such a way that protection from disk failure is built in. This isn't the cheapest form of backup, but it is one of the best. However, it doesn't necessarily protect you from disaster damage, such as fire or theft, and it may still need backing up remotely.

Somewhere between these two options is Apple's Time Machine, a standard feature of OS X since the 10.5 ("Leopard") edition. This takes advantage of an additional hard drive to make and organise backups for you. You can then simply look at earlier versions of Finder windows to locate files you've deleted, lost, or saved over. It goes without saying that this is Mac-only.

A final option is the purpose-designed backup tape system, but this type of solution might prove unviable for most users.

Ultimately, you may find that a combination of backup processes is what works best for you. For reference I use HDD in pairs, one acting as a mirror of the other, and also back up to DVD (mainly because I'm paranoid!).

Disaster recovery

In the unfortunate event that data is lost from your hard drive and no backup is available, it may be possible to recover it. There are several software packages on the market that will do the job, although, as fortune would have it, I've never had call to use any. I have read, however, that a shareware solution called PC Inspector (www.pcinspector.de) works effectively.

Online services

Though it's undoubtedly not practical for everyone, a number of services are springing up on the internet that make it possible to upload your images to password-protected web servers and make some accessible to the wider community. While there are certain bandwidth limits, it's certainly feasible to upload high-resolution JPEGs of your images after batch-exporting from a program like Lightroom or Photoshop's own Image Processor tool (*File > Scripts > Image Processor...*). Then, in the unlikely event that all your originals are destroyed, you can still access a backup (admittedly of a lower quality) from any location via the internet. If you choose to make the files viewable by the public, you can also receive feedback from the community, though whether this is a good thing is open to debate.

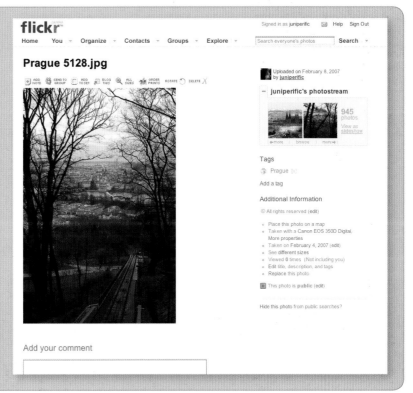

Managing hardware in Photoshop

Having considered every storage device that might be attached, or at least linked, to your computer, it's worth checking out how Photoshop relates to these devices.

Your computer's resources are controlled more directly by the machine's operating system—Mac OS X or Windows—than by Photoshop, but nevertheless the program can exert its own influence. The relevant settings should not be ignored; they can have a dramatic impact on the speed of your workflow. There are two key factors at work here—the size of what Photoshop likes to call your Scratch Disk, and the proportion of the live memory (the RAM, see page 17) that you're prepared to devote to the program.

Both of these settings can be adjusted via the Performance section of the Preferences window, which is accessed via *Photoshop > Preferences > Performance* (Mac OS X) or *File > Preferences > Performance* (Windows). (Here, incidentally, is one of the few differences between the Mac and PC versions, and it is only because all Mac applications have their preferences under their name in the menu bar, while Windows doesn't feature such a bar. The dialog still works in the same way.)

Scratch disks

The scratch disk concept is not unique to Photoshop, but generally goes by the name "virtual memory," and represents the freedom of being able to work with a great deal more data than is possible without it, even while strapping on the ball and chain of what computer users term a "hardware bottleneck." The bottleneck is the speed of the hard drive, which, even at the best of times, is an order of magnitude slower than the memory—it is, after all, a component with moving parts, not just a chip.

Flash based memory

Photographers (and indeed the iPod Nano generation) are familiar with the benefits of Flash based memory, which has no moving parts just like computer RAM but retains data when the power is off. Computer manufacturers are starting to implement this as a middle ground between hard discs and RAM, though it is in it's infancy and at the time of writing not directly supported by Photoshop.

By default, the scratch disk will be set as the drive on which you installed Photoshop. If your computer has only one drive anyway, then you will have no other choice, however many users find that it is preferable to use a second drive as Photoshop's scratch area since this minimizes conflict with the data flowing to and from the main drive (which the operating system will most likely be using as its own virtual memory device). I'd recommend using a second drive whenever possible, though it is a lot more convenient with an internal drive—you won't have to remember to turn it on when you boot up your computer and you can't accidentally trip over the cable. USB hard drive connections are probably too slow for this to serve any benefit.

Memory usage

Though there is little need to adjust it, if performance seems slower than you'd expect, make sure that the Memory Usage is set up to at least 70%. Photoshop can only address a maximum of about 3GB of RAM thanks to a technical limit imposed by 32-bit computing. 64-bit machines which can address far more RAM are beginning to emerge, and Mac OS X and some versions of Windows do support this, but we'll have to wait for another version of Photoshop before it is possible to address more memory. That's not to say RAM above 3GB won't speed up your computer, as other applications and of course the operating system can make use of it, as well as Photoshop comfortably using its maximum allocation.

History and cache

Setting a limit to the number of history states (how many steps you can undo) will reduce the amount of scratch space needed, though obviously it reduces your ability to go back and undo mistakes. Caching is storing data in anticipation of your returning to it, so the more you have, the faster your workflow. Sometimes, however, the screen will be drawn quickly from the cache but won't be quite accurate based on all the most recent changes you've made. Reducing the cache levels will give you a better quality preview on the screen, but this comes at the expense of speed.

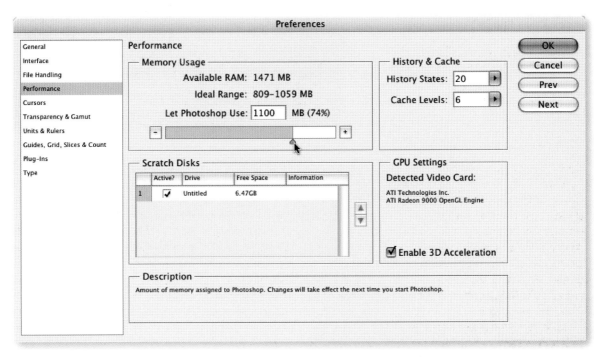

The Preferences pane's
Performance section, showing
settings for a computer with
one hard drive and 1.5GB of
physical RAM.

GPU settings

GPUs, or graphics cards, help to accelerate both 2D and 3D performance, and different cards may offer the option to disable this if for some reason you're not happy with the way 3D objects are drawn. Adding 3D objects is a very specialized feature in Photoshop, generally for architectural visualizations rather than photography, so that's the last I'll say on the matter.

The preferences pane, despite
slightly different access routes,
is identical in Windows Vista.

A graphics card, or "GPU." Enabling 3D
acceleration in the GPU settings dialog
will use your system's graphics card to
reduce strain on the main processor, but
sadly photography rarely benefits from
Photoshop's ability to import 3D objects.

TIP

Keep at least 10%, and preferably far more, of the space in your main hard drive free at all times. If you run close to the capacity then the virtual memory will not function properly, risking slow-down, hourglasses (or beachballs on the Mac) and even crashes.

Printers

Photographers will always need to see their work on paper, and printing technology has progressed rapidly. In many ways the printer is the end of the digital process, creating traditional prints for all to see.

For many, the digital workflow stops at the printer. The most popular choice is one of the many inkjet printers currently available on the market from manufacturers such as Epson, Canon, and Hewlett Packard. Printer technology changes so quickly, however, that it is impossible in a book like this to make any specific recommendation. However, there are certain considerations that should inform your decision-making.

Paper size

Firstly, you need to decide how large you want to make prints. All current digital SLR cameras will produce excellent quality photographs when printed to US Letter/A4 size, so this is your starting point. However, the larger Tabloid/A3 (approx. 16 × 11 inches) size looks good when mounted, and for poster-sized prints you will need Broadsheet/A2 (22 × 16 inches) format. Any larger and you are moving into the realms of roll-fed inkjet printers that vary in width, usually between 24 and 44 inches.

Inks

The number of ink cartridges used by the printer to create color will affect image quality. Entry-level printers typically use two cartridges, one of black ink, the other color. Better quality printers separate out the color inks into separate cartridges, usually the three colors used in printing—cyan, magenta, and yellow (CMY), but sometimes introducing

Branded inks

Branded inks can seem expensive compared to non-branded supplies. However, be very careful when choosing inks other than the manufacturer's own. It has been my experience—and that of other professionals I work with—that non-branded inks can cause the printer to malfunction. You pay your money and make your choice but, personally, I prefer the added cost of reliability.

Typical inkjet printers can print on a variety of paper formats and—where presentation is important—even onto discs.

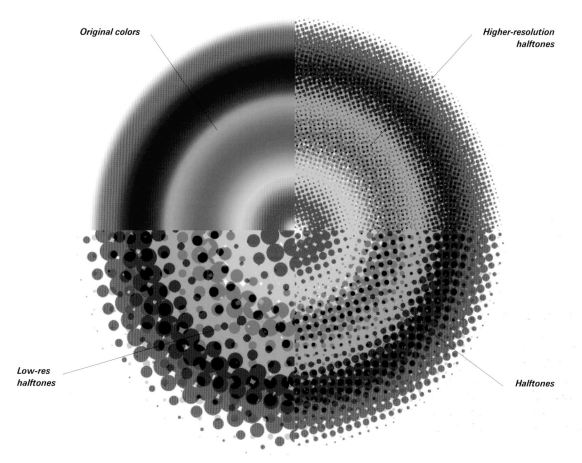

Original colors

Higher-resolution halftones

Low-res halftones

Halftones

This diagram shows how color is created from CMYK on traditional presses. Most inkjets use alternative pseudo-random dithering patterns to distribute dots.

variants such as photo (light) cyan and photo (light) magenta. These added colors enable the printer to reproduce color more accurately, so increasing print quality.

Print resolution (dpi)

The relationship between image resolution and print resolution is complex. In a nutshell, inkjet printers are relatively crude devices that require many ink dots for each individual image pixel. What this means is that you don't get anywhere near the dpi of image resolution from a color printer because the need for multiple printer dots per image pixel reduces significantly the printer's actual image resolution capability to a fraction of the advertised dpi. That's not to say that printer specifications are inaccurate and meaningless. However, they shouldn't be confused with image resolution. For this reason, a minimum 1,200 dpi printer (ink dots) is needed to print an image at 250 dpi (pixels). Indeed the latter is more correctly referred to as pixels per inch (ppi), but this is commonly confused, even by professionals.

Dye sublimation printers

Dye sublimation printers use a process in which solids are converted to gas to produce high quality, photorealistic continuous-tone prints. They result in prints much closer in appearance to traditional laboratory prints. However, they are expensive compared to inkjet printers and are currently limited in paper size.

Understanding color

Color matching is a perennial problem for digital photographers, with images looking different on the camera viewer, your computer display, and the printed page. The first step to fixing this is understanding the science.

Have you ever wondered why the colors in the print from your printer never match those of the image when it's displayed on the monitor? Or why the same vibrant on-screen colors don't look right when the image is printed in a book or magazine? The answer lies in how colors are interpreted and reproduced by the different devices used in the digital photography workflow.

In digital form color is nothing more than a numeric value, but different devices interpret these values in different ways. For example, in very simplistic and hypothetical terms, say that red has a numeric value of 100 in RGB color mode (the color mode used by a computer monitor) and that in CMYK color mode (as used by printers) the value 100 represents orange. When you print the RGB image, unless you somehow tell the printer that the value 100 equals red, the printer will reproduce its preferred orange. This is an extreme example, but the principle is the same for all color correction.

Another problem faced by photographers is the limit in the range (referred to as the gamut) of colors that different devices are able to produce. An RGB device (e.g. a camera or a monitor) can produce colors in the range indicated by the diagram below. On the other hand, a CMYK device (e.g. a printer) can produce colors in the range indicated by the diagram botttom right. If we merge these two diagrams to produce a third diagram

(lower large diagram) you will see that while many of the colors overlap, some from each fall outside of the range of the other, and these colors cannot be reproduced accurately by the respective device.

You can get a rough idea of on-screen colors that fall outside a specified CMYK gamut by opening an RGB image file and viewing the gamut warning (*View > Gamut Warning*). RGB colors that fall outside the CMYK color range will be highlighted in gray and may not appear in print as they do on screen.

So, in a digital workflow it is essential that all the devices used interpret and reproduce color in a consistent way. Or put another way, that they all speak the same "color language." This process we refer to as color management, and the following pages identify and illustrate how to manage color throughout the workflow so that what appears in print is as close as possible to what you want.

Choosing an RGB workspace

The RGB workspace defines the range of colors that the monitor can display when processing an image. What is important when deciding on an RGB workspace is how it relates to the output process. Prior to Photoshop 5, the monitor RGB gamut defined the editing RGB workspace. This setup had several limitations, including the clipping

To the right are a typical RGB device (camera, monitor) color space (top) and a typical CMYK printer's space (bottom). The larger diagram shows the areas that conflict.

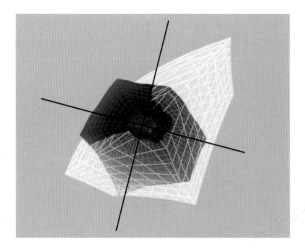
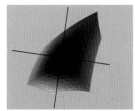
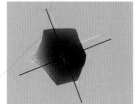

Why use RGB?

If printers use the CMYK process, why don't we edit image files using CMYK in Photoshop? Essentially, Photoshop provides more tools and functionality when working on an RGB image file. RGB is generally the medium in which images are acquired (camera and scanner technology is RGB) so there is little sense making the CMYK conversion until the end of the process. If your output medium is video or the web then you will never need to make any CMYK conversion anyway. Unless you are completely familiar with the CMYK device and know it'll be the only medium you ever use to output the image, it is usually preferable to allow the RGB-to-CMYK conversion to be made when printing.

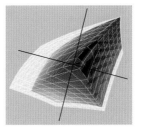
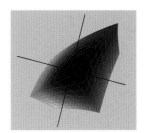

The sRGB IEC-61966-2.1 range is strong in terms of RGB but comparitively weak in CMYK colors, especially cyan.

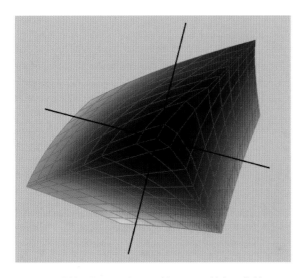

The Adobe RGB color space is one of the most widely available, and ideally suited to digital devices.

of some CMYK colors (particularly in the areas of yellow, cyan, and cyan/green), while the extensive range of blue and green colors available in monitor RGB fell well outside of the CMYK gamut. Since the introduction of Photoshop 5, the editing RGB workspace has been device-independent and is user-selectable. There are several RGB workspace options available and it is recommended that once you have adopted a particular workspace you keep it consistent for all image-editing work.

Adobe RGB (1998)

The most commonly used RGB workspace for digital files destined for use in print publication (i.e. to be converted to a CMYK color mode) is Adobe RGB (1998), which is also utilized by most digital camera manufacturers. Previously known by the catchy name SMPTE-240M, Adobe RGB makes better use of the available colors and minimizes potential clipping of the CMYK gamut, making it particularly suited to RGB-to-CMYK conversion. For all the professional photographers using Photoshop that I know, Adobe RGB (1998) is the RGB workspace of choice.

sRGB IEC-61966-2.1

The other RGB workspace commonly provided on digital cameras is sRGB. The idea behind sRGB is a multipurpose, standard color space for consumer digital devices, which can be matched by any camera, monitor, and inkjet printer. This makes it ideal for low-end, non-professional use, where significant image processing in the computer is not envisaged and high quality prints are non-essential. However, it is unsuited to professional reproduction because the CMYK gamut is severely clipped, particularly in the cyan range.

ProPhoto RGB

ProPhoto RGB has a very wide gamut space, significantly wider than CMYK. This has the advantage of making greater use of raw color data captured by a digital camera when converting the raw data to RGB. Other output options, such as when outputting to transparency emulsion, or when using a high-end photographic quality inkjet printer, can also benefit from the wider RGB gamut. However, the benefits of the wider RGB gamut can become more problematic in traditional print reproduction with its gamut limitations, making ProPhoto RGB a less suitable workspace for many RGB-to-CMYK conversions.

There are additional RGB workspace options with a gamma of 1.8—Apple RGB and ColorMatch RGB—that are particularly suited to working on 1.8 gamma files. ColorMatch RGB is preferable, as it is an open, known standard and more compatible with legacy Macintosh files.

Profiling

Color profiles are the perfect solution to the variety of gamuts that crop up in any workflow. Each device can have its own idiosyncrasies measured scientifically, and that information can be used to correct color shift.

Simply put, a profile describes the properties of a color space and defines the gamut of an output device such as a computer monitor or printer. Although a digital workflow can survive without profiling, it will be very inefficient. In reality, accurate and efficient color management is reliant on successful profiling. In essence, a profile is the basis of communication between devices and sets a standard for how color is reproduced throughout the digital workflow. With an accurately profiled monitor and printer, in particular, you will come close to achieving consistent color both on screen and in prints.

Eye-One Match is a calibration utility which guides you through the process of calibrating your screen, and works in conjunction with a colorimeter.

Advanced monitor calibration

Although it is possible to achieve a basic level of calibration and profiling visually, there are too many variables affecting this method to achieve any degree of accuracy. In a professional workflow the monitor should be calibrated using a hardware device in conjunction with an appropriate software package. For an inexpensive and highly accurate solution, I recommend the Gretag MacBeth Eye-One Display, which comes with proprietary software (Eye-One Match). This solution uses a colorimeter to build the monitor profile, and, although limited to use with monitors only, is regarded as equal to the more expensive spectrophotometers. Better still, the process is relatively straightforward—all that is generally necessary is to follow the steps on screen.

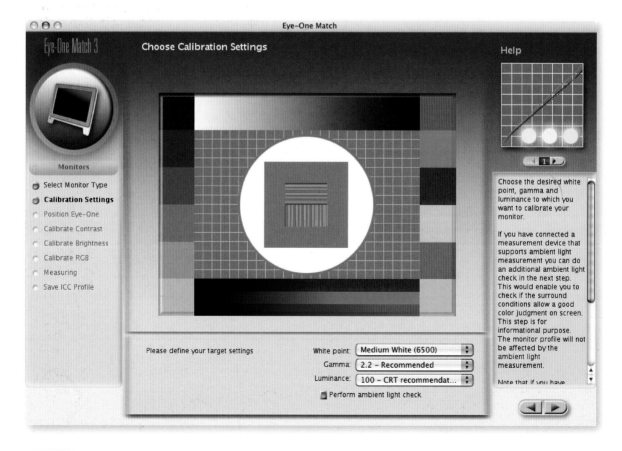

Profiling an input device

It is possible to profile an input device, such as a scanner or digital camera, although the value of doing so is less obvious. Profiling a digital camera, for example, would be particularly difficult if the camera was used in inconsistent lighting conditions, such as outdoors or in a studio where the lighting setup changes regularly. Where complete control over color is absolutely essential (for example, when a photograph is to be used as reference for an historic or valuable object) then the value of profiling the input device justifies the process. However, for most photographers, color assessment is primarily made via the computer monitor, and color management is most important between this point and the printing stage.

Before you begin monitor calibration you should be sure that monitor option settings are correct. The table below shows my recommended settings:

Monitor option	Recommended setting
Gamma space	2.2
White point	6,500
Profile (CRT)	Small
Profile (LCD)	Large
Luminance (CRT)	100
Luminance (LCD)	140
Contrast	100%

Also, if you are using a CRT monitor, it should be switched on for a minimum of 30 minutes before you begin calibration.

Once the colorimeter is placed on the screen, the supplied software will step through the calibration process. This involves a series of colors being displayed on screen, from which are taken measurements that are subsequently used to set the video card and fine-tune the monitor for a neutral display.

Once the screen is calibrated the software continues to build the profile. When the sequence is complete you can name the profile and save it to your hard drive. There is no specific naming convention but it is wise to include the date within the name you use, as this will enable you to easily locate the most recent profile. Macintosh computers automatically save the profile to a folder named Library/ColorSync/Profiles/Displays. PC users should save profiles in the Windows/System32/Spool/Drivers/Color folder. For the very best results you should calibrate your monitor on a weekly or fortnightly basis.

Printer profiling

Once you have a profile for your monitor, the next stage in the color management process is building a library of profiles for each combination of printer and paper that you use. The drivers provided with inkjet printers will provide a selection of profiles for use with proprietary inks and some of the better known brands of photo paper, such as Kodak, Fuji, and Ilford. As a starting point these profiles will produce acceptable results, so long as you match them accurately to the paper you are actually using.

When print quality is of the utmost importance it is best to build your own printer profiles using a color target test card, such as those available from Kodak, together with a spectrophotometer, such as the Gretag MacBeth Eye-One. This process involves making a non-color-managed test print on your preferred paper stock, with the patch measurements from the stable print being used to build the color profile.

Embedding ICC profiles

The ICC (International Color Consortium) was established with the aim of creating, promoting, and encouraging the standardization and evolution of an open, vendor-neutral, cross-platform color management system architecture and components. By embedding the ICC profile used in editing (e.g. sRGB, Adobe RGB (1998), etc.) when saving an image you are effectively saving with the image a color reference chart that any other program or device can refer to when attempting to recreate those colors accurately.

Color management in Photoshop

Color profiling is all very well, but conversion between devices is inevitable, especially since cameras are RGB and printers are CMYK. The Color Settings dialog allows you to manage your policies and maintain maximum quality.

Although Photoshop provides the option of a high level of sophistication with regard to color management, much of this is unnecessary for photographers, who can work in Photoshop quite adequately with some simple adjustments to the basic color settings.

The Color Settings menu and dialog box is accessed by clicking *Edit > Color Settings* from the main menu. In the Settings menu option, Photoshop has a number of preset options, which will vary depending on where the software originated (United States or Europe for example). The default setting will be a general-purpose setting and ideally should be edited to your requirements.

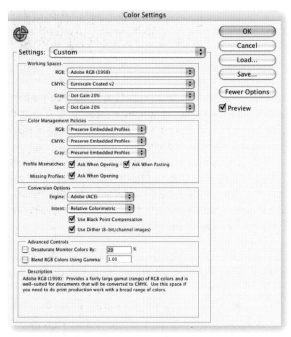

The Color Settings dialog with the More Options button pressed to reveal the choice between Adobe and Apple color correction.

Settings

If you don't want to configure your own custom settings, click on the More Options button to reveal a more extensive range of color setting options and choose one of the Prepress options, which will provide the basis for an effective color managed workflow. For example, if in the US, you would select North America Prepress Defaults; in Europe, select Europe Prepress Defaults; in Japan, select Japan Prepress Defaults, and so on.

Alternatively, you can choose to build custom settings by selecting the Custom option from the drop-down menu. Once you have selected the relevant options you can save the custom settings, which will then appear in the drop-down menu. When saving a custom setting you can also add a narrative to describe, for example, where the setting might be used. As a guide, my most frequently custom setting is named Chris ARGB-Euro.

Color management policies

You also need to tell Photoshop how to manage color in incoming image files. When you open an image in Photoshop it checks for an embedded ICC profile. The default option is to preserve the embedded profile. For example, when opening an image with an sRGB profile to a workspace with an Adobe RGB (1998) profile, the image will retain its original (sRGB) profile and the workspace will match the sRGB colors. This also allows several images with different profiles to be open on the same workspace,

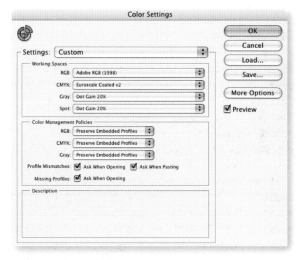

The Color Settings dialog as it appears via the Edit menu, or by pressing Ctrl/⌘+Shift+K

all viewed as intended by the originator. When resaving an image, the original, embedded profile will be retained.

The alternative is to convert the embedded profile to the workspace profile, in which case, where there is a profile mismatch, Photoshop will automatically perform a profile conversion, changing the embedded profile to the workspace profile. You may choose to do this with RGB mode images in order to gain some uniformity across several image files. However, I strongly urge against converting images in CMYK mode, as the image may be profiled for a specific press output and altering the numeric color values could potentially be disastrous. For either RGB or CMYK files, defaulting to preserving the embedded profile is the foolproof option.

Profile warning dialogs

In the Color Settings dialog box under the Color Management Policies drop-down menu are some options for enabling Photoshop to warn you when there is a profile mismatch or when a profile is missing altogether. Selecting all three options by checking the relevant boxes is recommended and will cause Photoshop to display a warning dialog. This gives you the option of manually deciding how Photoshop deals with files where the embedded profile differs to the workspace profile.

Conversion engines

In its default setting, the Conversion Engine, which is the color management module (CMM), is set to Adobe Color Engine (ACE). The alternative options are Apple ColorSync and Apple CMM. I recommend leaving this in the default setting, ACE, which uses 20-bit per channel bit depth when calculating color space conversions, making it by far the most effective of the three options.

Rendering intent

Your next option is to decide on the rendering intent. This is important because it determines the rules used by Photoshop when translating between the source and destination color spaces. Critically, it defines how Photoshop manages colors that fall outside the CMYK gamut but inside the RGB color space gamut (i.e. colors that are visible in the RGB color mode but are beyond the limits of a printer's ability to reproduce them).

When Photoshop performs a color space conversion, it is effectively translating between the values of individual colors in the RGB color space and their equivalent colors in the CMYK color space. In relative terms, it is like a language translator converting, say, English into French. But just as not all words in a language have a direct equivalent in another, not all colors in the RGB color

Original (in so far as it is possible to print in CMYK)

Absolute Colorimetric conversion

Perceptual conversion

space have a CMYK equivalent, and vice versa, and where this is the case Photoshop must decide on the closest equivalent. The rules governing how Photoshop performs this task are referred to as rendering intent.

For photographers, the two most common and most effective rendering intent options are Perceptual and Relative Colorimetric, with the latter being the default setting and typically the better of the two options for photographic image conversions.

Relative colorimetric vs. Perceptual rendering intents

When performing a relative colorimetric conversion, out-of-gamut colors in the source space are mapped to the closest in-gamut equivalent in the target space. For example, an RGB green that is outside the limits of the CMYK gamut will be given a color value equivalent to a green just inside the CMYK gamut range. This results in

---

TIP

When one of the Web/Internet preset color settings is selected, Photoshop Color Management is automatically switched off.

Rendering intent	
Perceptual	This is one of the better options for digital photography, since it aims to preserve the relationship between colors that fall inside or outside the new gamut, even if this results in inaccuracies for in-gamut colors. In other words, all the colors are adjusted so that the overall impression seems right. This is the best choice for images with a lot of color detail, like close-ups of flowers.
Saturation	The worst option for photographers, this method doesn't attempt to maintain realism but preserve saturated graphics. It's better used when converting, for example, charts from one RGB space to another.
Relative Colorimetric	Alongside Perceptual this is one of the two favorite options for the digital photographer. It aims to preserve the relationship between in-gamut colors as precisely as possible, and clips some out-of-gamut colors as a result. This is an ideal choice for images with fewer extremes of color, like some portraits or cloudy and foggy scenes.
Absolute Colorimetric	This is similar to the relative colormetric method, in that colors in both gamuts are preserved exactly. exactly. However, if the original white point (the lightest, brightest color in the space) is in a different place to the one in the new space, there will be a color shift because there is no compensation.

clipping of out-of-gamut RGB colors but tends to produce more vibrant separations.

Perceptual rendering conversions are managed differently. Rather than clipping out-of-gamut colors to their closest equivalent they are compressed, or squeezed into the target space. Depending on how far out-of-gamut the colors are, more or less compression is applied. This has the advantage that it retains more of the tonal separation but can result in less vibrancy. Certainly, where few colors fall outside the CMYK gamut (e.g. when the Adobe RGB color space is set), relative colorimetric rendering is the recommended option.

Black point compensation

The other advanced options available include setting on or off black point compensation, which affects how black tones are reproduced in print. Deselecting the Use Black Point Compensation option is likely to result in deeper blacks on paper but may be detrimental to accuracy. Activating the Use Black Point Compensation option will typically result in more realistic prints, with black tones truer to the original image.

Dither (8-bit/channel images)

It's possible that an RGB-to-CMYK conversion will result in banding. This is most likely where an image contains areas of gentle tonal gradation and saturated bright tones. Although on-screen banding may not be reproduced at the print stage, selecting Use Dither will reduce the likelihood of its occurrence. Note that this option is only available with 8-bit per channel images.

RGB-to-CMYK conversion

Digitally originated files, such as those produced by a scanner or a digital camera, start life in RGB mode. If they remain in a digital environment—for example, on the World Wide Web—then there is no need to convert them to any other color mode. However, if your images are destined for printing in books, magazines, or on some other medium that uses a commercial print process, then almost certainly they will be reproduced in CMYK mode, in which case a conversion from the original RGB file to a CMYK file must occur. Unfortunately there are many flavors of CMYK and unless you know the exact CMYK settings being used in the specific print reproduction, you may find it safer to allow the printing house to perform the conversion.

If you decide to take on the color mode conversion yourself (after consulting with the clients) then you will need first to select one of Photoshop's preset CMYK space settings, or build your own custom setting. The preset

Check it out

To compare the difference between RGB-to-CMYK conversions using the two rendering intents described above, you can perform a soft proof via your monitor. With an RGB image file open on screen, select *View > Proof Setup* from the main menu. From the fly-out menu, select Custom, which opens the Customize Proof Condition dialog box. You can switch between rendering intents using the relevant drop-down menu to make the comparison.

A photograph seen in its original RGB form in Photoshop (reproduced as accurately as possible, given that for this book the image must also undergo a CMYK conversion).

The same image with Photoshop's Gamut Warning mode turned on. All the areas highlighted in gray will not be converted exactly as the colors cannot be recreated in the target (CMYK) mode.

options are listed in the drop-down menu and include versions for coated and uncoated paper stock, as well as press setup. If you have a rough idea of the type of specification used in the specific print process, then you can select one of these, whichever is closest.

If you know the relevant CMYK separation information then you can set up and save a custom CMYK setting by clicking the Custom CMYK button at the top of the drop-down menu. This will open a new dialog box (shown right). I recommend entering a name that provides a suitable reference for the relevant print specifications. The additional options in the dialog box refer to the

information you will need to source from the print house, such as ink colors, dot grain, black generation, etc.

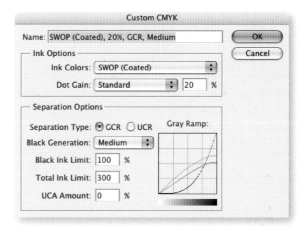

The default CMYK workspace

Whichever setting the CMYK workspace is set to in the Color Settings dialog will be the default setting used by Photoshop when running an RGB to CMYK conversion (*Image > Mode > CMYK*).

The Custom CMYK dialog enables you to make changes to details like GCR (Gray Component Replacement). The Gray Ramp curves show where a mixture of cyan, magenta, and yellow are mixed to form black, and where, as the shade nears 100% black, the black (Key) component takes over.

your way around

Despite its name, Photoshop isn't only the preserve of photographers. Photoshop offers a huge range of possibilities for everyone from graphic artists to prepress agents, so understanding how these tools are organized is crucial. This chapter explores the palettes, tools, options, and helper applications you'll need to keep your workflow smooth. That includes a good look at what might be seen as the child of Photoshop, Bridge, which has emerged from the File Browser in earlier versions of Photoshop to act as a fully fledged organizational tool. Creating an efficient workflow is all about getting your house in order.

The full extent of Photoshop's functionality is, thankfully, concealed behind a Toolbox which recognizes that you can only do one thing at a time. Following on from that, Photoshop—with a bit of help from you—can select what information to display and what it doesn't need to share with you. The thing is, you need to know what you're looking at before you decide whether or not you need it.

Workflows for photographers

The more you shoot, the more you'll find yourself dependent on a logical workflow. That way, should you forget a file, or need to start over with an original, you'll know exactly where to look.

Workflow is a term you hear a lot in digital photography. It refers to the process of taking a digital original to its final output, and achieving the most efficient and effective workflow is the digital photographer's Holy Grail. Although it is mentioned in books, it is rarely written about in depth, with good reason. The difficulty in determining an appropriate workflow is that there's no single right way to do things.

Take, for example, my own situation as a professional wildlife photographer. My images are sold through two agencies, and are used in books and magazines. Recently, I have begun printing images for exhibition and fine art sales. Each of these uses requires a different process. One of my agencies requires all images to be interpolated to 50MB, while the other doesn't. Both agencies require images to be unsharpened, but sharpening must be applied to images used in my books and magazine articles. Both agencies and publishers prefer that the CMYK conversion is done at the print stage and so request RGB files. However, when I print for exhibition work, the CMYK conversion is managed in-house. With so many variables it's easy to see why workflow has become such a hotly debated topic.

Another influencing factor is that software and technology are changing constantly. The launch of Aperture by Apple changed the way variations of the same image can be saved, significantly reducing the load on hard disk capacity. A similar process option is currently unavailable in Photoshop, Adobe Camera Raw, or the new sidekick Lightroom, although I have no doubt that it will be added at some point.

And so, the following workflow descriptions are given as examples only. They should be viewed with all the above caveats taken into account and adapted as necessary to your own circumstances. You should also be aware that by the time you read this, there no doubt will be another plausible variation on the theme!

Adobe Photoshop Lightroom is one of several tools on the market designed to take charge of much of the workflow shown opposite.

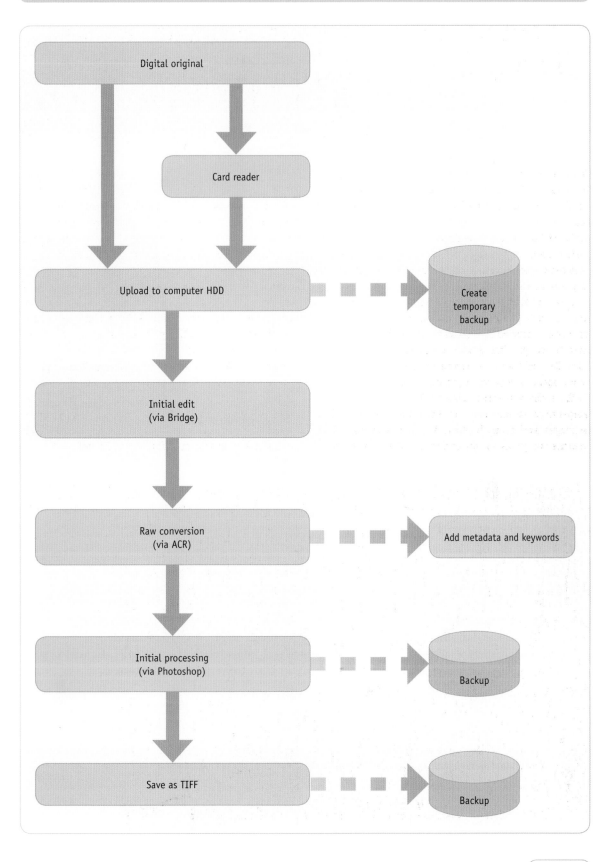

Image management

It's certainly not the most exciting aspect of photography, but it is necessary nonetheless. Much of your image management will take place on the periphery of Photoshop, but that doesn't stop Bridge getting involved.

Image management isn't unique to digital photography. Photographers have been managing images one way or another since the recorded image was first realized. Indeed, the basis for effective image management hasn't changed: images must be edited, sorted, named, and stored; and there should be a suitable method of retrieval. Of all these steps the only thing that has really changed with digital photography is the method of storage.

Older versions of Photoshop included a File Browser application. With CS2, File Browser was replaced by a standalone, bundled Adobe software solution called Bridge, upgraded to Bridge 2 with the release of CS3. Bridge's role is to ease the flow of image files between the various Adobe applications that make up the Creative Suite. These include Illustrator, GoLive, and InDesign, as well as Photoshop itself.

As such, Bridge is not an application designed specifically for photographers. That exists in the form of Lightroom (and there are several independent software packages already on the market). However, it is a tool that can be used effectively for some stages of the image management process, and to that extent it is included in this section. However, where applicable I have also made mention of some independent software solutions that I use in my own workflow.

Portable hard drive

Different devices available to the system

Uploading files

Before you can work on an image file in Photoshop, you have to upload it to an accessible Hard Disk Drive (HDD), or other storage media, such as a DVD or CD. If you have a large number of images I advise setting aside a HDD specifically for storing images. Otherwise, set aside a specific folder on your main internal HDD. See Storage and Disaster Planning (page 20) for more advice on the equipment available to store images.

For uploading of images I usually use a card reader, although images can be uploaded directly from the camera (which is equally convenient if you only have one memory card, but less so as your collection grows). If I have been on assignment, I store images on a portable HDD, which I then use to upload images to my main HDD via a USB2 connector. I have divided my image HDD into

two main folders, one for processed images and one for pre-processed images. In the first instance, as you might expect, I upload the new files to the latter.

Once my new images are on the HDD I immediately make a backup copy on DVD, which I then store separately.

Editing files

Once images are uploaded, my first step is to cull them in an initial edit, which I can do in Bridge. When I turn on my computer I have it configured to automatically launch both Photoshop and Bridge. Alternatively, you can launch Bridge from its desktop icon, or directly from Photoshop by clicking the Go to Bridge icon on the main menu bar (to the left of the palette docking well), or from the File menu (*File > Browse*).

The Bridge workspace is very flexible, but by default features docked palettes on either side of its main browser. The size of each palette can be changed by clicking and dragging with the mouse. Alternatively, use the two small arrow keys in the bottom left corner to hide or reveal this area of the workspace, or cycle through the various workspace defaults (Ctrl+F1 to F4). Typically, during an initial edit, I hide the palettes from view to increase the area of the viewing workspace (Ctrl+F2).

The top menu bar shows the location of the current image and, in a drop-down menu, the folder hierarchy on the left side. On the right side is a filter option, create new folder option, image rotate tools, Trashcan and an option to switch to compact mode, which folds away practically all but the header bar, revealing the computer desktop below.

The bottom menu bar shows the number of items in the current folder, together with the number of items selected in that folder. To the left of the menu bar there is a slider that determines the size of the thumbnails (sliding to the left makes them smaller, to the right larger) and the viewing mode. There are three viewing modes: thumbnails (tiled image layout with image name), filmstrip (thumbnails along the bottom and a larger view of the currently selected image above), and detailed (thumbnails with metadata).

For editing purposes I always use the filmstrip mode, which provides me with a row of thumbnails that I can quickly reference, as well as an image of sufficient size that I can make my initial culling decisions.

Rotating files in Bridge

Sometimes images shot in the vertical (portrait) format are shown in Bridge on their side, in the horizontal format (this is down to the camera settings). Images can be easily rotated in Bridge by clicking on the relevant Rotate arrows in the top menu bar. Making the relevant multiple image selection can rotate multiple images.

My initial cull is based on some obvious criteria: is the subject in focus, the image well exposed, and the composition strong? If I want to delete an item from the HDD I simply click on the Trashcan.

Bridge 2, included with Photoshop CS3, is divided into adjustable panes. Here the preview is small and the thumbnails occupy most space, convenient for browsing.

Top menu bar

Bottom menu bar

Thumbnail size slider

Sorting, arranging, and rating files

There is little sense in working on images which will never see the light of day, so arranging and rating files gives you the opportunity to select those that are worthy of further attention.

Before I begin the actual culling process I might want to arrange the files into some sort of order. This can be easily done in Bridge in one of two ways. The unsophisticated approach is to simply drag and drop files within the workspace. However, with a large number of files this can be unwieldy and inefficient.

A more efficient method of arranging image files is to use the star rating system in Bridge. For example, I recently returned from an assignment where I had been shooting for three separate projects and with multiple cameras. Once the images were uploaded I used the star rating system in Bridge to tag each image to its respective project, using 1 star for project A, 2 stars for project B, and 3 stars for project C. I then used the *View > Sort > By Rating* option to arrange the images by project.

Adding a star rating in Bridge is simply a matter of using the Ctrl/⌘ key with the relevant number key, i.e. 1 for one star, 2 for two stars, and so on up to five stars. Alternatively, use the Ctrl/⌘ key with the "." or "," keys to increase or decrease ratings respectively.

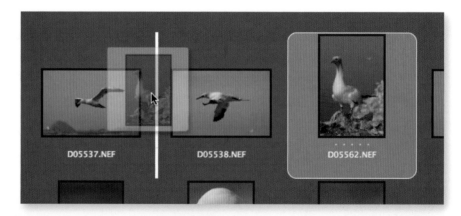

By clicking and dragging an image in the Bridge viewer you can move its position in the Thumbnail previews, a very natural way of organizing files.

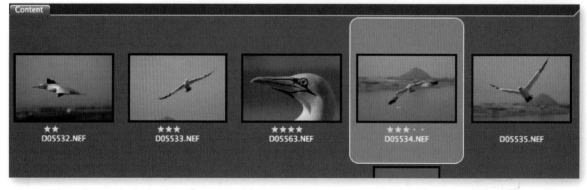

To apply a star rating, select a file and press Ctrl/⌘+1 to 5. Remember, you can enlarge the preview pane if you want a closer look before making your judgement.

Star ratings are a tried and tested system. The figures on the right are running totals of the number of files reaching each level.

Bridge also has a labeling system that can be used in much the same way. The labeling option uses colored labels to identify groups of images. Labels are applied by using the Ctrl/⌘ key with the numbers keys between 6 and 9, or

via the Label menu option. To show how this might work in practice, let's take another example. Say I'm sorting a batch of images into two separate groups, one for my main picture agency and one for my secondary agency. I can label all the images for the first group with a red label, and the others with a yellow label. I can then sort images (*View > Sort*) by label ready for shipping.

Renaming files

Once satisfied that the remaining images are "keepers" you may decide to rename the camera-generated image title. I use a simple numeric value, with each image having a suffix that determines whether it is a RAW file or a TIFF file, together with a five-digit number. The number of each new image is simply one higher than its predecessor. The RAW and TIFF files of the same image share the same numeric number. For example, if the RAW file is named D03115, then the TIFF file will be named P03115. This renaming I do via a Batch Rename process in Bridge.

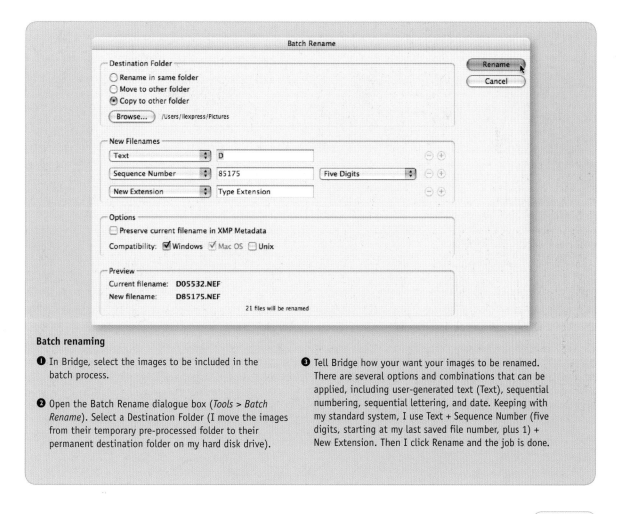

Batch renaming

❶ In Bridge, select the images to be included in the batch process.

❷ Open the Batch Rename dialogue box (*Tools > Batch Rename*). Select a Destination Folder (I move the images from their temporary pre-processed folder to their permanent destination folder on my hard disk drive).

❸ Tell Bridge how your want your images to be renamed. There are several options and combinations that can be applied, including user-generated text (Text), sequential numbering, sequential lettering, and date. Keeping with my standard system, I use Text + Sequence Number (five digits, starting at my last saved file number, plus 1) + New Extension. Then I click Rename and the job is done.

Adding Metadata and Keywords

Metadata is simply information about an image that is stored or embedded within that image. It is what helps us to catalog and retrieve image files effectively. The concept of metadata is nothing new—we have used it for decades. Remember, for instance, going to the library as a child and watching the librarian flick through a card index looking for the location of your favorite Dr Seuss book? Well, essentially, that librarian was using metadata.

Digital cameras automatically embed metadata into an image file, recording information such as the time and date, exposure settings used, lens data, flash information, and other shooting details. Once a file is uploaded, Photoshop embeds additional information, such as the file name and format, color mode, size, etc. All of this information can be further added to with additional user-generated information, such as an image caption, title, and copyright details.

In Bridge, metadata is shown in the Metadata panel which, by default, appears on the right side of the workspace (you can customize this by dragging the Metadata tab elsewhere, or using the numbered preset buttons at the bottom right of the window). The panel is split into three sections. At the top is the Photoshop-generated information (File Properties) and at the bottom is that generated by the camera, referred to as Camera Data, or EXIF. In the middle is a section called IPTC Core. In this section you can manually add details about the image by clicking on the pen icon to the right of the panel. This opens a text box for all options into which you can type the relevant details.

Of course, many images will use the same metadata and adding it over and again to individual files would become tedious. For example, I add my name, contact details, and copyright status to all my images, and I can assure you I don't do it one at a time. Fortunately, there are better ways. Still within Bridge you can add metadata to multiple files by selecting all the files you want to add it to. Then click on the field you want to amend and type in the relevant detail, e.g. your name. Then press Enter and the metadata will be added to all selected files.

Each frame—especially if they are Raw files—carries extensive metadata which can be viewed alongside the image in Bridge's metadata pane.

The metadata is divided into sections. Enter your copyright details into the IPTC Core sub-section, or look at the camera settings in the EXIF section.

Keywording

Keywords help to sort and filter images during retrieval and can be appended to the keywords field in the same way as other metadata. I have several keyword templates saved including a generic template (that includes my name, company name, etc.), as well as some more specific templates (one for wildlife images, a template for images of elephants, one for lions, and so on). Although these templates have taken time to build, doing so has saved me a lot of time in the long run. Once I have appended all the relevant keyword templates to selected images, I add one-off keywords to individual images as necessary.

Keywords are arranged in hierarchical structures, so Queens and Brooklyn would be subsets of New York, which in turn could be a subset of New York (state).

Retrieving files

Any retrieval system is only as good as the data it has to work with, so it's important that the metadata is accurate and comprehensive. Bridge's retrieval engine operates via the *Edit > Find* command. Accessing Find will open a dialog box from which you can choose where to look and the search criteria. Several options are available, including searching on Filename, Label, Rating, and, importantly, Metadata. You can also add filters such as contains, does not contain, starts with, and ends with.

Once you have entered the relevant search criteria, click Find and Bridge will search through the selected folders to locate matching images.

Metadata templates

To save even more time and effort, you can create and save a Metadata Template (and since CS3 arrived you don't even have to leave Bridge to do so). This can be use to append standard information to as many files as you like (or to replace it).

❶ Click *Tools > Create Metadata Template*, which can then be appended to multiple files in Bridge.

❷ Give your template a name which explains what metadata is included.

❸ Add the relevant, generic detail to each of the applicable text boxes (e.g. name, address, contact details, copyright notice, etc.), then press Save.

❹ To apply a template to a large batch of files, click *Tools > Append Metadata* and choose your new template from the options. Any blank metadata spaces in the selected files will be filled from your template. (The other option, *Replace Metadata*, uses the template regardless of whether the frame has individual data, so should be used with caution).

The true benefit of metadata lies in the ability to search. Bridge's search tool allows you to filter using multiple criteria, so this search finds pictures with the keyword "flight" which have more than three stars.

TIP

Collections
If you choose to save the search as a collection, you can then edit the files' ratings. When you reopen the collection, Bridge will update the files displayed based on the new metadata.

The Photoshop workspace

Familiarizing yourself with Photoshop's interface is only the first step. Once you're up to speed with the basics, it's easy to start customizing things to suit you.

You can think of the Photoshop workspace in terms of an office desk, with a tabletop and several items, some always useful, others less so, hidden away in various drawers and cabinets. And, just like your desk, the tidier and more organized it is, the easier it becomes to find what you need when you need to get the job done quickly and with the minimum of stress. Similarly, because we all work differently, how you organize the workspace is, to a certain extent, down to you. So here are some ideas to make Photoshop life easier.

When you first open Photoshop, you are presented with a screen layout similar to that shown below. Along

Tool Options Bar
This bar reflects the individual settings of the tool selected from the main Toolbox.

Histogram palette
The Histogram palette has been docked against the side of the screen.

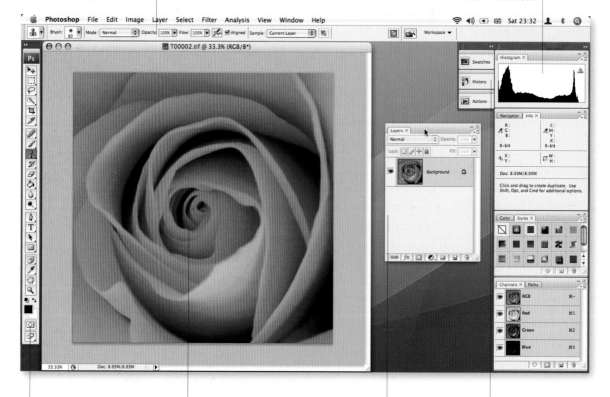

Toolbox
These tools give you the power to manipulate your image in different ways, changing the appearance of the cursor accordingly.

Image
The main image you are presently working on.

Layers palette
The Layers palette has been dragged away from the side of the screen so has become undocked.

Image
Since Photoshop CS3 it has been possible to minimize a group of docked palettes using the button at the top right of the column.

the top of the screen is the main menu bar. Options that are unavailable until an image file is open are grayed out. Down the left side of the screen is the main tool bar (see Photoshop tools, page 46). Clicking in the top bar (above the Adobe online icon) and dragging with the mouse will reposition the tool bar. The background is your main computer desktop and it is advisable for this to be uncluttered and set to a plain, neutral gray.

Image document window

When you open an image it is displayed in an image document window. This is the area in which you do all your work, so you will want to position this somewhere where your view isn't obstructed by the other tools—it is especially wise to avoid obstructing the scroll bars.

Duplicate image document windows

When you are working on an image it is often helpful to be able to view it at different scales. For example, when cloning you might want to work on the file viewed at, say, 300% while seeing the effects of cloning on the image at print size. CS2 enables you to open multiple, duplicate image document windows via the main menu (*Window > Arrange > New Window for* [document name]).

Any changes made to the main or duplicate image(s) are copied across all windows, so it is possible to see the effects of your actions at different scales. Also, scrolling and resizing of the image can be synchronized across all duplicate windows by pressing Shift while performing the scroll or resizing.

TIP

To quickly and easily arrange duplicate image document windows, use the Window > Arrange *option in the main menu. Document windows can be arranged as a cascade (one in front of another), or tiled horizontally or vertically.*

TIP

Title bar
If you are working on a Mac, then along the top bar you may find a proxy image icon, next to the filename. ⌘ + click on this icon to reveal the location of the image file. A neat option available with the proxy image icon is the ability to move the file to a new physical location: ⌥ + click and drag to a new destination.

Information displays

There are more information displays along the bottom of the window. At the far left is the current scaling percentage. You can type over this figure with a value between 0.9 and 3200% to change the scaling. The right side display is the Preview box, which shows whatever information is selected in the fly-out menu.

If you click on the Preview box, a display will appear showing the size and position at which the image will print using the current page setup settings. This is a useful guide if you regularly print images.

Alt/⌥ + clicking on the Preview box will reveal an information box displaying size and resolution information, while Ctrl/⌘ + clicking on the Preview box will display tiling information.

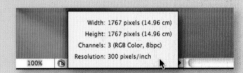

STATUS DISPLAY OPTIONS	DESCRIPTION
Document sizes	Shows the file size for the flattened image (first figure) and the layered image (second figure). If no layers are present these two figures will be the same.
Document profile	Indicates the current color profile assigned to the image.
Document dimensions	Shows the document's actual dimensions and resolution.
Scratch sizes	Refers to memory usage. The first figure shows the amount of RAM used, the second figure the amount of RAM currently available to Photoshop.
Efficiency	Indicates the level of efficiency at which Photoshop is operating. The higher the percentile value, the more efficient the software.
Timing	Marks the length of time taken to complete an operation. Timing starts over when a new tool is selected.
Current tool	Identifies the currently selected tool.

Palettes

Photoshop uses palettes to provide information on various workflow functions, such as Layers, Channels, Paths, History, and Actions. Typically, palettes are hidden until requested from the Window menu option. Once visible, palette size and position can be easily changed to suit your desktop. When using a two-screen setup, it is often useful to position all open palettes on the second screen, leaving the main screen clear for the image document window.

If there are certain palettes that you continually refer to it's possible to lock them together (dock them), making it easier to resize them when necessary. To dock palettes, first position them one above the other. Then drag the tab from the lower palette onto the bottom edge of the upper palette—the positioning needs to be precise. As the palettes dock, the bottom edge of the upper palette will change to a double bar. Release the mouse and the palettes will be docked together.

You will notice that some palettes are grouped with others. For example, the Navigator and Histogram palettes are grouped. Because I refer to these two palettes often, I prefer them to be separate. To separate grouped palettes, simply click on the relevant palette tab and drag it outside of the palette box.

Once you have a preferred workspace design, you can save it (*Window > Workspace > Save Workspace*) so that it appears in the *Workspace* menu listing. Multiple workspace setups can be saved for different workflows, making it easy to switch between one workspace setup and another.

Drag the Histogram palette away from the others to ungroup it. It can then be dragged into another group or screen edge, or dropped anywhere else on the screen. To return it, drag it back.

You can arrange the a palette within the stack by dragging it left or right.

Palette icons

New to CS3 are flexible palette icons. If you choose to use the "fast-forward" style button at the top right of any one column of palettes to reduce it to icons, you can adjust their size even further by dragging the side of the column. You can then temporarily open any palette you need simply by clicking on its icon.

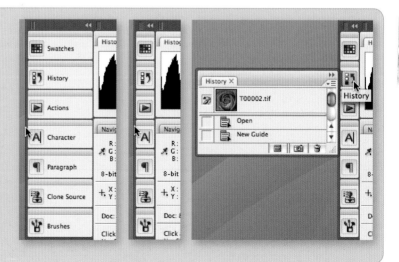

Some useful palettes

There are some palettes that you will use much of the time, such as the Layers palette and History palette. Of the others, some will prove more useful than others. I have described briefly below some of the palettes I refer to frequently.

Navigator palette
The Navigator palette enables you to zoom in and out and scroll around an image more quickly than by using the Zoom and Hand tools. To scroll, simply click and drag the red box. Sliding the scaling arrow left decreases the scale, sliding it right increases the scale. Clicking on the little mountain icon reduces scale in increments; clicking on the large mountain icon increases scale in increments.

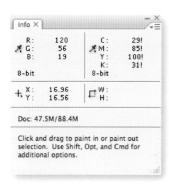

Info palette
The Info palette displays RGB and CMYK color information and coordinates for individual pixels. When editing in RGB mode, any colors that fall outside of the CMYK gamut are identified by an exclamation mark next to the CMYK value, making it easy to assess how image adjustments will affect print color quality.

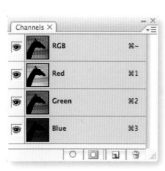

Channels palette
Individual channels are easily selectable with the Channels palette open.

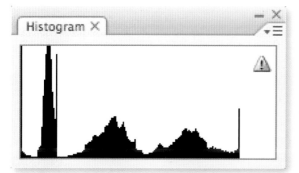

Histogram palette
The histogram is an essential tool for assessing tonality (see The Histogram and Levels, page 108). I use it extensively when making Levels adjustments in particular. Having the Histogram palette open allows you to see dynamically the effects of any changes you make.

TIP

All Photoshop palettes can be accessed by going to the Window menu option of the main menu bar.

Using rulers, guides, and grids

When selected (*View > Rulers*), vertical and horizontal rulers appear along the top and left side of the document window. A grid can be displayed over the image (*View > Show > Grid*) to help with object alignment and composition, for example when cropping. The grid format can be adjusted via the Preferences menu (*Photoshop > Preferences > Guides, Grid & Slices*). The default grid color is medium gray, which can make it difficult to distinguish, and I recommend changing to a more vivid color, such as red. Grid spacing and sub-division as well as line type can also be adjusted.

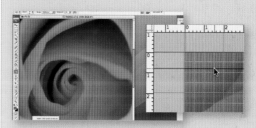

For more precise alignment, Guides can be drawn in the document window. Guides can be added via the menu (*View > New Guides*) but it is far easier to simply drag a new guide from the ruler bar. Click on the ruler bar and drag the guide across or down until it is positioned as desired. To move a guide to a new position, select the Move tool and drag the guide to the desired location. Once correctly positioned, guides can be locked in place (*View > Lock Guide*).

Photoshop tools and the Toolbox

The core of Photoshop's adaptability is the Toolbox, which enables you to switch between the cursor's many possible behaviors. Get to know it and you're well on your way to conquering the whole program.

By default, the Tools palette is located on the left side of the Photoshop workspace. It is made up of icons that relate to a specific tool type. Not all of the icons are immediately visible, as some are hidden. Hidden tools can be found by clicking on tool icons that display a small, black arrow in the bottom right corner.

To select a tool, click the relevant icon. The cursor will change appropriately and that tool's individual options will appear in the Tool Options bar at the top of the workspace. Each tool has also a keyboard shortcut, which is noted in the Tools palette shown opposite. Pressing the keyboard shortcut alone will select the relevant, visible icon. Press and hold the Shift key simultaneously with the shortcut key to access hidden icons that share a keyboard shortcut. For example, to switch between the Brush, Pencil, and Color Replacement tools, hold the Shift key and press B until the required icon is displayed.

Certain tools are unavailable under some circumstances. When this happens, click in the image document window for an explanation. For example, the Move tool is unavailable when the active image is in 32-bit mode, so an explanation dialog will be displayed.

GROUP 1
Move tool
The Move tool is used for dragging and dropping layers or selections between image windows or even between different software applications; to move the contents of a selection or layer within a layer; to select a layer; apply a transform operation to a layer; align or distribute layers; or to copy and move a selection (in conjunction with the Alt/⌥ key).

> **TIP**
>
> *You can change the Shift key/keyboard shortcut toggle option to a straight toggle option by changing the relevant preference in the Photoshop menu (In* Preferences > General, *deselect the Use Shift Key for Tool Switch option).*

Selection tools
Often it is preferable to adjust only selected image pixels, rather than the whole image. Photoshop provides three main selection tools: Marquee, Lasso, and Quick Selection (a new sister to the classic Magic Wand). Selecting an individual pixel or group of pixels is, in principle, much the same as highlighting text in a Word document. And, just as changes can be made to highlighted text without affecting the rest of the type, alterations can be made to selected pixels without affecting the rest of the image (for more on making selections see page 154).

Crop tool
Used for cropping images manually or to predetermined sizes (crop presets) or proportions (width, height, resolution). See Cropping, page 96.

Slice tool
The Slice tools are used in web design and divide an image into rectangular sections that can then be optimized individually for web use.

Adobe online link
Click here to start your browser and go to the Adobe website.

Move tool (V)

Rectangular Marquee tool (M) (also Elliptical, Single Line Horizontal & Vertical Marquees)

Lasso tool (L) (also Polygonal Lasso and Magnetic Lasso)

Quick Selection tool (W) (also Magic Wand tool)

Crop tool (C)

Slice tool (C) (also Slice Select tool)

Retro chic
Although the new CS3 single-column toolbar is actually more space efficient, you can return to the old two-column design if you prefer. Dock the toolbar against the side and click on the expand/ collapse column button.

Spot Healing Brush tool (J) (also Healing Brush tool, Patch tool, and Red Eye tool)

Brush tool (B) (also Pencil tool, Color Replacement tool)

Clone Stamp tool (S) (also Pattern Stamp tool)

History Brush tool (Y) (also Art History Brush tool)

Eraser tool (E) (also Background Eraser tool, Magic Eraser tool)

Paint Bucket tool (G) (also Gradient tool)

Blur tool (R) (also Sharpen tool, Smudge tool)

Burn tool (O) (also Dodge tool, Sponge tool)

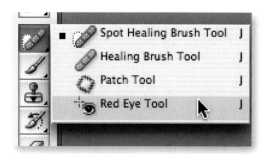

Pen tool (P) (also Freeform Pen tool, Add Anchor Point tool, Delete Anchor Point tool, Convert Point tool)

Horizontal Type tool (T) (also Vertical Type tool, Horizontal and Vertical Type Mask tools)

Path Selection tool (A) (also Direct Selection tool)

Rectangle tool (U) (also Rounded Rectangle tool, Ellipse tool, Polygon tool, Line tool, Custom Shape tool)

Notes tool (N) (also Audio Annotation tool)

Eyedropper tool (I) (also Color Sampler tool, Ruler tool, Count tool)

Hand tool (H)

Zoom tool (Z)

As the labeled Toolbar shows, there are more tools than icons. To access the hidden tools, click and hold an icon to open a flyout menu. All the icons with a black arrow in the lower right corner have alternative options.

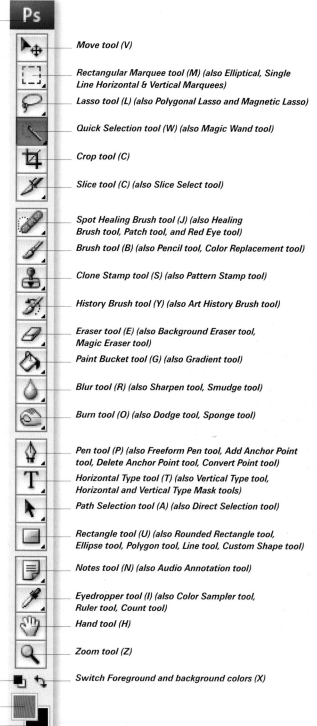

Revert to default foreground and background colors (D)   **Switch Foreground and background colors (X)**

Foreground color

Background color

Edit in Quick Mask mode (Q)

Change Screen mode (F)

GROUP 2

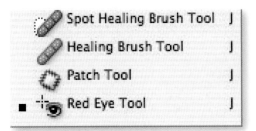

Spot Healing Brush, Healing Brush, and Patch tools

The Spot Healing Brush, Healing Brush, and Patch tools are all used to clone areas from an image and blend the texture from one area with the color and luminosity of another. The Healing Brush and Patch tools work in a similar way, although the Patch tool uses selections (see selections, page 154). The Spot Healing brush requires no source point (see page 150).

Red Eye tool

The Red Eye tool repairs the effects of direct flash in portrait photography, which can cause the eyes of the subject to appear red due to light reflecting directly off the retina (see page 171).

Clone Stamp/Pattern Stamp tools

The Clone Stamp is used extensively in retouching and repairing images. It works by copying pixels from one part of an image (right-click while holding down the Alt/⌥ key) and painting them in another (right-click/right-click and drag). Pixels can be copied (sampled) from the same image or from a separate image or image layer. Although the tool works without it, there is a Clone Source palette to help you select and switch between source areas (see page 149).

The Pattern Stamp operates in the same way except that the sampled pixels are a predefined pattern selected from the Clone Stamp tool's Options bar.

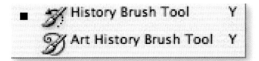

Color Replacement tool

The Color Replacement tool is used to colorize an area of the image with a color sample.

Brush tool

The Brush tool is used to paint areas of an image with a chosen color, much like painting with a paintbrush or airbrush. Brush size, mode, opacity, and flow can all be selected or adjusted via the Brush tool's Options bar.

Pencil tool

The Pencil tool can be used to draw hard-edged, aliased lines or drawings, much like using a pencil on a sheet of paper. Pencil (brush) size, mode, and opacity can be set via the Pencil tool's Options bar.

History Brush tool

Used simply, the History Brush can be considered an undo tool. However, it has a far more sophisticated use in retouching, and can be used in conjunction with the History palette to paint an area of an image using information from a history state (see page 168 for practical applications of this tool).

Art History Brush tool

Like the History Brush, the Art History Brush samples pixels from a history state. However, when you paint the sampled pixels they are reproduced showing abstract characteristics defined by the brush type chosen in the Art History Brush's Options bar.

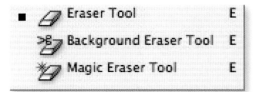

Eraser/Background Eraser/Magic Eraser tools

The three Eraser tools all remove pixels from the image space—just like rubbing out pencil marks with a traditional eraser. The Eraser tool removes pixels and replaces them with the selected background color. The Background Eraser removes pixels and replaces them with a transparent background. The Magic Eraser tool works in a way similar to the Paint Bucket tool but in reverse, deleting pixels of a similar color value to the sampled pixel. Brush type and size, opacity, and flow can all be selected via the Options bar.

Blur/Sharpen/Smudge tools

The Blur and Sharpen tools enable localized blurring or sharpening of pixels. Of the two, the Blur tool is by far the most useful and can be used, for example, to reduce apparent depth of field (see pages 134-137). The Sharpen tool is less useful, as there are better ways to achieve the same result (see Sharpening, page 140). The Smudge tool is used to give the appearance of smearing pixels in a manner similar to mixing paints.

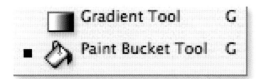

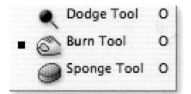

Gradient tool

The Gradient tool is used to add a gradient fill between two selected points on an image. It can be used, for example, to create an increasingly soft edge around a subject for artistic effect. Different predefined gradients are available via the Options bar. It's also possible to create your own custom gradient patterns.

Paint Bucket tool

Imagine buying a tin of paint and pouring it all over a sheet of paper. Well, effectively, that's what the Paint Bucket tool does. Based on a sampled color and Tolerance setting (selected via the Options bar), the Paint Bucket replaces pixels within the sampled value range with either the selected foreground color or a preselected pattern.

Dodge/Burn/Sponge tools

Dodge and Burn are toning techniques drawn straight from the wet darkroom and the days of film, paper, and chemicals. Dodging lightens areas of an image, while burning darkens them. Toning can be applied selectively by choosing shadows, highlights, or midtones in the Options bar. The Sponge tool affects color saturation, increasing or reducing saturation depending on the range selected in the Options bar (see page 120).

GROUP 3

Pen tools

The Pen tools are used to draw pen paths that can be converted into a selection. Standard and freeform pen types are selectable (see page 162).

Type tool

The Type tool enables you to add editable text to an image, either line by line or via a text box. Format options, such as font, pitch, and color, are available in the Options bar.

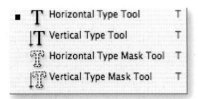

Path and Direct Selection tools

These tools allow you to manipulate the graphical structure of shapes, much like their equivalents in the drawing program Illustrator.

Shape tools

Shapes of varying forms, including regular and custom shapes, can be applied to an image in the form of a filled layer with a vector mask, a solid fill, or a path outline using the Shape tool.

GROUP 4

Annotation tools

Use the Annotation tools to add audio or text notes to Photoshop files.

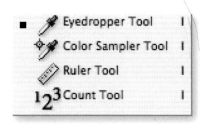

Eyedropper/Color Sampler tools

You can choose the foreground and background colors by sampling the color value of image pixels using the Eyedropper tool. With the Eyedropper tool selected, click on a pixel in an image window and that pixel's color is automatically selected as the foreground color. To select the background color, hold down the Alt/⌥ key while selecting the sample pixel. The Color Sampler tool provides pixel value information via the Info palette. It can be used in conjunction with the Curves tool to gain precise control over color.

Measure tool

The Measure tool measures distances and angles in the picture space. Perhaps one of its most useful functions is when used in conjunction with the *Image > Rotate* command (see Straightening, page 94).

Hand tool

The Hand tool enables scrolling of an image within the image window by clicking and dragging with the mouse.

Zoom tool

The Zoom tool magnifies or scales down the image as it appears on screen between 0.36% and 3200%. It doesn't affect the pixels of the image, and 100% is one image pixel to one monitor pixel—it is not based on print size.

Foreground/Background Color

The Foreground and Background Color boxes identify the currently selected colors. Clicking on either box displays a Color Picker dialog from which new colors can be selected. Foreground and background colors can also be set via the Color palette (see Palettes, page 44).

GROUP 5

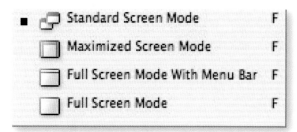

Selection Mode/Quick Mask

Use these buttons to switch between standard selection mode and Quick Mask mode.

Screen display modes

The Screen Mode button enables you to switch quickly between different screen layouts. The standard layout displays images in document windows, with all menu bars visible and other document windows visible. In Maximized Screen mode, the active document window is displayed full screen surrounded by a medium gray border (depending on the zoom). The desktop is hidden. In Full Screen mode, the active image is shown full screen with the main menu bar available or hidden, depending on your choice. The desktop is hidden in both Full Screen modes, though the Mac's Dock is only hidden by the former.

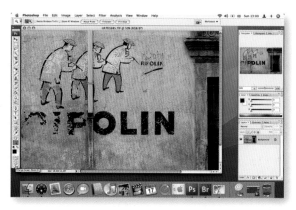

Standard Screen Mode

Full Screen Mode without menu bar

Tool Options Bar

Beneath the main menu bar is the Tool Options bar. Although this can be moved, it is advisable to leave it in its default position. The Tool Options bar shows the individual settings for each of the Photoshop tools. As you switch between tools you will notice that the settings options change relative to the selected tool. One useful feature of the Tool Options bar is the palette docking on the far right. Frequently used palettes can be docked here, making them easily accessible when needed. This particularly suits users with a small screen as it prevents palettes taking up valuable working space.

You can save tool configurations, which are stored in the Tool Presets palette. This is a particularly useful feature when certain tool configurations are used repeatedly—for example, preset crop sizes and resolutions, Brush or Clone Stamp settings, or type settings. Once a tool configuration is saved, it is a simple task to open the Tool Presets palette (which is best kept as part of your personalized workspace setup) and select the desired tool, making workflow more efficient.

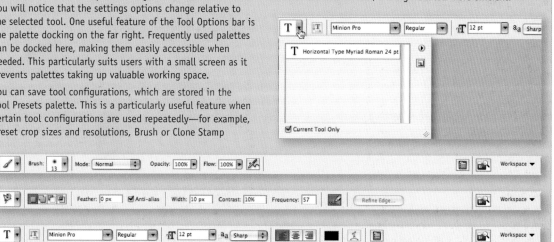

Actions

Sometimes you need to be freed from mindless, repetitive tasks in order to concentrate on the creative ones. Actions, like macros in other programs, record steps which can be repeated over and over again.

There are times when you need to make the same adjustments over and again to several different image files. To do this case by case would be time consuming and tedious in the extreme. The solution is to record a Photoshop Action that can be repeated on other images (or shared with other users). For example, when I process image files for use on my website, in all cases I have to resize the image within certain parameters and sharpen the image to overcome the loss of quality, before saving as a JPEG file. I can record this sequence of events as an Action and assign a function key to repeat the action, making it quicker and less laborious to complete the process.

There are certain limitations when recording Actions. For example, none of the painting tools can be recorded within an Action and, because many Photoshop steps require the image to be in RGB color mode, it is important to make sure any image for which an Action is played is in RGB mode. Also, it is important to make each step within an Action as unambiguous as possible. For example, if including Layers, make sure that naming the Layer is included as a step. Names should also be meaningful and not left to generic Photoshop-generated names. It is also advisable to create Layers (and similar Photoshop steps) from the main menu bar.

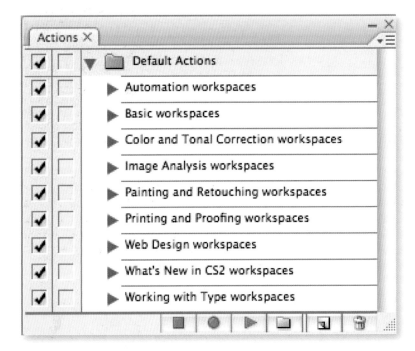

The Actions palette is organized into folders in which you can group your actions. The tools at the bottom are reminiscent of those on a cassette recorder and work in a similar way.

Adding menu items sometimes has to be achieved via the Insert Menu Items option. Click on the flyout button beneath the top-right close icon in the palette.

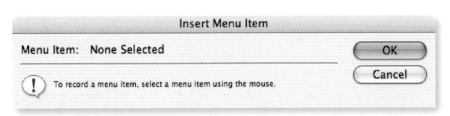

Recording Photoshop Actions

❶ Open the Actions palette (*Window > Actions*) and click on the small right arrow in the top right corner to open the flyout menu.

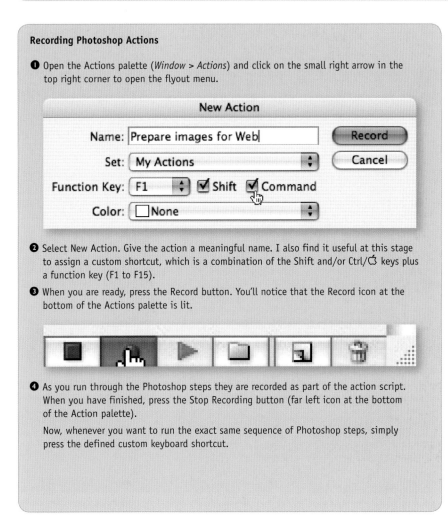

❷ Select New Action. Give the action a meaningful name. I also find it useful at this stage to assign a custom shortcut, which is a combination of the Shift and/or Ctrl/⌘ keys plus a function key (F1 to F15).

❸ When you are ready, press the Record button. You'll notice that the Record icon at the bottom of the Actions palette is lit.

❹ As you run through the Photoshop steps they are recorded as part of the action script. When you have finished, press the Stop Recording button (far left icon at the bottom of the Action palette).

Now, whenever you want to run the exact same sequence of Photoshop steps, simply press the defined custom keyboard shortcut.

New Action Sets

Action Sets categorize actions into groups. You can create a new Action Set from the Actions palette flyout menu (*Window > Actions > New Action Set*). Give the set a meaningful name and save relevant new actions under this set. This is a useful way of managing your Actions, as related actions can be grouped under a single heading, much like placing related folders into a single cabinet drawer.

Menu items

Some other Photoshop steps can only be included in an Action as a menu item, which can be inserted into an Action as you are recording. For example, the Zoom tool and Zoom options in the View menu can only be included in an Action as a Menu Item.

To insert a Menu Item, open the flyout menu from the Actions palette and select Insert Menu Item. Initially a dialog box will open, warning None Selected. Go to the relevant menu option and select the menu item you want to insert. The selected menu item will appear in the dialog box. Press OK to accept the insertion.

Adding alert dialogs

You can force Photoshop when playing an Action to display an alert dialog at any stage. For example, you might use this to remind you to convert any non-RGB files to RGB mode. To add an alert dialog, select Insert Stop from the Actions palette flyout menu. Enter the alert text you want to appear when the Action is played and select OK to add the Stop to the Action.

Record Stop

Message:

Hello

☐ Allow Continue

OK   Cancel

Actions and Batch Processing

When you want to play an Action, open the image and press the Play button on the Actions palette (the arrow icon third from right along the bottom of the palette). Photoshop will then run through each step of the Action. Alternatively, if you have assigned a function key to the Action, simply press this key to play.

You will notice that the Actions palette already contains a set of prerecorded (default) Actions. To see what these do, play them using a test image.

Batch processing

Actions can be processed as a batch using the Batch menu option, which can be accessed from the main menu (*File > Automate > Batch*). When the Batch dialog box is displayed, select the relevant Action Set and Action using the drop-down menus in the Play settings.

Then select a source (where the image is coming from) and destination (where the image is going to end up). The source can be all images currently open in Photoshop, selected image files from Bridge, or a specified

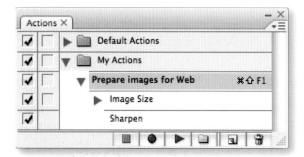

The Action's palette hierarchy is simple: Folder > Action > Step. You can record extra steps without starting again by pressing record and stop.

Your collection of actions can be used to full effect with the Batch tool. This complicated and relatively unfriendly dialog quickly becomes your friend once you overcome those first impressions though. The trick is understanding the language, for example, that "Override Action "Open" Commands" won't ignore any Open commands in the action, but will choose the Source folder you specify in this dialog instead.

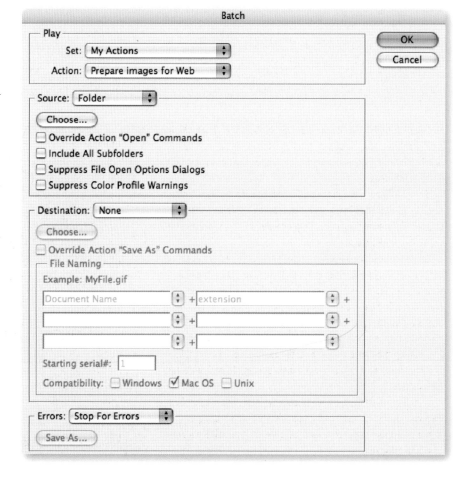

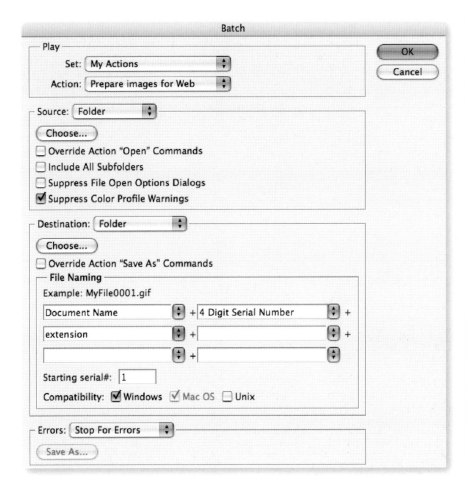

Batch

Play
Set: My Actions
Action: Prepare images for Web

Source: Folder
Choose...
☐ Override Action "Open" Commands
☐ Include All Subfolders
☐ Suppress File Open Options Dialogs
☑ Suppress Color Profile Warnings

Destination: Folder
Choose...
☐ Override Action "Save As" Commands
File Naming
Example: MyFile0001.gif

Document Name + 4 Digit Serial Number +
extension + +
+ +
Starting serial#: 1
Compatibility: ☑ Windows ☑ Mac OS ☐ Unix

Errors: Stop For Errors
Save As...

OK
Cancel

The Batch tool includes a very flexible file renaming facility, which can use not only the original document name, but append additional information and, if you choose, the file extension (extensions are not required by Mac OS but Windows relies on them).

TIP

As a precaution I advise saving an image file before executing an Action. If the result of the Action is not as intended you can revert to the saved file.

folder (including or excluding its subfolders, depending on whether the Include All Subfolders is checked or unchecked) selected via the Choose button in the Source settings.

If you want to stop color profile warnings being displayed (useful if you want to do something else while the batch process is running) then check the Suppress Color Profile Warnings box.

If you have included a Save or Save As command within an Action, Photoshop will perform the command unless you check the Override Action "Save As" Commands checkbox. The reason you may want to use this override option is in case the destination folder used in the Action no longer exists, which will cause the action to fail. As Photoshop provides an option for saving to a designated source folder in the destination settings, I advise using this option.

Finally, select a file name option in the File Naming settings. This can be the original image file name or a new naming protocol chosen from the various options available.

Creating a Droplet

Photoshop Actions can be saved as a Droplet (a self-contained mini-application) and stored on the main desktop (the recommended place) or on a specified HDD. Droplets make it very quick and easy to apply Actions to an image or selection of images by simply dragging and dropping the images over the droplet. To create a Droplet, select *Create Droplet* from the *File > Automate* menu. Choose a location to save the droplet (I recommend keeping droplets in a specific Droplets folder on the main desktop) and give it a meaningful name. Choose an Action Set and/or Action in the Play settings, and a destination. Choose the naming protocol and press OK to create the Droplet.

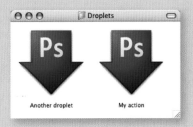

Layers

Layers are what makes using Photoshop a breeze, because with them comes what's known as "non-destructive editing." This is the ability to return to any change you've made without having to start again from the beginning.

If you edit directly on an image file, every change you make irreversibly alters the pixel data in what is known as destructive editing. To put it into perspective, let me describe it another way: you're sitting in your living room, which has white painted walls, when you wonder how the room would look painted blue. You buy a tin of paint and proceed to paint the walls blue. You sit back down to admire your handiwork and quickly realize that you preferred the original white. So you go about trying to paint over your mistake and, however hard you try and however long it takes, you just can't get the wall color back to exactly how it was. This is destructive editing.

Layer menu

MENU OPTION	DESCRIPTION	MENU OPTION	DESCRIPTION
New	Creates a new layer or layer group	Rasterize	Converts a Type layer to a work path or shape layer
Duplicate Layer	Creates a duplicate layer or group of layers, or duplicates of multiple layers or groups, of layer(s) or group(s) selected in the Layers palette	New Layer Based Slice	Creates a new layer-based slice
Delete	Deletes a layer, selected layers, or layers group(s)	Group Layers	Groups layers selected in the Layers palette
Layer Properties	Option to change a Layer name and/or add or change a Layer color code	Ungroup Layers	Ungroups one or multiple Layer Groups selected in the Layers palette
Layer Style	Applies layer effects	Hide Layers	Hides one or multiple layers or layer groups selected in the Layers palette
New Fill Layer	Creates a new fill layer (Solid color, Gradient, or Pattern)	Arrange	Enables repositioning of Layers within a stack
New Adjustment Layer	Creates a new adjustment layer (Levels, Curves, Color Balance, Brightness/Contrast, Hue/Saturation, Selective Color, Channel Mixer, Gradient Map, Photo Filter, Invert, Threshold, or Posterize)	Align	Enables exact alignment of Layers
		Distribute	Distributes linked Layers by edge or center
Change Layer Content	Enables changes to be made to the content of a Layer	Lock All Layers in Group	Locks all layers in a Layer Group
Layer Content Options	Enables selection of layer content options	Link Layers	Links layers selected in the Layers palette
		Select Linked Layers	Selects all linked Layers
Layer Mask	Creates a Layer Mask—see page 62	Merge Layers	Merges all layers into a single layer
Vector Mask	Creates a Vector Mask—see page 62	Merge Visible	Merges only visible layers into a single group, ignoring hidden layers
Create Clipping Mask	Creates a Clipping Mask—see page 162		
Smart Objects	See Smart Objects—see page 64	Flatten Image	Flattens layers into a single layer
Type	All type is added via a Type layer	Matting	Defringes, removes black or white matting

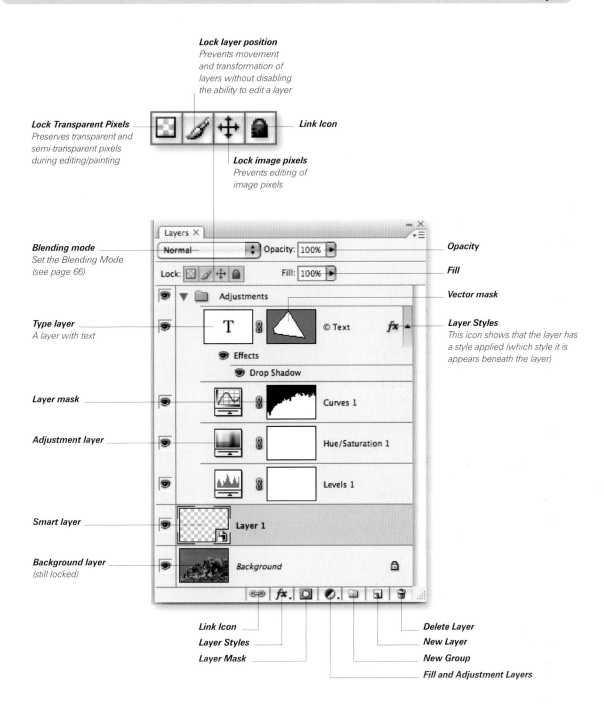

Lock layer position
Prevents movement and transformation of layers without disabling the ability to edit a layer

Lock Transparent Pixels
Preserves transparent and semi-transparent pixels during editing/painting

Link Icon

Lock image pixels
Prevents editing of image pixels

Blending mode
Set the Blending Mode (see page 66)

Opacity

Fill

Type layer
A layer with text

Vector mask

Layer Styles
This icon shows that the layer has a style applied (which style it is appears beneath the layer)

Layer mask

Adjustment layer

Smart layer

Background layer
(still locked)

Link Icon

Layer Styles

Layer Mask

Delete Layer

New Layer

New Group

Fill and Adjustment Layers

Fortunately, there is another way of editing in Photoshop that doesn't impact the original data in such a destructive manner—layers. Layers are instruction sets that contain editing instructions that can be applied to an image without changing the original data. Going back to my earlier analogy, rather than painting the walls blue, a plastic sheet is placed over the walls and the sheet painted blue. When it becomes clear that blue isn't the preferred color, the plastic sheet is taken down and discarded. The original wall color remains completely unaffected by the blue experiment. This is how layers work in Photoshop.

Layers are integral to Photoshop, so study these pages in detail to become acquainted with their functions.

Managing layers

Layers are the foundation that Photoshop is built on, and there are plenty of tools for keeping them organized, or reorganizing them to suit your particular purposes.

Layers have become an important aspect of working efficiently in Photoshop to the extent that a single image can contain many layers of various different types. Photoshop provides effective management of Layers through Layer Groups and Layer Properties.

To create a new Layer Group, click on the Create New Group icon at the bottom of the Layers palette, or select *New > Group* from the Layers menu. Using the Create New Group icon will add a new group above the currently selected layer. To add a new group below the currently selected layer, hold down the Ctrl/⌘ key while pressing the Create New Group icon. Once you have created a group you can click and drag with the mouse to add Layers to the Group. Another method of creating a Layer Group is to pre-select the Layers you want to group and hold down the Alt/⌥ key while clicking the Create New Group icon (or select *Layers > New > Group from Layers* from the main menu). This option automatically adds the selected layers to the new group.

Layer groups can be collapsed to hide the individual layers and expanded again when needed. This helps to make viewing and navigation of multiple layers quicker and easier. As with individual layers, groups can be hidden and revealed using the eye icon, and opacity, blending modes, and masks can be applied to whole groups in the same way they are applied to individual layers, although it is still possible to apply them independently to individual layers within a group.

It's also possible to assign a color code to different layers. For example, you could code all Adjustment Layers red and all healing layers blue. To assign a color code, select Layer Properties from the Layers palette flyout menu, enter a name (if applicable) and select a color.

Making layer selections

Hold down the Shift key and click on the first and last layers in the selection to select contiguous layers. Non-contiguous layers are selected by holding down the Ctrl/⌘ key and clicking on each layer to be selected individually.

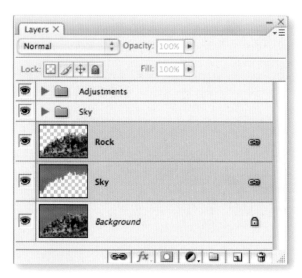

Linked layers
Notice the icon at the right of each linked layer.

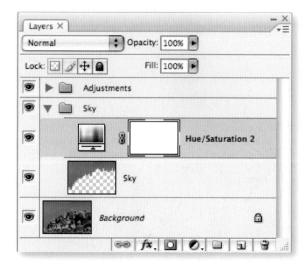

Layer Group
Although these layers have been moved into a separate group, the Hue/Saturation layer is still applied to all layers beneath it, including the Background layer.

Clipping Mask

If you want to create a layer which only applies to the pixels of the layer beneath it, choose *Layers > Create Clipping Path* (or hold Alt/⌥ as you create the layer).

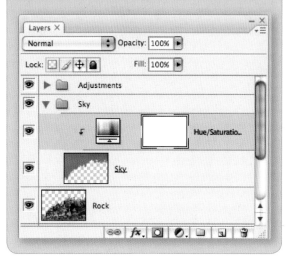

Linking layers

Layers can be linked so that any moves or transforms (for example scaling a layer's contents) are applied to the linked layers as if they were a single layer. Linking doesn't affect the individual nature of the layers, and they retain their own blending and opacity settings. To link layers, first make a selection and then press the Link icon (far left) on the bottom of the Layers palette. Pressing the link icon again will unlink a linked selection.

Duplicating layers
Make a quick copy of a layer by dragging it to the new layer icon.

PALETTE SETTING	DESCRIPTION
Blending mode	Select the blend mode—see page 66
Opacity	Set opacity—see page 67
▾≡	Open flyout menu (beneath close icon in palette)
Lock transparent pixels	Preserves transparent and semi-transparent pixels during editing/painting
Lock image pixels	Prevents editing of image pixels
Lock layer position	Prevents movement and transformation of layers without disabling the ability to edit a layer
Lock all	Locks all options
Fill	Set fill opacity (0–100%)
Type layer	A special vector layer for text
Shape layer	See page 162
Adjustment layer	See page 60
Background layer	The original image file
Layer styles	Style options for Layers
Layer group	Folder icon as described opposite
Linked image layer	Chain link icon appears
Linked layer mask	Black/white thumbnail
Eyeball icon	Hides and reveals Layers/Layer Groups
Color coding	Useful for reference, appears in the palette
Link icon	Applies links
Add layer style icon	At bottom, adds digital effects
Add layer mask icon	See page 61
Create new fill/adjustment layer	See page 60
Create new group	Create folders for layers
Create new layer	Doubles up as duplicate tool
Delete current layer/layer mask/vector mask/effect	Trashcan icon bottom right

Adjustment layers

While standard image layers allow you to add pixel information—for example, something not included in the original image—an adjustment layer allows you to apply an overall change, like a color shift, to the layers below.

O f all the layer types, the one used most frequently by photographers is the Adjustment layer. Image adjustments such as Levels, Curves, Hue/Saturation, and even the new Black and White function can be applied as a layer rather than directly to the image. Even better, in conjunction with a layer mask, adjustments can be targeted precisely to selected areas of an image only—all non-destructively. More on layer masks later.

To create an Adjustment layer, click on the Create new fill or adjustment layer icon (fourth from left) at the bottom of the Layers palette (or select *Layers > New Adjustment Layer* from the main menu bar) and select the type of adjustment you want to apply (Levels, Curves, etc.) You may want to add your own name for the layer.

You can now perform the adjustment in the same way you would if applying the adjustment outside of a layer. Once complete, in the Layers palette you will notice the new layer appear at the top. Remember that layers are hierarchical and will affect all layers below them in the hierarchy.

Here's an experiment to show the power of Adjustment layers. Choose an image and make a duplicate (*File > Image > Duplicate*). Open the original image and perform a Levels

Saving and preserving Layers

Layers are compatible only with certain file types. To preserve Layers when saving a file, save as either a TIFF, Photoshop native (.PSD), or PDF file type.

A Levels adjustment layer is used to give this image more contrast.

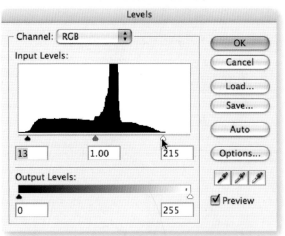

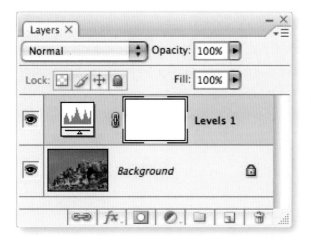

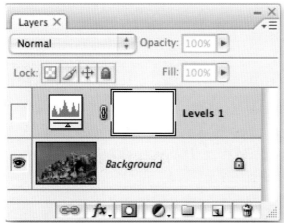

If you switch off the visibility of the Levels layer by clicking on its eye icon, the image is restored to its original, flat state.

adjustment directly to the image, without using layers. Save and close it. Reopen it and open the Levels adjustment dialog box. You will see that the histogram has changed and the black, gray, and white slider arrows have returned to their normal starting points.

Now open the duplicate image and create a Levels Adjustment layer. Recreate the levels adjustment you applied to the first image (it doesn't have to be exact) in the adjustment layer. Save and close the image without flattening it. Reopen it, open the Layers palette and click on the Levels Adjustment layer. The Levels dialog box will be displayed along with the exact changes you made.

If you want to readjust the Levels, simply modify your original settings. And, if you want to see what the image looked like before you made the Levels adjustments, just hide the Levels Adjustment layer.

Another advantage of using adjustment layers is the presence of an active layer mask. This means that adjustment effects can be hidden or revealed by painting or filling the mask with black or white respectively (or applied partially with a gray shade).

Clipping masks

Typically Layers are hierarchical in that they affect all Layers below them. By creating a Clipping Mask between the Adjustment layer and the Layer immediately below, the image adjustment will apply only to that layer. To create a Clipping Mask, select the appropriate Adjustment layer and select Create Clipping Mask from the Layers menu (or hold Alt/⌥ as you click the new adjustment layer button).

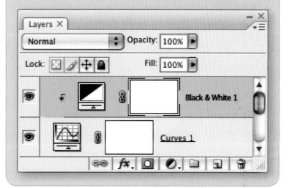

Applying image adjustments

Refer to the individual sections relating to image adjustments for advice on how to use particular Adjustment layers.

Layer Masks

Applying artwork from the layer above, or the tonal shift of an Adjustment layer to everything beneath, can be rather a blunt instrument. Masking restricts the application to your chosen areas.

Layer Masks are used to partially or completely hide or reveal the contents of a layer, making it possible to achieve selective adjustments only to those areas of the image that you want to affect. As the name suggests, Layer Masks don't add or remove pixels, they simply make visible or invisible the effects of the Layer to which they're related. There are two distinct advantages to Masks: first, they enable targeted adjustments; and second, they can be changed at any time to hide or reveal more of the Layer content.

Layer Masks use black and white to determine their effect. A totally black mask hides all Layer content, while a white mask reveals all Layer content. You will notice when you add an Adjustment Layer that a white Layer Mask is automatically appended. Because this mask is white it reveals all the contents of the Adjustment Layer.

However, masks are reversible and a white (revealing) mask can be converted to a black (hiding) mask by selecting *Image > Adjustments > Invert* from the main menu bar.

Layer masks can be applied to any Layer type, not just Adjustment Layers, so long as the layer isn't locked. To add a Layer Mask, click the Add New Mask icon (third from left) at the bottom of the Layers palette. Clicking once will add a white Layer Mask, clicking twice will add a white Vector Mask. To add a black mask (so no part of the layer shows through), hold down Alt/⌥ while clicking the Add New Mask icon. You can also add a Layer Mask from the main menu selecting *Layer > Layer Mask > Reveal All* (white mask) or *Hide All* (black mask).

Perhaps one of the most useful features of Layer Masks is the ability to paint on the mask to hide or reveal selected Layer contents. For example, say you had applied

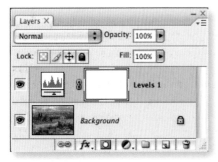

A Levels adjustment layer—as with all other adjustment layers—defaults to a white "show all" mask.

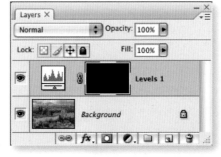

This Levels layer's mask is black, so the layer will have no effect unless some white is painted onto the mask.

TIP

Make sure that the Brush tool blend mode is set to Normal when painting a Layer Mask.

Fine-tuning the effects of masking

When you paint on a mask, if the opacity of the brush tool is set to 100%, then the full contents of the image adjustment is revealed. You can partially hide or reveal layer's contents by setting the opacity of the brush to a lower value.

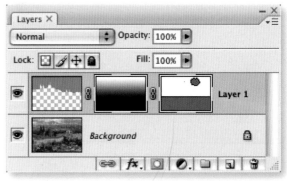

Each layer can have one pixel-based layer mask (with many possible levels of transparency) and one vector mask.

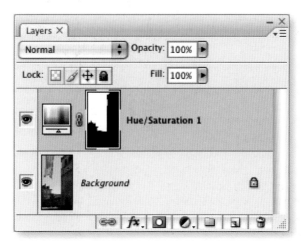

Viewing Layer Masks

To view the Layer Mask, press Alt/⌥ and click on the Layer Mask icon in the Layers palette. The screen will switch to Mask mode. Pressing Shift+Alt/⌥ while clicking on the Layer Mask icon will switch the screen to Rubylith mode (a Quick Mask-type overlay).

The original background image needs a boost to the sky and flag. Select them using the Quick Selection tool.

When you create a new Adjustment layer while a selection is active, a mask is automatically created revealing only the selected area.

The result is that the saturation of the sky and flag can be slightly boosted without affecting any original pixels, or changing the appearance of the image's foreground at all.

Saturation to an image of a landscape scene using a Hue/Saturation Adjustment layer, but you wanted the increase in saturation to apply only to the foreground and not to the blue sky. By selecting the Brush tool and selecting black as the foreground color (black hides layer contents) you could paint the area of sky to hide the effects of the saturation adjustment. If, at a later time, you decided to reverse the effects of the painted mask, you can simply brush over it with a white brush to reverse the effect.

You can delete a Layer Mask by highlighting it in the Layers palette and clicking the Trash icon (lower right corner of the palette). Alternatively, click *Layer > Layer Mask > Delete*. Other options are available via the main menu. You can elect to apply the mask to the layer's pixels before removing it (*Layer > Layer Mask > Apply*) or temporarily disable it (*Layer > Layer Mask > Disable*).

Layer Mask linking

By default, layers and their associated Layer Masks are automatically linked. Sometimes, however, you may want to perform movements or make changes to the layer independent of the Layer Mask. The link can be disabled by selecting the Layer and choosing *Layers > Layer Mask > Unlink* from the main menu.

Smart Objects

One of the biggest problems with pixel-based information is that you can't scale it up without losing information. Smart Objects are the best way to minimize information loss through scaling and rescaling.

For a long time, Photoshop insisted on changing pixels permanently when they were edited. This is very inconvenient if you make a mistake, and as the version numbers have rolled on—CS3 is the tenth version of Photoshop—solutions to this problem have gradually increased, layers themselves being the most obvious. Type layers, too, now remain fully editable even once styling and other effects have been added to the text.

Editing text after it has been typed might not seem too daunting a task for a word processor, but in an image editor, once you typed your words they would be converted into pixels, overwriting those beneath. Layers preserved the pixels beneath, then Type layers made it possible to change the text altogether.

The Smart Objects function brings the same principle to graphics which would otherwise lose information when edited. For example, if you were to scale a "dumb" object down and then up again, it would look grainy because the information lost when reducing wouldn't be available to scale up from. A Smart Object, however, will retain all the original data so it can be scaled and scaled again. An ideal tool when you're compositing for a tricky client (and is there really any other kind?). Just compare the boat in the example here.

While scaling might be the primary advantage of protecting data with the Smart Objects tool—indeed, remembering to convert a layer to a Smart Object should become a key part of your workflow—it is not the only one. You can also apply Filters (see page 182) to smart objects, once again preserving data where otherwise it would have been destroyed.

This image is a composite, with the boat having been added to the layer above the sunset background.

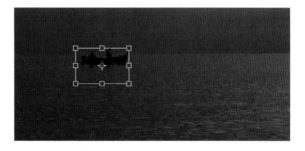

With the boat's layer selected, the Free Transform tool is activated (Ctrl/⌘ +T) and the corner point is dragged inward to reduce the scale of the boat. The green checkmark in the Tool Options bar is clicked on to complete the action.

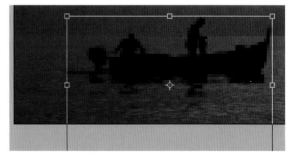

Using the Free Transform tool for a second time, the boat is scaled back up. It is clear that there is significantly less data to work from since all the previous detail was discarded when the previous scaling was accepted.

Vector graphics

Beyond preserving pixel data, Smart Objects can also protect the information in vector shapes like imported Illustrator files. This is less likely to be of use with photographs, but if your work includes graphics for any reason then be sure to make use of it.

When you click OK, the limited pixel data available to Photoshop is used to the best possible effect, which generally results in soft edges and a loss of detail.

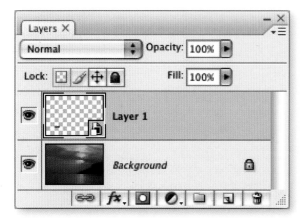

The alternative is to turn the object into a Smart Object as soon as you've imported it (or placed it on a separate layer). Do this by clicking Layer > Smart Objects > Convert to Smart Object.

Now when you scale the object using the Free Transform tool, all the original data is preserved. Here the image has been scaled down and back up again and all the original data is still visible.

Smart Filters

One of the best things about Smart Objects is the Smart Filters feature, which was added in CS3.

❶ Click *Layer > Smart Objects > Convert to Smart Object*.

❷ Now apply a Filter using the Filter menu. This follows the same process as you would with a non-smart layer, however the pixel information is not in jeopardy.

❸ You'll see that your filter appears beneath an inset Smart Filters layer. You may add additional filters to this layer and they will be listed below.

❹ The white box is a mask, just like those that accompany Adjustment Layers (see page 60).

Blending modes

Not only are there many types of layer, but you can change the way they interact, too. Blending modes can be quickly turned to the advantage of the photographer and offer a create alternative to some adjustment layers.

The blending mode determines how multiple layers are mixed. Modes are set via the Blending Mode drop-down menu in the Layers palette (directly below the Layers tab). It's also possible to adjust the opacity of Layers by reducing or increasing the Opacity setting. There are 25 blending modes in the menu and, although you probably won't use them all, their functions are described in detail on pages 70-71.

Using Blending modes to correct exposure

An image can be quickly and easily lightened or darkened simply by changing the Blending mode to Screen (lighten) or Multiply (darken). Corrections to exposure can be managed in this way as if a Curves adjustment had been made.

Normal
Dissolve

Darken
Multiply
Color Burn
Linear Burn
Darker Color

Lighten
Screen
Color Dodge
Linear Dodge (Add)
Lighter Color

Overlay
Soft Light
Hard Light
Vivid Light
Linear Light
Pin Light
Hard Mix

Difference
Exclusion

Hue
Saturation
Color
Luminosity

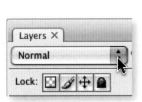

The Blending mode menu is opened via a drop-down menu at the top left of the Layers palette, and applies the choice to the selected layer.

A practical application of Difference blending

You can use the Difference blending mode to analyze variations in two seemingly identical images or layers. For example, to determine whether compressing an image when saving has had any effect on image quality, open the uncompressed image as the background layer and drag and drop the compressed image on top of it, making sure they are aligned. Select the compressed image layer and change the blending mode to Difference. If compression has had no impact on image quality, then the image on screen will be pure black. If image quality has been compromised by the act of compression, any artifacts will show clearly.

Advanced blending techniques

Blending modes are easily applied. However, it's possible to take blending to a whole new level, particularly when working on montages. These advanced blending techniques are described in more detail in Chapter 5.

Blending modes are not an easy concept to understand in the abstract, but that is not to negate their power in image editing. As the table on pages 70-71 demonstrates, they can have remarkably different effects on different shades and colors, but don't let the science put you off. Blending modes can be put to use in any number of ways by photographers, especially when a layer's Opacity slider is used to fine-tune the impact to something more visually palatable.

In the example shown here, an exceedingly dark night shot is given a boost by duplicating the layer and setting the new blending mode to Screen. This mode lightens pixels where those beneath are also light, but ignores the darker ones, so only areas of the image which have a shade other than complete darkness will be affected. The problem is that simply duplicating the layer produces far too strong an effect, which is where the Opacity slider is useful. This isn't necessarily a recommended technique, but it is sometimes a quick alternative to applying adjustment layers.

The final image has more light than the original, but not the excessive amount present in the second image (at which point the layer's opacity was set to 100%).

Opacity or Fill?

You may have noticed that at the top of the Layers palette there are two apparently similar sliders, one logically entitled Opacity and the other slightly more confusingly called Fill. On many occasions they function identically; however, if you have applied a Layer Style to the layer in question, the results will be very different. Opacity affects the whole layer, while Fill only affects the pixel information, so in these two examples (where the moon has been superimposed over a dark background) the former looks generally darker while the latter looks as if it has been lit from behind (as in an eclipse).

Moon layer at 50% Opacity (100% Fill).

Moon layer at 50% Fill (100% Opacity).

Blending Modes comparison

It's impossible to visualize every possible combination of blending modes, but here, two identical layers, the top one rotated by 90°, have been placed on top of one another. Unless otherwise noted, the layers are at 100% Opacity, so where the vertical graduated colors show through it is a result of that blending mode's particular behavior.

Normal

The default mode. Pixels are simply overlaid one on top of another. Adjusting opacity fades the intensity of overlaying pixels using a formula that averages the pixel values of the blend and composite layers.

Dissolve

As opacity is decreased from 100%, the pixels of the top (blend) layer are increasingly and randomly dissolved to reveal the base layer.

Darken

Applies color in the blend layer only if the value of color pixels determines they are darker than the color pixels in the base layer.

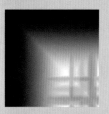

Multiply

Pixel values in the base layer are multiplied by pixel values in the blend layer. With the exception of white, this always results in darkened colors.

Color Burn

Uses the colors in the blend layer to "burn" (darken) the image. The effect is more distinct the darker the color, with white having no effect.

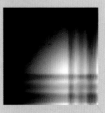

Linear burn

Another method of darkening the image with a more marked effect even than Multiply or Color Burn. Very dark pixel values may be clipped and, as with Color Burn, white has no effect.

Darker Color

The darker of the colors in either layer wins out.

Lighten

Has the opposite effect to the Darken mode. Applies color in the blend layer only if the value of color pixels determines they are lighter than the color pixels in the base layer.

Screen

Has the opposite effect of the Multiply mode. The inverse of the base and blend pixel values are multiplied to produce a lighter image (except where the blend color is black).

Color Dodge

The opposite of Color Burn. Uses the colors in the blend layer to "dodge" (lighten) the image. The effect is more distinct the lighter the color, with black having no effect.

Linear Dodge

You've guessed it, the opposite of Linear Burn. A more marked method of lightening than either Screen or Color Dodge. Very light pixel values may be clipped and, as with Color Dodge, black has no effect.

Lighter Color
The lightest of the colors from either layer wins out.

Overlay
Superimposes the blend image on the composite image, while preserving the highlight and shadow areas of the composite. Colors are either lightened (screened) or darkened (multiplied). Blending with 50% gray has no effect.

Soft Light
Similar to Overlay but with a milder effect. Think diffused lighting.

Hard Light
Again, similar to Overlay but with a more marked (hard) effect. Think harsh, direct lighting.

Vivid Light
Creates a more pronounced effect than Hard Light by applying a Color Dodge or Color Burn blend, depending on the color values of the pixels in the composite layer. Blending with 50% gray has no effect.

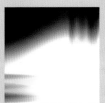

Linear Light
Going a step further, Linear Light mode creates a mildly stronger effect than Vivid Light mode. The process is the same, but the results are more pronounced. Again, 50% gray has no effect.

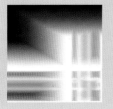

Pin Light
Creates a stronger effect than Soft Light by carrying out a Lighten blend to the light colors and a Darken blend to the dark colors. As with the other light-type blend modes, blending with 50% gray has no effect.

Hard Mix
Creates a posterized image made up of a maximum of eight colors (red, green, blue, cyan, yellow, magenta, black, and white) by combining the colors in the base layer with the luminosity of the blend layer.

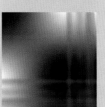

Difference
Based on the difference between pixel values, colors in the base layer are subtracted from colors in the blend layer or vice versa, depending on which has the higher value. Changing the opacity markedly affects the outcome.

Exclusion
Similar to Difference but with a less pronounced effect.

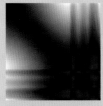

Hue
In Hue mode, luminance and saturation values in the base image are preserved but hue values in the blend layer replace those of the base layer.

Saturation
In Saturation mode, luminance and hue values in the base image are preserved, but saturation values in the blend layer replace those of the base layer.

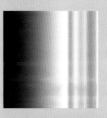

Color
In Color mode, luminance values in the base image are preserved but hue and saturation values in the blend layer replace those of the base layer.

Luminosity
In Luminosity mode, hue and saturation values in the base image are preserved but luminance values in the blend layer replace those of the base layer.

Paths and shapes

Paths and shapes are examples of vector graphics, which could almost be considered the opposite of photography. Despite this, the two technologies regularly cross paths for any photographer with print-based clients.

Paths are a means of defining the outline of an object or shape, often in order to create a very precise selection. Of course, there are other tools that do this job, which we have already identified (Lasso, Magic Wand, and Marquee), but none provide such an accurate method of defining an outline, particularly of irregularly shaped objects, as Paths. This is especially true when you're working on high-resolution files. Paths are also used to create a Vector mask that can be applied as a layer, or a clipping path (used predominantly in conjunction with a page-layout program such as InDesign).

Paths are drawn with the Pen tool and drawing accurate paths is a skill that takes some mastering. When you're starting out, it will help to turn on the Rubber Band option from the Pen Options in the Options bar. This will enable you to see path segments take shape as you draw them. I also advise that you learn all the various keyboard shortcuts for amending and reversing path segments, particularly if paths are relatively new to you. Drawing Paths is described in more detail in Chapter 5, on page 162.

The Pen tool and other vector drawing tools can generally be regarded as bolt-on functionality to Photoshop which you may not use a great deal, at least for pure photographic work. They appear in features which either don't impact the photographer's workflow at all—Shape layers, for example—or ones which can at best be described as infrequently necessary. Complete familiarity with them is therefore unnecessary, but the structure is still worth knowing, especially as you might well be asked to produce a clipping path by a client.

Vector-based lines are drawn using the Pen tools or the Shapes tool, and can be edited with the Path Selection and Direct Selection tools. They can either be drawn as shapes, which will appear on their own shape layer, or simply as Paths, which will live only in the Paths palette. The final choice is to draw the shape directly as pixels, though these cannot be edited later (there's an obvious comparison here to the difference between Smart Objects and ordinary ones). Three buttons to the left of the Shape layer's options bar offer this choice.

Shape layers are better for incorporating graphics into objects, and are very similar to Type layers (another kind of vector graphic). If you choose to save your vector shape in the Paths palette, however, you cannot directly use it in the document window. What you can do is give it a useful name. Then, if you choose to include clipping paths when you save, this name will appear in your client's copy of InDesign or QuarkXPress. The Paths palette also offers useful tools at the bottom, including one to create a path from a selection (and vice versa), and the ability to use the path to fill or draw pixel-based shapes.

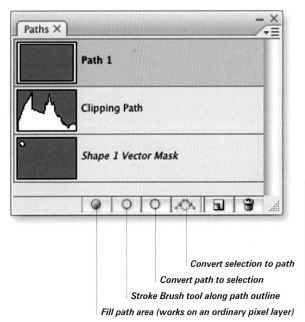

Convert selection to path
Convert path to selection
Stroke Brush tool along path outline
Fill path area (works on an ordinary pixel layer)

Converting Paths to selections

It is usual for paths to be converted to selections. However, the opposite can be achieved (converting a selection into a path) by selecting Make Work Path from the flyout menu in the Paths palette, or by clicking the Make work path from selection icon (third icon from right) at the bottom of the Paths palette.

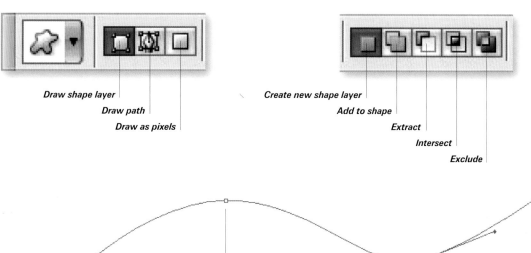

Draw shape layer

Draw path

Draw as pixels

Create new shape layer

Add to shape

Extract

Intersect

Exclude

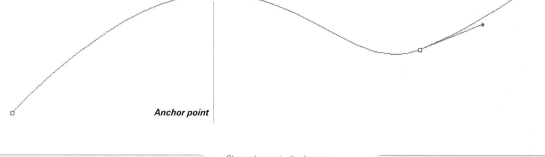

Anchor point

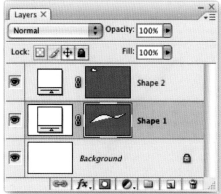

Shape layers in the Layers palette can be treated like any other layer. Double-click on the left icon to change the color of the shapes (or apply styles and effects as you see fit).

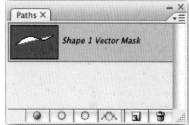

If the Path above is being edited, a representation of it will appear in the Paths palette, as shown.

SHAPE BEHAVIOR	DESCRIPTION
Create new shape layer	This option is only available if the Draw Shape Layer button is highlighted. It will create a new shape layer in the Layers palette as you begin to draw.
Add to shape area	As you start to draw a second shape, any overlaps with the first will cause the two to join into a single filled shape (both remain individually editable).
Subtract from shape area	With this button pressed, any new shape will remove filled area from the first shape (again, it remains individually editable).
Intersect shape areas	With this button pressed, the new shape is only shaded in the area where both new and old shapes intersect.
Exclude overlapping	The opposite of the Intersect button, leaving a gap at intersecting areas.

first steps

So far this book has been largely theoretical, and it's a testament to the breadth and depth of Photoshop that we can be more than 70 pages in without getting down and dirty with a file. In this chapter we'll begin tentatively with a look at those first changes that you need to make once you've brought your image into Photoshop.

The first thing we'll discuss is the various file formats and how Photoshop handles them—not least RAW files, which are opened using a special program called Adobe Camera Raw (which could be thought of as a one-at-a-time version of Lightroom).

Secondly you'll find solutions to all the most straightforward photographic problems—those that you can usually blame on the equipment (or an inability to hold the camera level). Getting these things right is always a good start.

File formats

Given Photoshop's standing as the dominant graphics package it isn't surprising that it offers a number of different ways to save your image. Each of the major formats has its advantages and disadvantages.

Photoshop enables image files to be saved in many different file formats. For photographers, the two most commonly used are JPEG and TIFF, as well as a variety of RAW formats (see pages 80-85). Each has advantages and disadvantages and which is the most appropriate depends largely on how you intend to use the image.

One notable aspect of image processing in Photoshop is the ability to process an image using all of the program's features irrespective of whether they are supported by the source file format. However, where an image is saved in a file format that doesn't support features such as layers (e.g. JPEG) the image will be flattened before saving to disk. Such features are preserved when saved in a supporting file format, such as TIFF.

JPEG

JPEG stands for Joint Photographic Experts Group (not that you really need to know that) and provides the most effective means of substantially compressing image data to reduce file size. It does this using a form of "lossy" compression, which means that once data has been discarded during the compression process it is irretrievable (see JPEG/TIFF comparison box). The JPEG file type is widely used for web design work as it enables quick downloads of photographic content over the Internet (see Save for Web, page 207). For example, an 18MB, 10×8 inch file at 300 dpi resolution (i.e. a typical print size) can be reduced in file size to around 1MB without any immediately discernible loss of image quality.

JPEG at 100%

JPEG at 1%

This series of images show a file saved at different compression settings. Even 100% is technically a "lossy" save, but the difference between it and 1% is very clear.

> **Saving TIFF files using JPEG compression**
>
> Where a TIFF (or EPS) file is saved using JPEG compression technology it's possible for problems to occur when sending the file to some older PostScript devices. When saving TIFF files, use LZW compression instead, or leave them uncompressed wherever possible.

JPEG at 10%

JPEG at 20%

	ADVANTAGES	DISADVANTAGES
JPEG	• Smaller image files take up less capacity on the hard disk drive • Smaller image files are more quickly transferred electronically, particularly over the Internet and by e-mail • Smaller image files speed up the process of downloading web pages containing photographs • At minimum compression ratios (i.e. high quality) the visible differences between JPEG and TIFF files are negligible for general photographic applications	• Lossy compression reduces image quality and increases the likelihood of artifacts occurring • Continued processing and resaving of data in JPEG mode will further reduce image quality • Doesn't support Photoshop features such as Layers • Upsizing image files is better done from a TIFF file than a JPEG file • Ordinary JPEG files must be saved in 8-bit per channel mode
TIFF	• Lossless compression reduces the likelihood of degradation of image quality and the occurrence of artifacts • Can be resaved any number of times with no loss of image quality • Supports Photoshop features such as layers • Upsizing is best done from a TIFF file • Can utilize both 8-bit and 16-bit per channel modes	• Larger image files take up more capacity on the hard disk drive • Slow to transfer electronically and generally unsuitable for use on the Internet • "Tagged" approach means some advanced features (like Layers) are not supported by all programs that can read TIFF files

JPEG 2000

JPEG 2000 is an advanced coding system that uses state-of-the-art compression techniques based on wavelet technology, and is available only from the Adobe Bridge plug-ins folder. It has some distinct advantages, including the ability to save images in 16-bit per channel mode (not possible with standard JPEG) and it's possible to save alpha channels and paths. Camera EXIF data and other metadata can also be preserved. The downside of JPEG 2000 format is that it requires any user attempting to read JPEG 2000 encoded files to be using JPEG 2000 compatible software, which, at the time of writing, isn't widely available.

Resaving JPEG files in Photoshop

Photoshop differs from some alternative image processing software packages in that data loss from continued resaving of JPEG files is minimized where pixels remain unmodified between repeated expansions and compressions. However, repeated processing and resaving of a JPEG file should be avoided, as image quality will quickly deteriorate.

JPEG at 40%

JPEG at 60%

JPEG at 90%

TIFF

Tiff, or Tagged Image File Format, is the most universally recognized file format used in publishing. Although far larger in size than JPEG files, they can be compressed using lossless compression technology, where compressed data is retained rather than discarded (see Compression box, page 77). TIFF files are easily imported into graphics and desktop publishing applications such as QuarkXpress and InDesign. Better still (from the client's perspective), adjustments to how the image will appear in print can be made to TIFFs by these layout programs. This is more convenient than the formats like EPS, and if supplying images for print purposes, TIFF is usually the safest option. Remember that you too might be the client, if you offer album creation using one of these applications.

Photoshop native file format (PSD)

The PSD format is the one used most frequently as an alternative to TIFF. It's a universal format that preserves and recognizes all Photoshop features. The main advantage of the PSD format over TIFF is faster save times and more efficient compacting of data for layered image files.

Photoshop support for 16-bit mode editing

Although all Photoshop's adjustments under the *Image* menu support 16-bit images in Photoshop CS3, that has not always been the case and some of these options are grayed out in earlier versions. Moreover, some of the filters (notably those under the Artistic, Brush Strokes, Pixelate, Sketch, Stylize, and Texture submenus) are still not suited to 16-bit editing. It may seem a long list, but these are filters which remove almost all of an image's bit depth in any case.

JPEG support for 16-bit

With the exception of JPEG 2000 file type, JPEG images are fixed at a bit depth of 8-bits per channel. This makes processing of JPEG files less accurate than when working on a 16-bit TIFF file, for example, and is another argument for saving files as a type that supports 16-bit processing.

File format compatibility

Of all file formats supported by Photoshop, only TIFF, PDF, PSB, and native Photoshop (PSD) support all Photoshop features, such as layers and vector masks. For a summary of supported Photoshop features, refer to this table.

FILE FORMAT	RGB	CMYK	INDEXED COLOR	GRAYSCALE	LAYERS	ALPHA CHANNELS	PATHS	ICC PROFILES	ANNOTATIONS
Adobe Photoshop	●	●	●	●	●	●	●	●	●
Adobe Photoshop 2.0	●	●	●	●	○	◗	●	●	○
FlashPix	●	○	○	●	○	○	◗	○	○
CompuServe GIF	○	○	●	○	○	○	○	○	○
JPEG	●	●	○	●	○	○	◗	●	○
Photoshop EPS	●	●	●	●	○	○	●	●	○
Photoshop DCS 1.0	○	◗	○	○	○	○	◗	◗	○
Photoshop DCS 2.0	●	●	○	●	○	●	●	●	○
Photoshop PDF	●	●	●	●	●	●	●	●	●
PICT	●	○	●	●	○	○	◗	●	○
PNG-8	○	○	●	●	○	●	◗	○	○
PNG-24	●	○	○	●	○	●	◗	○	○
Scitex CT	●	●	○	●	○	◗	○	○	
TIFF	●	●	●	●	●	●	●	●	●

KEY: ● = Fully compatible   ◗ = Compatible on Mac OS only   ○ = Incompatible

Large Document Format (PSB)

The PSB format is used to save image files up to 10 times the standard Photoshop limit of 30,000 × 30,000 pixels. This is rarely required outside of certain very specific professional applications.

Photoshop PDF

Photoshop PDF format is used to save Photoshop image files that are then readable in Adobe Reader (previously Acrobat Reader). The advantage of this format is that it can be read by anyone using Adobe Reader, irrespective of whether they have any other image editing software.

EPS

The EPS format is used for placing large color-separated files within a page layout or desktop publishing software application. Because EPS image data is encapsulated, unlike the TIFF format files, images cannot be manipulated within the application itself.

Bit depth

In digital photography variations in tone are referred to as levels, and bit depth relates to the maximum number of levels per channel. Typically photographic image files are saved in either 8-bit or 16-bit per channel mode. Some scanners and some digital cameras operate at other bit depths, such as 12-bit, but Photoshop always interprets any image captured above 8-bits per channel as a 16-bit per channel file.

In 8-bit per channel mode, each color channel (RGB) has a maximum of 256 tones (2 to the power of 8 = 256). When all three color channels are combined, this equates to a 24-bit color image and a possible 16.7 million colors. So what is the purpose of 16-bit mode and why is it important that many of the processing operations you undertake are done at 16-bit per channel bit depth?

To answer that question, let's look at an example of how Levels adjustment might affect a digital image. If you start with an image file that contains 256 levels per channel and you subsequently adjust Levels to increase contrast, then you will end up cutting the number of levels present in the processed file and stretching those levels that remain. In 16-bit per channel mode, each channel contains 4,096 (2 to the power of 16 = 4,096) levels. Not only does this make any adjustment to those levels more accurate, but also it reduces the amount of tonal data lost in the process.

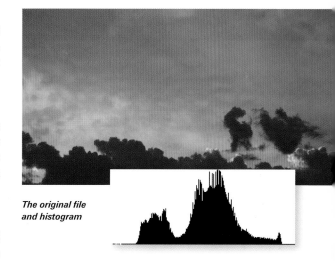

The original file and histogram

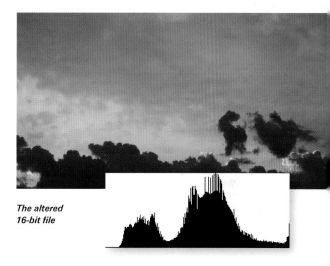

The altered 16-bit file

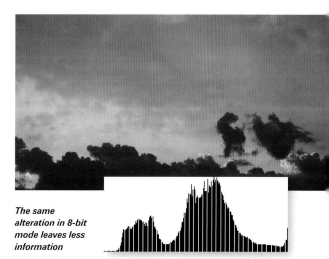

The same alteration in 8-bit mode leaves less information

Quality in, quality out: Using Raw

Raw files have rapidly established themselves as a mainstay of digital photography, preserving as much data as possible the moment the shutter is released. Here we'll examine how to use all that data to best effect.

Nowhere has the axiom "garbage in, garbage out" been truer than in digital photography. Achieving the best quality output from Photoshop begins in-camera by capturing a high quality original image. One of the key differences between a digital camera and its film counterpart is the level of processing that happens inside the camera. Film had none, but digital cameras can create close to a ready-processed image. The level of processing completed in-camera, however, should be consistent with the amount of processing you intend to do via a computer. The camera settings in the table below are an indication of the optimal settings to produce a digital original best prepared for post-capture processing in Photoshop.

RAW files contain the maximum amount of data available from the camera (including ISO, white balance, and other readings from the camera's meters) so should be your preferred choice when shooting. However, before

it can be used, a RAW file must be converted to another format (e.g. TIFF or JPEG). There are now several RAW conversion software applications available, but Photoshop users will probably find themselves choosing between the built-in program called Adobe Camera Raw (ACR) and its stablemate, Adobe Photoshop Lightroom.

Adobe Camera Raw

When you open a RAW file into Photoshop you are presented with the Adobe Camera Raw utility, as shown opposite. At first sight it appears daunting but it's simpler than it looks. Your initial step is to set up the workflow options (shown at the bottom). Once you have set these parameters they will remain the default for all subsequent RAWs opened.

At the top left of the ACR screen you will see a set of icons representing the ACR toolbox. While not as extensive

CAMERA CONTROL	RECOMMENDED SETTING	COMMENT
File type	RAW	RAW data is unprocessed in-camera and so provides the best starting point for post-capture processing.
File size	Large or Maximum	The more data you have to work with, the better the image is likely to be. Also, it is less intrusive to make a large file smaller than vice versa. Typically file size is set at Large when file type RAW is selected.
Compression	Off	Although RAW compression is virtually lossless, I prefer to work with an uncompressed file whenever possible. However, this is one setting, when shooting in RAW mode, on which you can compromise with minimal impact on image quality.
Color space	AdobeRGB	The AdobeRGB color space is capable of expressing a wider gamut (range) of colors.
Sharpening	None	While practically all digital-original files require sharpening, this is best done post-capture to suit different applications and/or markets.
Tone/ Saturation/Hue	None or Normal	All of these controls can be managed during post-processing, when it is typically easier to tweak single images than constantly accessing camera menus.
Noise reduction	On during long-time exposures (>= 1 sec) and at high ISO-E ratings (> ISO-E 400)	The occurrence of digital noise will degrade image quality and becomes most apparent during exposures of 1 sec or longer (caused by heat) and at high ISO-E ratings (caused by amplification).

as Photoshop's, the principle is the same, and indeed some tools (like the Retouch tool) add an additional subset of options in a second bar when activated, much like Photoshop's Tool Options bar. Healing work, however, is best left to Photoshop—Camera Raw's real power lies in the adjustments to the right of the window.

Under a series of eight tabs represented by small icons are image adjustments, from color temperature through noise reduction to lens correction, a set of processing options shared with Lightroom. Since they act directly on the RAW file, this is the best place to extract the maximum date from the original file and balance colors before opening the file in Photoshop. There is also an RGB/composite histogram (top right of screen), which will also change dynamically (when the Preview box is checked) as you make adjustments to RAW image.

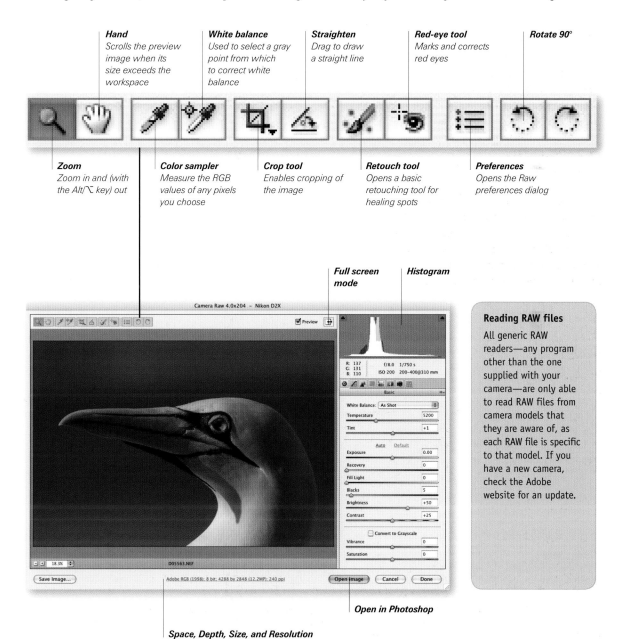

Hand
Scrolls the preview image when its size exceeds the workspace

White balance
Used to select a gray point from which to correct white balance

Straighten
Drag to draw a straight line

Red-eye tool
Marks and corrects red eyes

Rotate 90°

Zoom
Zoom in and (with the Alt/⌥ key) out

Color sampler
Measure the RGB values of any pixels you choose

Crop tool
Enables cropping of the image

Retouch tool
Opens a basic retouching tool for healing spots

Preferences
Opens the Raw preferences dialog

Full screen mode

Histogram

Reading RAW files

All generic RAW readers—any program other than the one supplied with your camera—are only able to read RAW files from camera models that they are aware of, as each RAW file is specific to that model. If you have a new camera, check the Adobe website for an update.

Open in Photoshop

Space, Depth, Size, and Resolution
The settings here are those that the converted file will contain when opened into Photoshop. Click to open a dialog allowing you to choose alternative settings (preserving 16-bits per channel for editing in Photoshop is sensible, for example, but creates larger files)

Adjusting RAW files

Adobe Camera Raw provides a wealth of options for adjusting images, and the incentive to use them at this stage—when you still have all the original camera data at your disposal—is high. Don't miss a trick.

On the right side of the ACR screen are the adjustment settings that you will use to make alterations to a RAW file before completing the conversion. There are eight tabs, each with their own settings. The principal settings used are found under the (default) Basic tab.

When you open a RAW image in ACR you will notice that, with the exception of White Balance and Saturation, the four main settings (Exposure, Shadows, Brightness, and Contrast) are all preadjusted automatically by Camera Raw (indicated by the check in the box against each setting). This is the software's best guess at how the image should look and, in many cases, is a pretty good starting point. However, as with most things automatic, you will nearly always change these settings—either slightly or significantly. This is particularly true when you have intentionally applied under- or overexposure,

for example when photographing a silhouette or when bracketing exposures.

White balance (WB)

The WB setting allows you to alter the white balance recorded in-camera. There is a drop-down menu with preset values that are similar to those found on the camera (Daylight, Cloudy, Shade, Tungsten, Fluorescent, Flash, and Custom). Click through these to see how

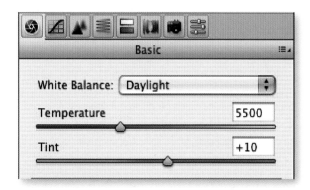

White balance is one of the most basic adjustments, and is found at the top of the Basic pane in Adobe Camera Raw.

As shot

Auto

Daylight

Cloudy

Shade

Tungsten

Fluorescent

Flash

different settings affect the image. The As Shot setting reverts to the setting applied in-camera. The Auto setting is Photoshop's best guess for the appropriate white balance, and not necessarily that of the camera.

There are also two sliders that can be used independently or in conjunction with the preset values. The Temperature slider sets the bias between yellow and blue. Moving the slider to the right will increase yellow (effectively warming the image, as when using an 81-series optical filter in the field), while shifting the slider to the left will increase the level of blue (cooling the image as when using an 80-series optical filter in the field). To gauge the effect of the Temperature slider, make exaggerated adjustments before settling on the optimal setting.

The Tint slider controls the bias between magenta (slide to the right) and green (slide to the left). A possible application for this control is to manage color shifts between natural-looking skin tones (magenta) and the vivid natural colors of nature (green). Again, experiment with different settings before settling on a preference.

Exposure, Shadows, and Brightness

Together these three controls act like the Levels control in Photoshop, with Exposure controlling the white point, Shadows the black point, and Brightness the mid-tone point. With all three the histogram will change dynamically (when Preview is checked) to show the effects of any adjustments made.

By sliding the Exposure control to the right the image lightens, while sliding the control to the left darkens the image. Move the control to position the white point on the composite histogram close to the far right of the horizontal axis, avoiding clipping where possible.

By sliding the Shadows control to the left the image lightens, while sliding the control to the right darkens the image. Move the control to position the black point on the composite histogram close to the far left of the horizontal axis, avoiding clipping where possible.

Adjusting the Brightness control will lighten (right) or darken (left) the image without significantly changing the black and white points.

Contrast and Saturation

Adjusting contrast using the Contrast control will alter all the pixels to increase tonal range. It is the global nature of the adjustments that make this a less than satisfactory method of managing contrast and, as such, it's best to make only very slight adjustments, if necessary, and opt to process contrast using the Curves tool in Photoshop (see page 112), where select adjustments can be made.

Clipping

It is easy to become a slave to trying to remove any element of clipping from an image. In reality this is often impossible and usually unnecessary, as a small amount of clipping in one or even two channels is often acceptable. The key is to avoid totally burning out large areas of highlights.

Image with some areas clipped.

The clipped areas revealed by checking the clipping box at the top right of the image area.

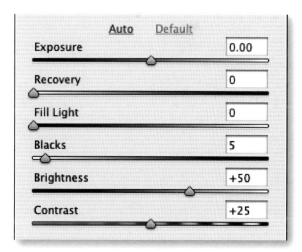

Exposure and other adjustments under the Adjust tab in Adobe Camera Raw. The Recover slider is especially useful, allowing you to pull back detail lost in highlight areas. Fill Light works the opposite way.

Like the Contrast control, the Saturation control in ACR applies any adjustments globally to all colors and all pixels. Again, then, my advice is to leave this setting alone and manage saturation in Photoshop itself.

The original image is a little flat, so the lights and darks have both been enhanced using the Parametric curves function.

Parametric curves

Under the second tab you'll find Adobe Camera Raw's interpretation of the Curves tool—a Photoshop mainstay that we'll come across on page 112. Here, however, two alternatives are offered; parametric and the traditional point curve. The latter will be covered later, but the parametric approach—introduced in Lightroom—is younger and works differently.

In either case the shades of the image are remapped so that lights become lighter or darker, midtones lighter or darker, and so on. This is represented by a curve; no change produces a straight line from the bottom left to the top right. The left end of the line represents dark tones, the right end highlights. Moving the line above the perfectly straight corner-to-corner diagonal lightens those tones, and pushing it below darkens them.

When you're working with parametric curves (you can choose alternative methods via the tabs beneath the Tone Curve pane's title bar), you do not work on the curve directly, but begin by moving the sliders beneath the graph to lighten or darken the respective tonal areas. The curve above will be redrawn to reflect the change (the gray area beneath is a histogram of the source image).

Once you've adjusted the lower sliders to your satisfaction, you can refine your changes by moving the goalposts that are the boundaries between the areas defined as highlights, lights, darks, and shadows. Do this by moving the sliders directly beneath the histogram.

Healing

As I've said before, there is little sense making extensive use of the rudimentary healing tools offered in Camera Raw when your next step is going to be a program with the power of Photoshop, but there are benefits to

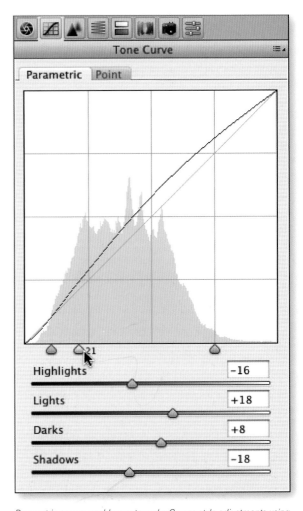

Parametric curves enable you to make Curves-style adjustments using a two-stage process. First the sliders at the bottom of the screen are adjusted, then each of the three mid-point sliders beneath the curve can be tweaked to redefine the areas.

highlighting image flaws, especially dust spots that will appear in the same place in a whole series of images.

The procedure is simple, and it doesn't change the pixels of the RAW file. Instead the computer just records the target area (the spot) and the location of a suitable replacement area. With the Retouch tool selected and Healing mode selected, click once on the spot and then, if necessary, drag the green and white outlined circle which shows the source area. This should be moved to a clean area of the image which has a similar texture. You can click on as many marks as you like and give each a different source location.

Lightroom, Camera Raw, and Photoshop

There are many more options available in Camera Raw, all of which have a parellel in Adobe's image organization tool Lightroom since they use the same underlying image processing mathematics. All changes are non-destructive—instructions that are processed as you view the image rather than applied to it. Lightroom keeps these in a seperate database, while Adobe Camera Raw saves them as a "Sidecar" file and applies them as it hands a copy of the file over to Photoshop (at which point it ceases to be RAW).

All that said, many of the changes have parallels in Photoshop proper, and will be covered alongside those later in the book. It is up to you at which stage to make the changes, but it is logical to make wider ones here in Camera Raw (or better still Lightroom) and more specific ones later when you have Photoshop's full range of features at your disposal.

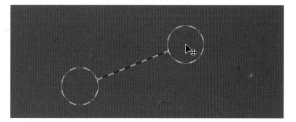

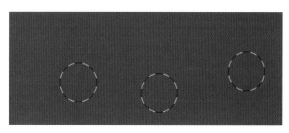

The three steps to repairing a spot in Camera Raw. Identify your spot and click on it, drag the source marker to an appropriately clean area, then repeat for other spots (finished ones are marked as shown).

TIP

Clipping warning
To show you where the image has lost all detail in either the shadows or the highlights it is helpful to view the clipping warnings. These will light up yellow or red if there are clipped areas of the image, and pressing U or O will highlight the problem areas on screen.

Shadows	**Highlights**
Press U	*Press O*

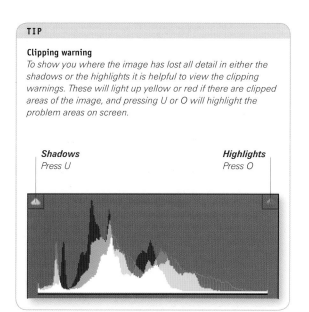

Saving default settings

If you have a number of images shot in identical conditions (for example a studio setup) then you can set new defaults and save them. These default settings then can be applied automatically to all relevant images. To save new default settings, open one of the images in Camera Raw and make the necessary adjustments. Open the drop-down menu by clicking the flyout to the right of the Settings box and selecting Save New Camera Raw Defaults. Then press Done in the bottom right of the ACR screen. Any subsequent images will open with these custom settings applied until you deselect them via the same flyout menu.

Chromatic aberration and vignetting

Flaws in lens technology are unavoidable, but should be fixed as soon as possible in your workflow. Everything else depends on getting the cleanest possible image into Photoshop.

Color fringing (chromatic aberration) can occur in the corners of an image and around the edges of objects within the image. These can be easily fixed using the Chromatic Aberration and Vignetting controls in the Lens tab on the Adobe Camera Raw screen.

Open an image and zoom in so that the image is shown at around 200%. Use the Hand tool to scroll to the corners of the image and also to review any distinct edges to objects. Check the fine detail for signs of color fringing. Where color fringing occurs use either or both the Fix Red/Cyan Fringe and/or the Fix Blue/Yellow Fringe controls to eliminate it by adjusting the relevant slider until it disappears. For example, where blue fringing is apparent, move the Fix Blue/Yellow Fringe slider to the left (toward yellow) until the blue fringe disappears.

Vignetting

Vignetting is caused by light fall-off at the corners of the image. Use the Vignetting control to reduce or eliminate vignetting, moving the Amount slider to the right to lighten dark corners. To add vignetting or to make vignetting more pronounced, move the Amount slider to the left.

Once you have completed making adjustments in ACR you are given four options via the buttons in the right corner of the screen. Selecting Open will open the file in Photoshop with all your adjustments applied. To save the changes you have made, either press Done, which saves the settings and closes ACR, or Save, which preserves your adjustments and saves the RAW file as a PSD, TIFF, JPEG, or DNG file. Otherwise, to cancel your adjustments and close the RAW file without saving, press Cancel.

Although it isn't immediately obvious in every shot, color fringing can be an irritating distraction in areas of high contrast, like the sharp edge of the subject against the background.

Why make adjustments in ACR?

The advantage of image processing in RAW mode using ACR (or any other RAW conversion software) is that the adjustments made are non-destructive. That is, they don't change the physical nature of the pixels, as occurs when processing a TIFF, JPEG, or other file type. What this means is that when you open the file in Photoshop to complete image processing, you are working with original data, which improves the potential quality of your processing work. Remember, however, that the aim of processing in ACR is not to produce a print-ready digital image—that's the job of Photoshop.

> **TIP**
>
> **Adding or eliminating**
> *To reduce vignetting, drag the sider to the left (creating a negative number). To create a more pronounced vignette effect, move the slider to the right.*
>
> *Amount -100*   *Amount +100*

> **TIP**
>
> **Lens correction filter**
> *If you're working on a non-RAW file, you can find equivalent functionality in Photoshop's Filters menu. Go to* Filter > Distort > Lens correction.

This bright sunny image is the simple result of applying a strong vignette correction to the original, right. Adjusted correctly and the flowers have the same shade sccross the image.

Vignette settings

Different lenses begin to vignette at different distances from the center.
Adjust the Midpoint slider from the default 50% to change the area affected.

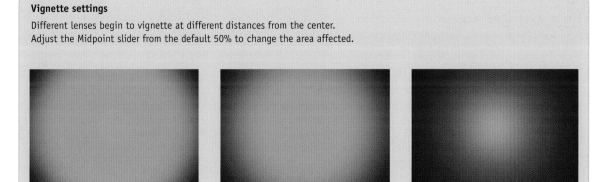

Midpoint slider 0%   *Midpoint slider 50%*   *Midpoint slider 100%*

Resizing images

It is vital to be clear about image size, resolution, and the difference between the two. That's not to say you won't encounter people who are confused by these issues, but at least you will be confident.

Digital photographs are made up of pixels and, as such, are resolution-dependent. That means they contain a fixed and finite amount of information, which, when resizing upward, can be stretched only so far before individual pixels become overtly visible. It is important to understand this before attempting to resize an image in Photoshop (or any independent interpolation software).

The image size dialog box

The pixel dimensions, document size, and resolution of an image can be altered via the Image Size dialog box. When you first open the Image Size function the following default values will be displayed in the dialog box:

- Pixel Dimensions: as per the captured image
- Document size: dimensions are set in preferences
- Resolution: expressed in pixels per inch
- Constrain proportions: checked
- Resample image: checked

Photoshop's Image Size dialog can be used to change the pixel size or—if you uncheck the Resample Image button at the bottom—just the resolution.

This series of images shows how an image with the same number of pixels appears when the resolution is changed. A lower resolution means the same pixels take up more space, but there is no more detail than in the small image.

236 pixels wide at 300ppi

236 pixels wide at 150ppi

236 pixels wide at 72ppi

When Constrain Proportions is checked Photoshop will automatically adjust height when width is changed and vice versa, to maintain the scale of the image (a link symbol appears next to the relevant fields in the dialog box). When Constrain Proportions is unchecked (the link symbols will disappear) both height and width must be adjusted manually and independently, allowing the image to be squashed or stretched.

When Resample Image is checked Photoshop will automatically and simultaneously adjust overall image size when pixel dimensions, document dimensions, and/ or resolution are changed. What Photoshop is actually doing is adding or removing pixels to make the image size bigger or smaller respectively. When Resample Image is unchecked, Pixel Dimensions are grayed out and remain unchanged even when document dimensions and/or resolution are altered. In this instance the total pixel dimensions will remain constant but the relationship between document dimensions and resolution will alter. In essence, Photoshop is spreading pixels, resulting in a larger image space, or squeezing pixels, resulting in a smaller image space.

Resizing an image

To resize an image using Photoshop, open the dialog box (*Image > Image Size*). To maintain the scale of the image make sure that Constrain Proportions is checked. To increase (or decrease) the physical number of pixels (and therefore the byte size of the image) check Resample Image at the bottom of the dialog. Choose your measurements by clicking in the drop-down menu to the right of the Width menu at the top, then adjust the image or document dimensions accordingly by typing the

> **Interpolation**
>
> Image resizing is also referred to as interpolation, though to be technically accurate, this is the name for the method by which the image is resized. Some interpolation methods produce sharper results than others (see page 90).

required image size into the relevant field. For example, to increase an image from 3000×2000 pixels to 6000×4000 pixels (i.e. doubling its size), type 6000 into the Width field and 4000 into the Height field. (Note: if Constrain Proportions is selected, one of the fields automatically changes as the other is adjusted.) Overall file size (in MegaBytes) is displayed at the top of the dialog box.

What is the correct resolution?

Many clients will ask for 300ppi images for print, or 72ppi for web. This is something of an archaic request in the days when images can be scaled easily to fit any gap, but the convention holds. Indeed this is a good way of understanding how far you can scale your image and still get a clear print (important for print clients). To change the physical dimensions of the image without affecting the number of pixels (or, by extension, the file size), deselect Resample Image and adjust either the document size or the resolution accordingly. For example, if the current document size is 10×8 inches and the resolution is 200 ppi, halving resolution to 100 ppi will double the document size to 20×16 inches. The opposite will occur when increasing resolution.

IMAGE SIZE OPTIONS	DESCRIPTION
Pixel Dimensions	The pane at the top of the dialog shows the image filesize in the title bar (M stands for megabytes) and allows you to change its size in different ways by altering the values in the drop-down menus.
Document size	This pane allows you to alter the image based on the ultimate size you want to print it at. The Resolution is an issue here, since it is this value which tells—for example—a print or design program what size the image should appear on the page.
Document dimensions	Shows the document's actual dimensions and resolution.
Scale styles	With this option checked then any values in Layer Styles (graphical effects) applied to the image will be scaled proportionally. Otherwise the absolute value (say 5 pixel drop shadow) is left.
Constrain Proportions	If this box is unchecked you can stretch or squash the image.
Resample Image: (method)	The algorithm used to interpolate the image when scaling (see page 90).

Methods of interpolation

Photoshop provides five methods of interpolation.
That is, five different ways of up- or downsizing an image.

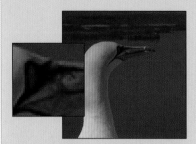

NEAREST NEIGHBOR

This is the simplest form of interpolation
and arguably the least accurate, so it is
not recommended for resizing photographic
images. However it does have its uses. For
example, it is a fast and simple means of
resizing screengrabs.

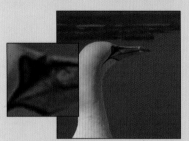

BILINEAR

When resizing using bilinear interpolation,
Photoshop uses data from the pixels
immediately above and below, and to the
left and right, to calculate the value of
new pixels. This method is fast but now
a little outdated.

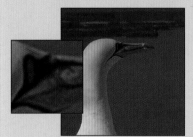

BICUBIC

This is the better option when resizing
photographic images. Rather than taking
data from just the neighboring pixels on the
horizontal and vertical axes (as in bilinear
interpolation), Photoshop uses the data
from all surrounding pixels (including those
on both diagonal axes) to calculate the
value of new pixels.

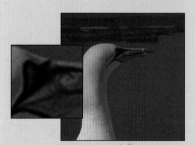

BICUBIC SMOOTHER

Works on the same interpolation basis as
bicubic and is geared towards increasing
the size of the image substantially.

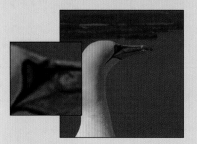

BICUBIC SHARPER

Works on the same interpolation basis as
bicubic but is geared towards decreasing
the size of the image, for example when
reducing pixel resolution in images intended
for web use.

Step interpolation

You may have heard of the step interpolation method of resizing, which is sometimes recommended when significant interpolation is required. The principle behind step interpolation is to gradually increase or decrease the size of the image in small percentages. This process was talked about often in the early days of digital photography but it is questionable whether today it adds any value. Indeed, a well-respected colleague of mine tested the theory and found little difference in image quality up to ten steps, and beyond that image quality degraded quickly using this method. My advice? Stick to Bicubic Smoother or Bicubic Sharper for significant interpolations.

Bicubic scale (close up)

Bicubic Smooth scale (close up)

Bicubic Sharper scale down (close up)

Pixel dimensions and print size

This table shows the relationship between document (print) size and pixel dimensions at 200 ppi and 300 ppi resolutions. (Document dimensions are approximate.)

PIXEL DIMENSIONS (SIZE)	MB (RGB)	MB (CMYK)	DOCUMENT DIMENSIONS (@200 PPI)	DOCUMENT DIMENSIONS (@300 PPI)
3000 x 2000 (6 MP)	17.5	23.5	15 x 10 inches (38 x 25.5 cm)	10 x 6.5 inches (25.5 x 16.5 cm)
3500 x 2500 (8.75 MP)	25	33.5	17.5 x 12.5 inches (44.5 x 32 cm)	11.5 x 8.5 inches (29 x 21.5 cm)
4000 x 2850 (11.4 MP)	32.5	43.5	20 x 14 inches (51 x 35.5 cm)	13.5 x 9.5 inches (34 x 24 cm)
4500 x 3200 (14.4 MP)	41	54.5	22.5 x 16 inches (57 x 40.5 cm)	15 x 10.5 inches (38 x 26.5 cm)
5000 x 4000 (20 MP)	57	76	25 x 20 inches (63.5 x 51 cm)	16.5 x 13.5 inches (42 x 34 cm)

Scaling images with plug-ins

Numerous third party plug-ins—programs sold separately to extend Photoshop's functionality—are on the market. Upscaling is one area in which they certainly offer more than the program itself.

In the past there has been much debate about the quality of Photoshop's resizing facility. While the algorithms now used for resizing in Photoshop are a vast improvement on earlier versions of the software, some users prefer to use third party software when interpolating images. Some professional image libraries even insist on it.

Of all the non-proprietary software solutions available, one in particular has come to prominence—Genuine Fractals. It can be bought from OnOne software as a Photoshop plug-in, which has made it significantly more useful for photographers. I have detailed below how to incorporate it into your workflow.

It's worth noting, however, that fans of Photoshop argue, with some justification, that the resizing engine in CS3 will produce results equal to Genuine Fractals and other similar software applications. No doubt the debate will continue!

The most common method of image resizing used in Photoshop is the bicubic method, which samples a single pixel and then assesses surrounding pixels to determine the color value of interpolated pixels. On the whole the bicubic method produces smooth tonal gradations and high quality upsizing.

Genuine Fractals, on the other hand, assesses a larger sample and examines the color values in a range of pixels rather than an individual pixel. It then calculates the new color values to be applied when the image is scaled based on this larger sample. By basing its calculations on a wider color value range, the results from Genuine Fractals can appear truer to the original image.

As I have said, the results are often debated and the differences in small-scale interpolations are arguably so slight as to be meaningless. However, personally, when I am performing high-percentage interpolations, I choose to use Genuine Fractals.

Performing a Genuine Fractals resizing

Early versions of Genuine Fractals required a prolonged process of saving and resaving images in different file types and was far too long-winded a process to incorporate into a smooth workflow. Fortunately, things have improved and Genuine Fractals resizing can be completed simply and easily.

From the File menu choose Automate, then choose Genuine Fractals. The active image opens in the Genuine Fractals work area. You can view and change scaling information in the Image Scale panel of the Genuine Fractals work area.

The workspace is divided into specific sections. The left portion is a preview window. A navigation pane in the upper right corner shows a smaller view of the entire image, with red lines marking out exactly what portion of the image the Preview window is displaying. On the right side of the workspace, below the navigation pane, are panels for image scale and crop options. A toolbar is found below the option panels.

The original image (whole)

Genuine Fractal scale (close up)

Original (close up)

PhotoZoom Professional is another of the growing number of fractal-based interpolation tools. Available as both a Photoshop plug-in and a standalone application, the program makes a much better job of scaling up images than Photoshop itself. The downside is the relatively slow speed (note the visible bar as the image is processed).

Straightening

The tilting horizon is an all too common problem, but one that is easily resolved. The only difficulty is in choosing between making the correction in Photoshop or Camera Raw.

If you forgot to take your spirit level into the field and your landscape photos have an unwanted sloping horizon, there's no need to panic. Photoshop provides the necessary tools for straightening either horizontal or vertical lines. The technique is simple to master.

This strong structural image is let down by the slight lean to the left. It's a common problem when shooting and needs to be corrected.

Straightening by prescribed amounts

Image > Rotate Canvas offers three prescribed rotation values: 180°, 90° CW (clockwise), and 90° CCW (counter clockwise). To make more subtle adjustments, follow the instructions below.

Straightening crooked photos

1 *From the Tools palette, select the Ruler tool (it's grouped with the Eyedropper tool) and draw a line running parallel to the line you want to correct. The longer the line, the more accurate it will be.*

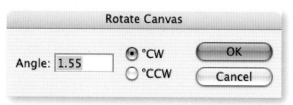

2 *Select* Image > Rotate Canvas *and select Arbitrary from the drop-down menu. A dialog box will appear with a rotation value (in degrees) and direction (clockwise (CW) or counter clockwise CCW)) automatically applied, based on the line you drew with the Ruler tool.*

3 *The image is rotated on the canvas by the prescribed amount. If you want to check the amended alignment for straightness, bring up the grid* (View > Show > Grid) *or insert a new guide* (View > New Guide) *and compare the angle of the relevant line in the image to the grid or guide line.*

4 *To clear the areas of blank canvas now visible in the background, use the Crop tool (see Cropping, page 96).*

Straightening using Camera Raw

Camera Raw, and its bigger brother Lightroom, are both capable of recording crop information which is applied as the Raw file is moved into Photoshop. In Camera Raw, click the Straighten button then draw a line just as in Step 1 in the main example. The change is automatic but reversible.

Straighten

Straightening using the Crop tool

Crooked photos can also be straightened, albeit less accurately, using the Crop tool (see Cropping, page 96).

Flipping photos

Using the Rotate Canvas menu option, images can be flipped either horizontally or vertically. This can be especially useful when changing the horizontal format is appropriate, for example to better fit a book design or magazine layout. Remember, though, that this can pose certain dilemmas when it comes to representing reality; faces, buildings and—most obviously—any writing or designs can all look wrong when flipped.

To flip a photo, select *Image > Rotate Canvas* and choose *Flip Canvas Horizontal* or *Flip Canvas Vertical* from the resulting menu.

The result of flipping a photo can be dramatic. Culturally, people often like to see subjects moving in the same direction in which they are used to reading.

Cropping

Cropping became something of a lost art while photographers concentrated on 35mm film, but digital makes it easy to recreate stately square formats and many more besides, as well as the chance to trim out any unwanted mistakes.

There are several reasons you may want to crop an image, and basic cropping in Photoshop is a relatively simple task. The result can be markedly different images, whether you're looking to create a panaroma, crop to a television frame for a presentation, or simply choose a shape better suited to the original image. Beyond using the Crop tool in its simplest form, which simply discards the pixels outside the crop area, there are several other cropping features that make the process either faster or more accurate. The ability to rotate your crop is especially useful, since it sidesteps the problem of leftover trim when straightening (see page 94).

The Tool Options bar's extended functionality turns the Crop tool into an image scaler too, albeit one that is

Performing a basic crop

❶ Select the Crop tool from the Toolbox.

❷ Move the cursor into the picture space and drag out a crop border. The exact dimensions of the border can be adjusted later. You will notice that the image area outside of the crop border is shaded to separate it from the part of the image that will remain after cropping. You can toggle off this shading function by pressing the forward slash (/) key on the keyboard.

The original uncropped image.

❸ If you need to make a precise adjustment, do so by dragging the handles again.

❹ When you're happy with the crop, click OK on the Tool Options bar.

The final crop is a traditional square format image concentrating on the main subject and eliminating unnecessary foreground and background detail.

The Crop tool's functionality is identical in Camera Raw. Here the crop area is being rotated by dragging the cursor in the area outside the crop.

forced to use the default scaling method (defined in the Preferences dialog) rather than any plugins you might prefer. By specifying the dimensions before choosing your crop, you can define the shape and insist on Photoshop scaling the cropped pixels to fit. Whatever the dimensions of the area you choose to crop, the size of the image is set at the parameters originally entered. The smaller the crop area, the more the image must be interpolated to maintain the specified crop size and the greater the extent of image degradation. Beware... don't crop too small!

The Crop tool has another trick up its sleeve, too. While the crop border is in place you can rotate it by dragging the cursor outside the border (the cursor will change into a two-point arrow) and using the mouse to drag the entire crop border in any direction around its axis. This is especially useful in horizon correction when using the Adobe Camera Raw tool to import files, since your correction will be recorded with the original RAW file without discarding pixel data, but the crooked original will never be imported into Photoshop at all.

Cropping and rotating is very useful, but don't become dependent upon it. Every rotation (except those by 90° increments) lose some detail as the old pixel grid must be remapped against the new one. It is no substitute for getting it right in camera.

Performing a specific crop

1 Select the Crop tool, but instead of dragging a crop across the page enter the dimensions of the crop into the Tool Options bar. The dimensions can be entered in inches, centimeters, millimeters, or pixels.

2 Drag the cursor across to mark the crop on the original.

3 Adjust the crop with the anchor points or by dragging it around the image area, then press Return to accept it.

The Front Image button allows you to borrow the dimensions of another open document.

These Tool Options bar settings will crop the image to the exact size, 5x7 at 300ppi. This will always be 3.15 megapixels, no matter which area of the image you highlight.

Advanced crops and tool presets

If the flexibility of the Crop tool is at odds with the paper sizes at your disposal, you can keep things tidy with tool presets.

If you regularly crop images to a specific size, say 10 × 8 inches or 7 × 5 inches, then you can make the process quicker and simpler by creating one or more custom settings, which are then saved as presets. These Tool Presets are quick to build and become a staple of any regular Photoshop user's workflow, and there is no better illustration than with crops.

Whether it's because of paper sizes or your client's preferences, you'll inevitably find yourself needing to create identically proportioned crops time and time again. While you could do this by typing in the same few sets of dimensions into the Tool Options bar each time, it is far more convenient to have a few readymade standard options and the possibility of more. And as you've probably realized by the title of this page, that possibility has already been realized in the form of the Tool Presets drop-down menu.

Every tool has its own set of options, though some are more complex than others. Some it makes little sense to save at all (the Eyedropper tool only has one drop-down menu of its own anyway), but for sake of cleanliness the presets drop-down is always accessed via the Tool's icon at the left end of the Tool Options Bar. At the bottom of the menu is a checkbox which allows you to suppress or reveal all of the other tool presets which have been

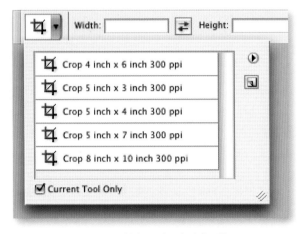

These are the tool presets which are already defined for the Crop tool with a standard installation of Photoshop.

defined (if you select a preset for a tool other than the one you're currently working with, that tool will automatically be selected from the Toolbox).

Given how easy it is to create them, it's all too easy to end up with more tool presets than you can handle. When you need to rationalize or reorder your presets, you can call upon the Preset Manager, which allows drag-and-drop sorting as well as renaming and deletion.

Defining a Crop tool preset

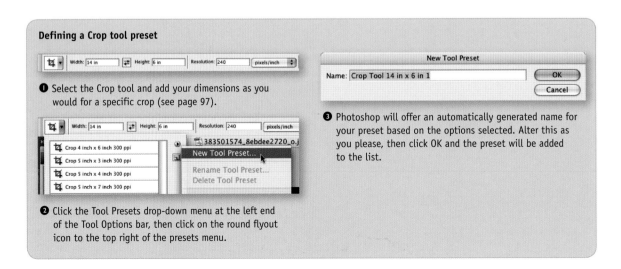

❶ Select the Crop tool and add your dimensions as you would for a specific crop (see page 97).

❷ Click the Tool Presets drop-down menu at the left end of the Tool Options bar, then click on the round flyout icon to the top right of the presets menu.

❸ Photoshop will offer an automatically generated name for your preset based on the options selected. Alter this as you please, then click OK and the preset will be added to the list.

Trim

To remove large areas of blank canvas surrounding a subject you can use the Trim tool to automatically crop to the smallest size possible. This crop technique can be useful when working on product shots that have been shot in a studio against a plain background, although it does require a completely pure background to function properly—there is no Tolerance option as there is with tools like the Magic Wand.

Trimming also has many uses in graphical work, since it can look for transparent pixels and, for example, crop an image around a subject from which you've already eliminated the background.

Increasing image area

When you crop you are not constrained to working within the image area. If you needed to create a square format image from a horizontal one without losing any of the information in the original, you can actually expand the crop area beyond the bounds of the image. Since this leaves Photoshop with no information to base the new image on, it uses the presently selected background color, which works well for the nighttime shot shown.

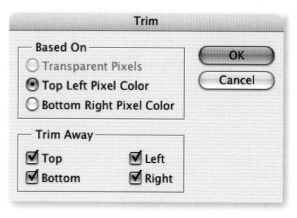

Trim the image via the Image > Trim *dialog. The Based On options allow you to choose which color Photoshop assumes is the background and the lower checkboxes can be used to avoid trimming from one or other of the sides.*

Image cropped despite the crop area being drawn outside the original frame.

Preset Manager

The Preset Manager is accessed from the same flyout menu used to add presets (see Defining a Crop tool preset). Highlight the tool you want to change and then simply drag it to a new position or click on the Delete button to remove it for good.

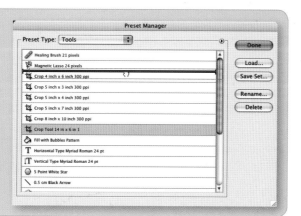

TIP

Tidy presets
Tick the Current Tool Only box at the bottom of the Tool Presets palette to reveal the tool presets for one tool only. This will make it quicker to locate your preferred tool preset when you come to use them. This applies to any tool for which you have created presets.

99

Converging verticals

It took painters until the Renaissance to understand perspective, and even now they can pick and choose. Thanks to Photoshop, photographers can manipulate perspective in their images in a fraction of the time.

When a photograph of a tall structure, such as a building, is taken at an angle, the vertical lines in the picture space visually converge. The greater the angle, the greater the level of convergence. Converging verticals can be overcome in-camera to a greater or lesser extent by using special lenses (known as "tilt and shift" lenses) or by using a camera with moving front and back elements, such as a large format field camera. Otherwise, it is possible to correct the appearance of converging verticals using Photoshop tools.

The simplest method of dealing with converging verticals is to use the Transform command in the Edit menu, as detailed here, although a more accurate and preferable method is described later (see Lens Correction Filter, page 102).

1 *With your image open, select all pixels by choosing* Select > All *from the main menu. At this point I also recommend extending the image space and creating a working area around the image. This will make it easier to drag the image outward.*

2 *In the Edit menu, select* Transform > Distort. *Drag points will appear in the corners and on the edges of the border.*

3 *To help with alignment when performing the Distort, open the grid* (View > Show > Grid) *or draw a new guide* (View > New Guide).

4 Click and drag the relevant drag points one at a time until the converging lines are vertical. Here, I have dragged the top left and top right drag points to pull the top of the building outward.

5 When you're happy that all lines are vertical, click the Commit button to confirm the transform (or click the Cancel button to cancel the transform).

6 Deselect the pixels by going to Select > Deselect.

The reason for dragging outward rather than inward is to preserve the original image size. If you drag the image inward, it will result in areas of blank canvas. These can be cropped after committing the transform but this will reduce the overall image size.

Lens Correction filter

The Lens Correction filter is the photographer's friend, a one-stop shop for eliminating those problems that occur despite your best efforts. To an extent, it can also compensate for the limitations of your equipment.

A relatively recent addition to Photoshop—arriving with version CS2—is the Lens Correction filter (*Filter > Distort > Lens Correction*). As well as providing a more accurate and better means of correcting converging verticals (vertical and horizontal perspectives) compared to the simple technique described on pages 100-101, it also enables users to correct other optical imperfections such as pin cushion and barrel lens effects; chromatic aberrations, which sometimes appear around distinct edges and at the corners of an image; and vignetting, the darkening of the image corners caused by light loss. These are discussed in more detail on pages 104-105.

For any photographer who seeks optical perfection I recommend spending some time mastering this particular Photoshop filter, as it's an indispensable tool for overcoming the limitations of cameras and their optics. In any other book, this might belong some way deeper in, but for a photographer correcting lens issues should come before any other work (see page 100). Once again flouting traditional top-down sequence, I'm going to start with the Transform option, as I've just been talking about converging verticals.

The Transform option enables you to correct both the vertical perspective (e.g. converging verticals) and the horizontal perspective (converging horizontals caused when a building, say, is photographed from a position other than head on). This tool is particularly useful in architectural photography, the genre of photography where perspective can be most problematic.

The first step is to set the dialog options. At the bottom of the dialog box, select Preview so that any changes you make appear on screen dynamically. Next select Show Grid. This will open a grid that overlays the image, aiding alignment. You can change the size of the grid squares by adjusting the figure in the Size field, as well as the color of the grid. I would recommend choosing

The first stage to any conversion is to switch on the Grid.

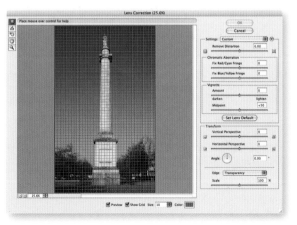

The Lens Correction filter showing a cylindrical column tapering away with perspective into the sky.

TIP

Before using the Lens Correction filter, it's sensible to convert the image layer to a Smart Object (see page 64).

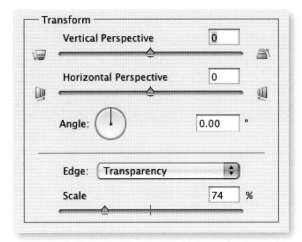

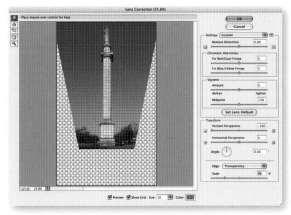

The lower pane on the left of the Lens Correction filter features corrections for perspective. I prefer to reduce the image scale (to leave a transparent area around the image) before starting.

The transparency makes it easier to see the extent of the effect that can be created by dragging the Vertical Perspective slider. Use the grid to guide you.

a bright grid color (the default is mid-gray) to make it more apparent onscreen. To do this, click on the color box and select a color (red is my preference) from the color wheel.

You can also move the grid within the picture space by selecting the Move Grid tool (third icon down on the left of the dialog box), enabling more accurate alignment.

Adjusting vertical and horizontal perspective

When the image perspective is adjusted using the Lens Correction filter the image will be distorted (cropped) to within and/or outside of the picture space. This has the potential of clipping detail (outside the frame) and reducing image size (inside the frame). To minimize the effects of the corrections you can increase or decrease the scale of the image (to overcome the reduction in image size or clipping, respectively) via the Scale slider.

The edge pixel mode, i.e. the type of pixel Photoshop places around the edge of the image when the image is scaled down or when the image is distorted to within the picture space, can be set via the Edge field. When Transparency or Background Color are selected, Photoshop will fill blank space with either a transparent or colored pixel, respectively. When Edge Extension is selected, Photoshop fills blank space with pixels that match the edge pixels of the image. Depending on the type of image and the existing edge pixels, Edge Extension can be more or less accurate. For example, it tends to be relatively accurate with flat tones, such as a blue sky, but less so when there is significant detail in the image. The Edge Extension option is likely to make it easier to apply the Healing Brush.

The final image, once cropped, shows the statue standing tall with no hint of the perspective effect (whether eliminating the effect 100% is artistically successful is another matter).

Once you have set the lens correction screen appropriately you can use the Vertical Perspective and Horizontal Perspective sliders to adjust the image perspective. For example, to correct converging verticals where the camera has been pointed upward, move the slider to the left to bring the bottom of the subject inward. Moving the slider to the right has the opposite effect.

Horizontal Perspective can be used to make an angled shot of, say, a building appear as though it has been shot from head on, almost as if you were rotating the building around a vertical axis. Shifting the slider to the left will "rotate" the subject anti-clockwise, while shifting to the right produces a clockwise "rotation."

Remove Distortion

No lens is perfect, and some are less perfect than others. For that reason the Lens Correction filter offers a full array of photographer's tweaks.

When using inferior quality lenses, images can become distorted to reveal a pin cushion or barrel effect. Extreme wide-angle lenses can also cause a slight curvature at the very edge of the frame. These distortions can be corrected using the Remove Distortion control.

Shifting the slider to the left (barrel) corrects pin cushion distortion. Shifting the slider to the right (pin cushion) corrects barrel distortion. Again, using the grid display will aid alignment.

Chromatic Aberration

Chromatic aberration, such as edge fringing, which often occurs at the edge and corners of the image frame, and along high-contrast edges, can be corrected using the Chromatic Aberration controls.

There are two sliders that control red/cyan fringing and blue/yellow fringing respectively. Shifting the Fix Red/Cyan Fringe slider to the left is effective in making the red tones more apparent, while shifting it to the right will similarly affect the cyan tones. It achieves this by adjusting the scale size of the red channel relative to the green channel. The Fix Blue/Yellow Fringe slider operates in the same way with its respective colors. You will need to balance the two together for accurate correction and often it is simply a case of experimenting until you get the best result.

Vignetting

Vignetting occurs due to light loss at the corners of the picture space. It can be caused by physical obstructions, such as a lens hood, as well as when using extreme wide-angle lenses. The problem of vignetting is often particularly apparent in panoramic image formats.

Where vignetting occurs, shift the Amount slider to the right to lighten the dark tones. With the Preview option selected you can calculate the ideal amount of correction visually. If you're feeling particularly artistic, you can even add vignetting by shifting the slider to the left.

Correcting chromatic aberrations and vignetting in RAW files

Adobe Camera Raw provides similar controls for correcting chromatic aberrations and vignetting, which can be found under the Lens tab. From experience I tend to prefer to use the ACR option for these two corrections in preference to using the Lens Correction filter. They also have the advantage, discussed before, of being non-destructive (although if you use a Smart Object the same is true of this correction).

	TOOL	FUNCTION
	Remove Distortion tool	Provides the same functionality as the Remove Distortion slider to the top right of the dialog box, but you can use it by simply clicking and dragging in the image area.
	Straighten tool	Like a faster version of the straightening method described on page 94, simply click and drag to draw a line along the correct horizon.
	Move Grid tool	The grid is essential to correcting lens distortion, but if the lines cover the edge you need to examine, select this tool and click and drag the grid to move it.
	Hand tool	Moves the image around within the preview area, just like the Hand tool in the main program.
	Zoom tool	Zoom in by dragging or clicking and zoom out by Alt/⌥-clicking anywhere.

Saving corrections

If you have several images all requiring the same level of correction you can save the most recently made corrections by opening the flyout menu from the Settings option and selecting Save Settings. When you want to apply those settings to successive images, select Previous Correction from the Settings drop-down menu.

Archiving

Any correction settings applied to an image can be archived in the EXIF metadata by pressing the Set Lens Default button. These settings are then available to use in the future by selecting Lens Default from the Settings drop-down menu.

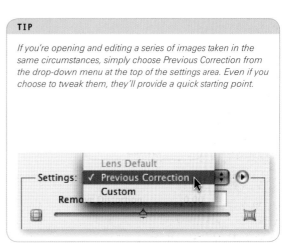

TIP

If you're opening and editing a series of images taken in the same circumstances, simply choose Previous Correction from the drop-down menu at the top of the settings area. Even if you choose to tweak them, they'll provide a quick starting point.

Removing chromatic aberration requires patience and judgement. It's also a good idea to switch off the grid while you work.

Image magnification

You have greater control over chromatic aberration corrections when the image on screen is magnified to around 200%.

enhancement tools

Photography has always been a two-part process. Part one happens in the camera when we capture an image. But all cameras have limitations. They cannot "see" with the flexibility and sophistication of humans and so rarely record the world exactly as we perceive it. And this is where part two comes in. For many photographers, the primary purpose of any image processing software, Photoshop included, is to help overcome the limitations of the camera. In this respect, Photoshop is essentially a more convenient and less messy way of achieving what was previously managed in the darkroom. This chapter covers precisely this—enhancement tools: Photoshop features that enable precise control over exposure, color, and sharpness.

The Histogram and Levels

Understanding the histogram is the key to understanding digital photography. The Levels tool builds upon that, using the histogram as a straightforward visual tool to manipulate the tone of your work.

The histogram is one of the most useful aids for managing exposure in digital photography. Essentially it is a bar graph representing the range and extent of tones in a digital image (sometimes known as Levels for reasons which will be clear). Each vertical bar in a basic 8-bit per channel histogram graph represents the number of pixels having a specified value between 0 (black) and 255 (white) with various shades of gray in between, as represented by the horizontal bar. It is an indicator of tonal range and can help to identify under- and overexposure, as well as the tonal quality of the image.

The first screengrab here shows an example of a histogram for a (technically) well-exposed image. The graph identifies the existence of tones in both the extremes (white and black) and an even spread of tones throughout the gray scale. There are no clipped pixels (pixels that fall outside of the histogram scale) indicating that detail exists in all areas of the photograph.

In general, then, a histogram graph that is skewed heavily to the right is an indication of overexposure, while a histogram graph skewed heavily to the left indicates underexposure. The exceptions would be scenes under- or overexposed on purpose, for example silhouettes

The Histogram palette

After making adjustments to an image with the Histogram palette open, click on the Refresh button to make sure the histogram is showing an up-to-date and accurate representation of the image tones. If the warning triangle appears in the top right corner it is indicating that the histogram needs refreshing.

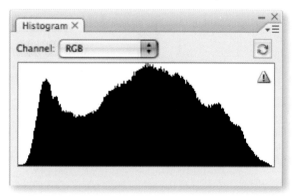

The histogram of a technically well-exposed image, as seen in the Histogram palette.

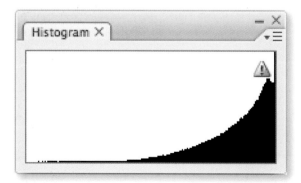

Here you notice a significant peak towards the right of the graph, indicating a likelihood of clipping. Clipped pixels have no value at all, indicating a total loss of detail. In this example, the highlights are badly clipped, a circumstance we often refer to as washed-out highlights.

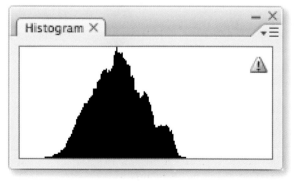

In this example, the range of tones indicated by the histogram is very narrow and there are no pixels at the extremes of the histogram (blacks and whites). The extent of this graph is indicative of a scene with very low levels of contrast, which may result in an image lacking in form (also referred to as being flat).

An image like this, with relatively few light colors, will show a histogram biased to the left, but in this case it's not a sign that the image has failed in any way.

(underexposure) and high-key images (overexposure). A histogram showing a narrow graph reveals a lack of contrast, resulting in formless, flat images.

The histogram also reveals information about the quality of the digital image. The occurrence of clipping is an indication of over- or underexposure, and the presence of pixels falling outside the dynamic range (latitude) of the sensor. Where this is apparent, the loss of detail is irretrievable. Gaps in the histogram indicate a lack of smoothness in the gradation of tones, representative of a poor quality scan or a heavily manipulated image.

It is inevitable when manipulating digital images that quality is degraded and that the histogram will appear less smooth after editing. A small loss of detail is undetectable at print stage but it's worth bearing in mind that a poor original histogram won't get any better with processing and when this is the case you are better off starting over.

Levels adjustment

The main purpose of the Levels adjustment tool is to enable the remapping of pixels so that they better fit the available tonal range (0–255). For example, to increase contrast to its fullest extent we adjust Levels so that the darkest tones are equal to black (value 0) and the lightest tones equate to white (value 255).

Directly below the histogram in the Levels tool you will see the three input sliders controling shadows (left side, black slider), highlights (right side, white slider) and midtones (middle, gray slider).

Adjustments and Layers

When making image adjustments I advise using Adjustment layers whenever possible (see Adjustment layers, page 60) or—failing that—duplicate Background layers where a suitable Adjustment layer is unavailable. A layer can be duplicated by dragging it's thumbnail to the Create New Layer icon at the bottom of the Layers palette.

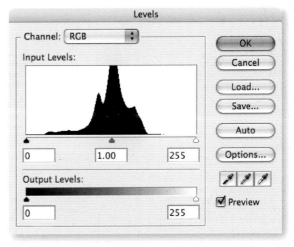

To adjust levels, open the Levels dialog box (Image > Adjustments > Levels) *from the menu bar, revealing the representative histogram.*

To set the darkest pixels to black (value 0), click on the shadows slider and drag it to the point on the histogram indicating the current darkest pixel value. To set the lightest pixels to white (value 255) click on the highlights slider and drag it to the point on the histogram indicating the current lightest pixel value.

The midtones slider can be used to lighten (slide to the left) or darken (slide to the right) the overall image without affecting the shadows or highlights. What we are doing with Levels is telling Photoshop to change (remap) original pixel values to a new value in order to adjust the tonal range of an image. For example, the photograph at the top of the opposite page looks flat and lacking in contrast. Opening its representative histogram, we see that indeed the tonal range extends only between Levels 28 (medium dark gray) and 205 (light gray). There are no pixels with a value of 0 (black) or 255 (white). In order to increase contrast we need to extend (stretch) tonal range, which we achieve by dragging in the input levels, setting the darkest image pixel to black (0) and the lightest image pixel to white (255).

Setting Levels for printing presses

I have talked mostly about remapping image pixels so that the darkest pixels have a value of 0 (black) and the lightest pixels have a value of 255 (white), which is what you will want to do on the majority of occasions. However, pixel values can be remapped to any value depending on the effect you are trying to achieve. In particular, when you are editing a grayscale or CMYK image file that is destined for a printing press.

Because of the way printing presses operate it can be beneficial to slightly amend the remapping process. When you execute an RGB to CMYK conversion Photoshop automatically compensates the shadow point by the exact amount necessary for the type of output selected (see page 26 for more on color theory). However, the highlights have to be set manually. Often pixels with a value ranging between 240 and 255 are printed as pure white and it is therefore advisable to set the Levels value to no more than 245.

The Output Levels slider can be used to notch away from absolute blacks or whites.

The appropriate method for setting Levels for printing presses is to use the Output Levels box, which sits underneath the Input Levels in the Levels dialog box. There are two Output Levels sliders representing shadows (black arrow, left side) and highlights (white arrow, right side). By dragging the white arrow slider to the left and setting an Output Levels value of 245 you effectively reset the available tonal range to between 0 (black) and 245 (near-white) making sure that no pixel value can be greater than 245, irrespective of what adjustments you make to the Input Levels values.

To clip or not to clip?

We are constantly told that clipping highlights must be avoided at all costs and so we become slaves to the highlights screen on our digital cameras. However, not only does this potentially greatly degrade image quality but it is often unnecessary. For example, a lit bulb at night will invariably cause highlights to be clipped if the image is exposed to retain detail in the shadow areas. But as the light at the center of the bulb has no detail anyway, why bother trying to preserve it? Similarly, reflected light from a shiny object is likely to be devoid of detail and therefore unworthy of preservation. In these and similar instances you should not get too hung up about highlight clipping.

Reducing tonal range

In general, Output Levels controls are used when retouching a pre-press file in CMYK or grayscale. However, it is possible to reduce levels of contrast using the output sliders. For example, by shifting the black arrow (left side) slider to the right you can set Levels so that the darkest image pixel value is never greater than, say, 50 (effectively lightening the image), and shifting the white arrow (right side) slider to the left so that the lightest image pixel value is never more than 225 (effectively darkening the image). What we are really doing by adjusting the output sliders is reducing the available tonal range from its usual 0–255 levels to something less than that, and if you experiment with the output sliders, you can see how dragging them inward reduces levels of contrast.

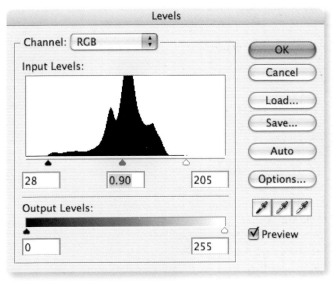

A Levels adjustment where both the highlights and shadows sliders have been moved toward the detail area of the histogram.

Curves

The photographer's favorite tool has received a small but useful revamp in Photoshop CS3, and remains as efficacious as it's always been for contrast and color adjustments.

The Curves tool is used for making contrast and color adjustments. Although both contrast and color can be adjusted using other Photoshop tools, such as Levels, the Curves tool provides the user with the greatest amount of control and accuracy. The downside is that Curves is less easy to apply and takes more practice to master.

The Curves dialog box shows a square grid, with the vertical axis representing the Output values and the horizontal axis representing the Input values. The line running at an angle of 45° is the linear curve line (used to make the Curves adjustments) representing tonal range. The black point (0) is at the bottom left corner and the white point (255) at the top right corner. By placing the cursor over a point in the grid the Input, Output (x, y) coordinates are shown in their respective value boxes below the grid.

Above the grid is the Channel selector, with an RGB composite and red, green, and blue channel options. (In CMYK mode the Channel selector shows a CMYK composite along with cyan, yellow, magenta, and black channels.)

Next to the Input and Output value boxes are the curve tools. The left box is the point tool (the default option and the one used most regularly), which enables you to drag the curve line and add curve points along the line. The right box enables the freehand tool, which enables the drawing of a curves line by hand in a manner similar to using the Pencil tool. This can be used in conjunction with the Smooth button, which smoothes curves drawn freehand.

The black (left), white (right), and gamma (middle) eyedropper buttons enable you to map pixels to their respective values.

A Curves adjustment. The Curves tool plots the image's histogram behind the tone curve to help you.

Curves or Levels?

The Levels tool enables you to maximize tonal range, and this is often all that is needed to improve contrast. When it's necessary to further refine contrast—for example, by adjusting midtone contrast without affecting shadow and highlight areas—a greater level of user control is provided by the Curves tool.

Curves adjustments

The Curves tool can replicate Levels adjustments (although if that's all you need to do you might as well just use Levels). Dragging the curve line from its bottom point straight across to the right, you mimic the action of dragging the black slider in Levels to remap the black point. Similarly, dragging the curve line from its top white point straight across to the left mimics dragging the white slider in Levels to remap the white point.

What happens next is what separates the Curves and Levels tools. Because using the curve line you can now control overall contrast for either the composite or any individual color channel.

Here, a very simple application of the Curves tool—moving only the corner points inward—has had a dramatic effect.

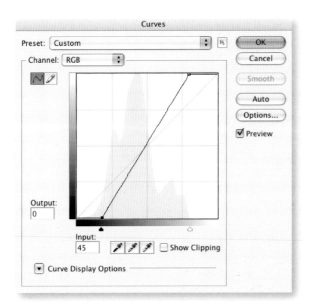

Contrast adjustments using Curves

To adjust contrast levels using Curves you need to create an "S" shaped curve to steepen or flatten the curve line. The main point to be remembered is the steeper the curve the greater the contrast. Conversely, a flatter curve will soften contrast.

Work through the following example to increase image contrast. The values chosen were for example only, but notice how the level of contrast has increased, with the highlights brighter and the shadows darker.

Working from the image above, a curve point was added about one-fifth of the way up from the black point (Input value = 52, Output value = 52) by placing the cursor over the curve line and clicking once. A second point was added about four-fifths of the way up from the black point (Input value = 203, Output value = 203). With the Preview box checked, the curve line was dragged up until the Input value equalled around 110 and the Output value equalled around 140.

The resulting image with the "S" curve applied.

TIP

Accurate curve point placement
If you scroll the mouse inside the image space while pressing the Alt/⌥ key, you will notice that a hovering point appears along the curves line indicating the Input, Output coordinates of the pixel covered by the mouse pointer. If you then Ctrl/⌘+click the mouse, a curve point will be added at the relevant point along the curve line. This is the most accurate way to position curve points.

Points about one-fifth of the way up from the black point and about four-fifths of the way up from the black point form the basis of this curve.

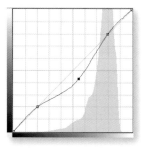

The final touch to the curve below was to drag the curve line downward until the Input value equalled around 140 and the Output value equalled around 110.

TIP

Saving Curves adjustments
Any adjustment made in Curves can be saved and applied later to other images. Once an adjustment has been made, click on the Save button and give the adjustment a meaningful name. Then choose a location to save the adjustment. It's a good idea to create a folder specifically for Photoshop adjustments with subfolders for different tools. When you want to reuse the adjustment, simply click on the Load button and select the relevant setting.

TIP

Color adjustments
The Curves tool can also be used to perform color adjustments, as described on page 128.

Curve workflow

Now do the opposite to see the effect of a flatter curve line. Notice how the level of contrast has decreased.

When you make a contrast adjustment using Curves you may notice a color shift. This is because as well as changing the tonal balance you are also adjusting color saturation. To prevent a color shift, after performing the Curves adjustment open the Fade Curves option in the Edit menu (*Edit > Fade Curves*) and select Luminosity in the drop-down menu. This will cause the Curves adjustment to apply to luminance only, without affecting color saturation.

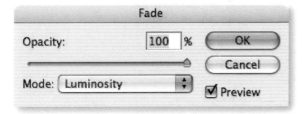

Selective contrast adjustments using Curves

So far I have described how to use the Curves tool to adjust overall levels of contrast. However, one of the advantages of the Curves tool is the ability to affect contrast in more defined areas of the images.

For example, say I wanted to increase contrast in the shadow to midtone range, while preserving detail in the highlights. Here are the steps I would follow:

❶ Add a curve point close to the white point (Input and Output values = 229) to anchor the highlights.

❷ I then add two further curve points, one at coordinates 179, 179 and another at coordinates 76, 76 that I use to create my "S" shaped curve.

❸ I then drag the curve line upward (Input value = 105, Output value = 130), steepening the curve to increase contrast in the desired darker tones.

Once again, the Input and Output values used are for example only. Notice, however, how the level of contrast in the highlights has remained much the same but the shadow and midtone areas have increased levels of contrast.

Shadow/Highlight tool

While Levels and especially Curves are great for adjusting the tone of a whole image, they can be a blunt instrument. The Shadow/Highlight tool offers a more subtle solution.

Hidden away about two-thirds of the way down the list of tools in the image adjustments menu is a gem of a Photoshop tool called Shadow/Highlight (*Image > Adjustments > Shadow/Highlights*). Using this tool, it's possible to enrich detail in areas of shadow or highlight independently (not unlike Camera Raw's Recovery and Fill Light sliders). It is particularly useful for revealing detail in well-exposed images with a good tonal range, but where the extent of the tonal information is too tightly compressed to be fully visible.

In practice, Photoshop makes an analysis of neighboring pixels within a predefined radius of the sample pixel, and then applies a compensating adjustment based on the average of the analyzed pixels.

Basic settings

The Shadow/Highlight tool can be used in either basic or advanced modes. The basic options enable you to set independently the amount of adjustment for the shadows and highlights areas. The default level is 50%, which is a relatively arbitrary setting and I recommend that the first thing you do is change this by adjusting the levels for each setting and then clicking the Save as Defaults button (which can be found at the bottom of the Shadow/Highlights dialog box when Show More Options is selected). For the record, I have my values set to 5% for shadows and 10% for highlights. With the Preview box checked it is possible to visually assess any fine-tuning adjustments you make to an image on screen.

Even in its simplest form, the Shadow/Highlight tool has a amazing ability to recover detail from either end of the tonal range.

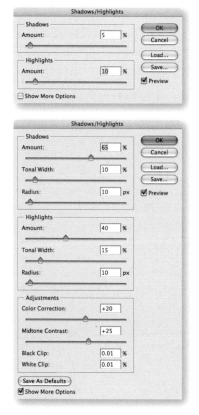

Advanced Shadow/Highlight settings

By checking the Show More Options box, the advanced Shadow/Highlights control settings are displayed. This adds Tonal Width and Radius to the Shadows and Highlights control options, and a new section called Adjustments for making color corrections, adjusting the midtone contrast and setting the Black Clip and White Clip percentages.

To be honest it would make little sense to use the Shadow/Highlight tool and ignore these settings, so I suggest that you keep them displayed. As with the Amount values you can also change the default values for each of the advanced settings. I suggest setting a value of between 5 and 10 for all Shadow and Highlight values, then click the Set As Defaults button.

White and Black Clipping

By setting a clipping percentage in the Black Clip and White Clip boxes at the bottom of the Shadow/Highlight dialog box you can tell Photoshop to ignore the specified amount of either extreme when identifying the lightest and darkest pixels in the image. This clipping of pixel values ensures that white and black values are representative areas of the image content rather than extreme pixel values.

Adding Shadow/Highlight as a Layer

The Shadow/Highlight adjustment tool is not available as an Adjustment Layer. To make Shadow/Highlight adjustments in a Layer, create a duplicate Background layer.

Tonal Width	Tonal Width refers to the range of pixels affected by the adjustment, starting from 0 for shadow adjustments and 255 for highlight adjustments and going through to middle tones. For example, if the Shadows Tonal Width value is set to 100% then any adjustments made will affect all pixels from black to midtone gray. By setting Tonal Width to 50% then shadow adjustments will affect only those pixels that fall between black and halfway towards middle tone. The same theory applies to the highlights. By adjusting Tonal Width you can define the range of pixels that are affected by Shadow/Highlights adjustments.
Radius	The Radius control setting determines the width in pixels of the area that Photoshop analyzes when calculating its corrections. As these corrections are based on data gathered from neighboring pixels, the wider the area the greater the number of pixels that are taken into account. This can be a good or bad thing. If the radius is too narrow then the adjustment will have little effect other than to produce a flat-looking image, as all pixel values between black or white and middle tone become lighter (thereby reducing contrast).
	Similarly, if the Radius value is set too high then more of the pixels are taken into account, increasing the likelihood that any adjustments affect too wide a range of pixels, lightening the whole image and reducing contrast.
	The optimum amount is somewhere between too few and too many, which is perhaps the least useful statement in this book. The difficulty is it depends entirely on the image being enhanced and the only way to tell the best value setting is by trial and error. However, as a starting point, set a value of around 10 pixels for Shadows and 20 pixels for Highlights.
Avoiding radius halos	One possible consequence of adjusting the Radius values is the occurrence of radius halos, typically around hard edges of stark contrast. When making adjustments to the Radius values make sure the Preview box is checked and watch carefully the pixels around sharp-edged objects. If halos become too apparent, reduce the Radius value.
	Alternatively, you can apply a Fade Shadow/Highlight edit (*Edit > Fade Shadow/Highlight*) and reduce the effects of the Shadow/Highlight adjustment by reducing opacity.
Color Correction	Another consequence of making Shadow/Highlight adjustments is a possible shift in color saturation. This usually only occurs in extreme cases and the Color Correction control can be used to compensate for any noticable changes in color.
Mid-tone contrast	As I noted earlier, one of the effects of making Shadow/Highlights adjustments is a possible loss in contrast, as the midtone pixels are affected by the changes you apply. Use the Midtone Contrast control to restore or increase contrast to affected areas of medium gray.

Brightness, Contrast & Exposure

Photoshop's Brightness/Contrast control has been given a welcome overhaul for CS3, but there are still more effective ways to do the same job.

Practically every book or article you read on Photoshop will advise against using the Brightness/Contrast tool. That said, practically every book you've read was written before Photoshop CS3 changed the rules in that department. The new Brightness/Contrast tool uses a different algorithm to process the image, with much more pleasing results than legacy versions of the program, finally elevating it to the status of a useful tool.

The old approach was to remap each pixel's value by an equal amount, either darker (Contrast) or lighter (Brightness). Because of this equal and non-discretionary shift, the Brightness/Contrast tool could easily cause pixels to be pushed from the ends, resulting in poor quality images with patches of solid black or white rather than deep shadows or highlights.

Looking at the table below it's clear that the new approach treats the image substantially differently, remapping according to predetermined curves that result in more photographically pleasing images. If, for some reason, you want to use the older method, check the Use Legacy option to the bottom right, but this would only seem useful in graphic rather than photographic work. Another bonus is that Brightness/Contrast works as an adjustment layer.

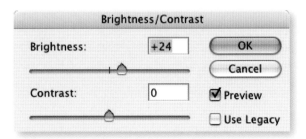

Brightness/Contrast in CS3—note the option at bottom right.

Adobe Camera RAW

When you open a RAW image in Camera Raw you are presented with a setting for adjusting exposure (under the Basics tab). By adjusting exposure here you are effectively using a Curve on the RAW file. One of the advantages of using this exposure control is that the adjustment values are given in photographic terms (i.e. in reference to f/stops) making them easy to relate to. For example, dragging the slider arrow to plus .50 is the equivalent of increasing the exposure by half an f/stop. Similarly, dragging the slider to, say, minus 1 is equivalent to closing the exposure by one f/stop. And, because adjustments can be made in increments of 1/5th of an f/stop, they can be quite accurate.

New Brightness/Contrast

Applying Brightness and Contrast adjustments to an image with the new tools reveals significant differences in the way the images are processed. Sure, they all leave gaps (all processing on 8-bit images does), but the new methods introduced in CS3 don't leave so many gaps so close together.

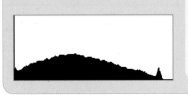

Legacy

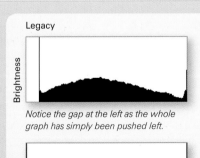

Notice the gap at the left as the whole graph has simply been pushed left.

Here the information in the image has simply been stretched over the ends.

CS3 and later

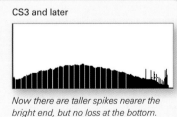

Now there are taller spikes nearer the bright end, but no loss at the bottom.

There is still a full range of data, with more at each end than before.

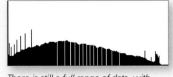

Levels and Curves

I have already identified Levels as a powerful tool for managing contrast and tonal range. However, Levels can also be used to adjust the relative brightness of an image using the midpoint gamma slider (the middle, gray arrow slider used to control the middle tone input values).

Dragging the gamma slider to the left (towards the black point) increases the relative brightness by placing more of the levels to the right (brighter) side of the middle point. Conversely, dragging the gamma slider to the right, toward the white point, increases the relative darkness of the image by placing more of the pixels to the left (the darker side) of the midpoint. See also Levels, page 108.

A side effect of correcting exposure using the Levels tool is a reduction in overall contrast and you may find it necessary to use some of the contrast adjustment techniques described earlier in this chapter.

Similarly, the relative brightness of an image can be lightened or darkened using the Curves tool by dragging

> ### Dealing with digital noise
>
> One of the likely outcomes of correcting underexposure in Photoshop is an increase in the visibility of digital noise in the lightened shadow areas of the image. Review the section on reducing digital noise (page 132) to minimize its effect on image quality.

A duplicate blending mode set to Screen improves contrast, and the strength is adjustable via the Opacity slider.

the curve upward to make the image relatively brighter, or downward to make the image relatively darker. For more details about using the Curves tool see Curves, page 112.

Blending modes

Another quick and simple technique for dealing with under- or overexposed images is to use the blending modes in conjunction with Layers.

Open an underexposed image and create a duplicate layer (*Layer > Duplicate Layer*). Select the duplicate layer in the Layers palette and change the blending mode to Screen. Instantly you will see the whole image brighten.

If the effect isn't sufficient to deal completely with the underexposure then add a new duplicate layer, changing its blending mode to Screen. Repeat the process until the image brightness is as you want it.

If you find that the correct level of brightness falls between two layers (i.e. not bright enough with the current number of layers but too much when you add an additional layer) then you can use the Opacity setting to reduce the effects of a layer. For example, reducing opacity to 50% will reduce the brightening effect of the Screen blend by half. Simply adjust opacity until the relative brightness of the image appears the way you want it.

The same technique can be used to deal with overexposure using the Multiply blend mode.

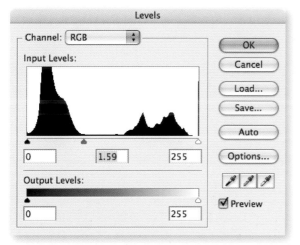

The Levels tool, also an adjustment layer, can be used to adjust contrast by dragging the midpoint slider beneath the histogram.

Dodging and burning

Dodging and burning are classic techniques from the black and white era. The tools are replicated in Photoshop, but there are better ways to achieve the same results.

The terms dodging and burning will be familiar to any photographer who has experience of operating in a "wet" darkroom. They are selective exposure techniques, used to lighten (dodge) or darken (burn) selected areas of the image space without affecting the overall tone.

Photoshop provides specific tools for applying a dodge and/or burn adjustment, which are selectable from the Tools palette. Although it would seem perfectly normal to use these tools for making selected tonal corrections (after all, that's what they're for) few photographers I know, me included, who use Photoshop extensively find them the best tool for the job and we prefer to use a slightly different technique to achieve the same results.

If you want to use the Dodge and Burn tools, the following example describes how to produce professional-level results. If you prefer to do it the way most of us do, skip this example and go straight to the opposite page, which fully harnesses layers for added flexibility.

Using the Dodge and Burn tools

The following example describes a professional technique for making selective tonal corrections using Photoshop's Dodge and Burn tools.

Dodging and Burning

❶ Create a new layer (*Layer > New*). You may want to give it a meaningful name, such as Dodge & Burn.

❷ In the New Layer dialog box, change the Mode to Soft Light via the drop-down menu. Then check the Fill with Soft-Light-Neutral color (50% gray) box, under the Mode setting.

❸ Select either the Dodge tool (to lighten the image) or the Burn tool (to darken the image) from the Toolbar.

❹ Set Exposure to 1-3% in the Tool Options bar, which will create a smooth result. Make sure the Sample from all Layers box is checked.

❺ Click and scroll the Dodge/Burn tool over the area you want to lighten/darken until you have achieved the desired tonal correction.

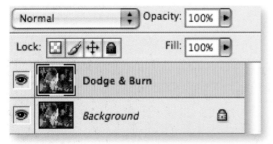

Tonal range

When applying the Dodge and Burn tools, you can define the range of tones most affected by the adjustment by selecting Midtones, Shadows, or Highlights from the Range drop-down menu in the Options bar.

The default setting is Midtone, which causes Dodge and Burn adjustments to apply to most pixels except those at the extremes of the tonal range. By selecting Highlights, adjustments have a greater effect on the lightest pixels and a reduced affect on the dark and midrange pixels. The opposite applies when the Shadows option is selected, with the darkest pixels affected the most.

A variation on the Dodge and Burn technique is to replace the Dodge and Burn tools with a Brush tool, as shown in the Tonal Correction example.

Tonal Correction

❶ Create a new layer (*Layer > New*). You may want to give it a meaningful name, such as Tonal Correction.

❷ In the New Layer dialog box, change the Mode to Soft Light via the drop-down menu. Then check the Fill with Soft-Light-Neutral color (50% gray) box, under the Mode setting.

❸ Select a soft-edged Brush from the Toolbar. Set Brush opacity to between 5-10%.

❹ To lighten tones, set the foreground color to white (using the keyboard, press D and then X). To darken tones, set the foreground color to Black (press D).

❺ Click and scroll the Brush tool over the area you want to lighten/darken until you have achieved the desired tonal correction.

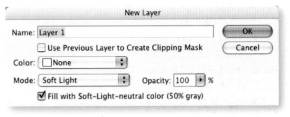

You must create the new layer via the menu (either the fly out or Layer > New) to open this dialog box with the neutral fill option.

> **TIP**
>
> **Different mode**
> *For a more pronounced effect when making tonal corrections, select the Overlay Blend mode in place of the Soft Light mode.*

> **TIP**
>
> **Adjustment method**
> *Select the area you'd like to darken then create a Curves adjustment layer to do the job (the mask is automatic). Double-click the layer to open and tweak the adjustment.*

High Dynamic Range (HDR)

An emerging style of photography suited to still subjects with wide dynamic range, Photoshop can merge a series of exposures to retain detail in both shadow and highlight areas.

One of the greatest challenges photographers face is managing exposure for a scene that has a high subject brightness range (i.e. excessive contrast). This is due to the limited latitude of film and dynamic range of digital sensors (that is the ability of film/sensor to record simultaneously detail in areas of shadow and highlight). One solution to narrow latitude (including dynamic range) is called Merge to HDR (High Dynamic Range).

This tool enables you to take two or more images, exposed separately for the shadow and highlight areas of a scene, and merge them to produce a single image that reveals detail in all areas of the image space, however wide the prevailing subject brightness range.

Before I begin this section it is worth pointing out that the HDR process has its own limitations. Firstly, each of the images used for the Merge must be composed identically, which requires that the camera must have been set on a tripod (or similarly solid support) and be unmoved between exposures, and that the subject be absolutely still. These limitations rule out subjects such as wildlife, sport, and reportage. Even outdoor photographers shooting a still scene in wind may find subject movement too great for HDR. There is an option in the Merge to HDR menu that forces Photoshop to align the images, but I have found that even slight changes can degrade the quality of the final image. To fire the shutter, I also recommend using an electronic cable release to minimize camera movement.

When setting up the camera to take a set of images for HDR I recommend using the camera's auto-bracketing function. For best results, first measure the subject brightness range (SBR). To do this, take a meter reading of the darkest area of the scene, followed by a meter reading of the brightest area of the scene. Using the Exposure Values of the two readings (or the f/stop scale) calculate the difference in brightness in stops. This will tell you the extent to which you need bracket your exposures. In the example, the SBR was five stops. I therefore set auto-bracketing to five exposures at 1-stop increments from the median exposure.

It is also important that any variation in exposure is managed using the shutter speed only, as adjusting lens aperture will affect depth-of-field, making it impossible to create identical images. Therefore, set the camera to aperture priority auto-exposure, which will cause the camera to adjust the shutter speed, leaving the aperture setting fixed.

Once you have the necessary set of images, follow the steps opposite to create your HDR image.

This HDR project uses a series of three original frames, the darkest exposed to favor the detail in the highlights...

...and the brightest exposed to favor shadow detail, which also serves to soften any motion in the water.

The resulting merged image.

HDR Merging in Photoshop

❶ Open all three images to be used in Adobe Camera Raw.

❷ Make sure the Auto settings in ACR are deselected (*Settings > Deselect Use Auto Adjustments*). Turn off all adjustments in ACR.

❸ Select all the images in the set. Then, select Synchronize (the button below Select All) to synchronize ACR settings across all images. A Synchronize dialog box will be displayed—check all the boxes to synchronize all settings. Press the Done button to apply the synchronization.

❹ Open the Merge to HDR Selection dialog box (*File > Automate > Merge to HDR*) and use the Browse option to select the set of images. You may find it simpler if the HDR images have been separated to a specific location.

❺ At the bottom of the dialog box is an option to Attempt to Automatically Align Source Images. This is particularly suited to images taken without the aid of a tripod. But you may choose to select it anyway. A word of warning—the alignment process isn't a fast one. To open the main Merge to HDR dialog box, click OK.

❻ Select the source images to use in the Merge by selecting the check boxes under each relevant image.

❼ When all the relevant images are selected, press OK to perform the HDR Merge. The single merged Preview image will appear on screen. Don't be surprised if at this point not all of the detail is showing. A standard computer monitor is incapable of displaying all the data in a 32-bit image, and so some will be hidden from display.

❽ Save a copy of this Preview HDR image in Portable Bit Map file mode to a suitable location. This can be kept as a master HDR file for this set of images.

❾ Now, and only now, change the bit depth to 16-bits/channel (*Image > Mode > 16-bit/channel*). This will open the HDR conversion dialogue box.

❿ There are four HDR conversion options available from the Method drop-down menu; Exposure and Gamma, Highlight Compression, Equalize Histogram, and Local adaptation. The latter is the most controllable (Highlight and Equalize have no options) but the choice of method is yours.

⓫ For the ultimate in control, choose Local Adaptation with Curves and adjust the curve to suit. When you click OK, a new, non-HDR image is created which can be used in Photoshop just like any other file.

Correcting color

Color is an artistic decision as well as a technical issue, and like so many others it is one that has been passed from one that must be made when film is chosen to one that can be tweaked on the computer.

So far we have looked at standard image adjustments in terms of gray tones and enhancing contrast. More often than not, however, we are working on color images. This section examines how Photoshop enables enhancements and corrections to be made to color, from the overall color of an image to selective color adjustments.

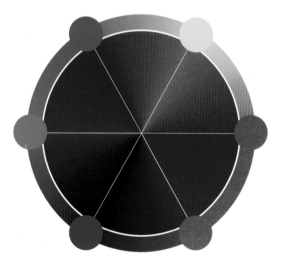

The color wheel shows the relationships between the colors—notice how the printers' primaries lie opposite those of the computer monitor.

Color is such a complex subject that whole books have been written about it. Earlier in this volume we looked at how to set up your computer correctly and considered color correction in terms of display and printed results. Now it is time to consider making changes for artistic reasons. To accomplish this it is useful to understand the relationship that colors share, which will help when having to make color correction decisions. The three colors that form an RGB image (red, green, and blue) can be mapped, together with the CMY(K) colors (cyan, magenta, and yellow) onto a chart known as a color wheel. Opposite colors (e.g. blue and yellow, red and cyan) are called complimentary colors, and it is this relationship that's worth getting to know. For example, if you want to make the colors in an image less red, then

applying a corrective amount of cyan will achieve that. Adding yellow reduces blue tones, magenta reduces greens, and so on. In a nutshell, it's useful to understand that the concept of color correction in Photoshop is based on these color relationships.

There are some basic tools for enhancing and correcting color that you will probably use more often than some of the more advanced and selective techniques that can be applied to specific images. Let's consider those first.

The Hue/Saturation tool

One of the most useful tools for color enhancement is the Hue/Saturation tool, found in the Image menu (*Image > Adjustments > Hue/Saturation*). It is the color tool that I use most regularly and, for reasons I'll explain in a moment, most frequently.

The Hue/Saturation dialog box contains three control sliders that manage Hue, levels of Saturation, and relative Lightness respectively. Above these is an Edit drop-down menu that, in default mode, is set to RGB. Open the menu and you will find the six color channels that form the color wheel mentioned above (red, green, blue, cyan, magenta, and yellow).

Below the Lightness scale are three color eyedroppers, used for making and fine-tuning color selections, and to their right, Preview and Colorize checkboxes.

The Hue/Saturation dialog, available as an adjustment layer, is a very natural tool for correcting a photograph's color, and has the advantage of being non-destructive.

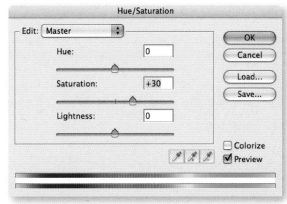

A Hue/Saturation adjustment layer was added to this image, with the Saturation slider moved to +30. The results were a vast improvement on the original.

At the bottom of the dialog box are two color bars, which provide a useful guide when performing adjustments. The upper box represents the input color values, or the color values as they appear in the original image. The lower box represents the output values, i.e. how the input values will be interpreted after adjustments have been made.

In it simplest form, the Saturation setting increases or decreases overall saturation of the image colors, making them more vivid when saturation is added (slider pulled to the right), and increasingly less vivid when saturation is reduced (slider pulled to the left). Pull the slider all the way to the far left and your color image will become grayscale.

This simple operation can be used to boost the colors in an image in much the same way that film users might have chosen a very saturated film to reproduce vibrant colors. For example, nature photographers, like myself, typically chose Fuji Velvia film for its vivid rendition of colors. Now we can use Photoshop to create a similar effect (a useful tool considering that the original Velvia film is now out of production). Compare the two images shown above to see the Saturation tool in action. The original flat colors have been brought to life with a simple boost to the Saturation slider.

Monitor settings

It shouldn't need to be said, but before you start making strong changes to the saturation make sure that your monitor is correctly calibrated (see page 28). Even if you do not have a colorimeter you will find useful tools in your computer's System Preferences (mac) panel or Control Panel (Windows) which will help you tune your monitor as best possible by eye.

Saturation and color channels

On the last page, I used saturation globally over the whole image. Sometimes, however, you may want to a adjust individual color channels. Let's take another example, this time an image of a hippopotamus. From experience I know that the hippo's dark gray hide reflects a lot of blue light, which can give an image an unnaturally cool color cast, so I apply the adjustment shown here.

To edit the blue areas only, create a Hue/Saturation Adjustment Layer (Layers > New Adjustment Layer > Hue/Saturation) then select the Blue color channel from the Edit drop-down menu.

Applying a Saturation adjustment of –40 removed some of the striking blue reflections and gives the hide of the animal a more natural appearance.

Applying Photo Filters

The use of color correction filters has been common in photography for many years. Now they can be replicated in Photoshop. For example, let's take a landscape scene photographed during the middle of the day, when the color of the light is naturally very cool (due to the blue cast).

From the Photo Filters options (*Image > Adjustments > Photo Filters*) I select a Warming Filter (in this case a mild 81) set to a medium strength (Density) of 32%. Comparing the two images, the second image has a much warmer tone than the original.

The Photo Filters menu has several filter-type options to choose from. However, if you click on the Color option you can manually select any of the multitude of colors that Photoshop supports.

When applying Photo Filters make sure the Preserve Luminosity box is checked in order to avoid adversely affecting the relative lightness of the image.

With the Hue/Saturation tool it's also possible to make more drastic color changes. Take this example of a fall landscape scene made to look more summery.

Color correction using Levels

Levels can be used quickly and simply to correct color casts using the gamma slider (the middle, gray slider) to make adjustments to any of the color channels independently. For example, to correct a yellow color cast caused by shooting an image under tungsten-type lighting with a non-corrected white balance setting, you can select the blue channel and drag the slider left to add blue.

The gamma slider works the same way in each color channel, adding color relative to the color wheel (see page 124). For example, in the blue channel, dragging the slider to the left adds blue, while dragging it to the right adds yellow (the complimentary color of blue). In the red channel, dragging the slider to the left adds red, while dragging it to the right adds cyan (the complimentary color of red), and in the green channel, dragging the slider to the left adds green, while dragging it to the right adds magenta (the complimentary color of green).

Alternatively, with the Levels Channel set to the composite channel, you can use the gamma (gray) eyedropper to click on an area of the image that should be a neutral gray. Using this method the gamma setting in each color channel will be set automatically to remove the color cast. However, this often results in an unnaturally colored image that requires further adjustment.

In itself, this option is limited and Levels can be used to apply more precise color corrections, as the lion example below shows.

Working under the Reds drop-down in the Levels tool, the shadow and highlights tools are moved to the point where they just start to clip. When making this adjustment I recommend using the Threshold Display Mode by holding down the Alt/⌥ key while dragging the sliders. In this instance, drag the sliders until any clipped pixels disappear from view and the screen is pure black. Repeat this procedure independently with the other two color channels (green and blue). This technique can be used to very precisely correct color casts in areas of highlight and shadow. Using the Threshold Display Mode increases the accuracy of your highlight and shadow point positioning.

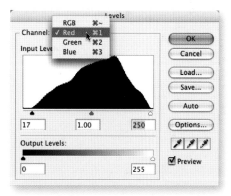

Color correction using Curves

Color corrections made in Levels will be sufficient in many cases, obviating the need to use the slightly more involved Curves procedures. However, there are times when what's needed is a more precise color correction than Levels can manage. In these instances, just as the Curves tool provides a more precise management of tones, so it does with color. As with most things in Photoshop there's more than one way to crack this particular egg. The process detailed opposite makes use of the program's ability to measure and temporarily record values.

In the bottom half of the Info palette you will see the respective RGB color values for each of your Color Sampler Targets (I'm assuming that this edit is being done in RGB color mode) numbered 1, 2, and 3. Against each RGB channel for all three Targets you will see two values. The first figure is the before (prior to remapping) value, the second figure is the new, remapped value. At this point the two values will match. However, the individual values for the red (R), green (G), and blue (B) channels are likely to differ.

The purpose of the remapping process is to match all three values for the Black point (Color Sample Target no. 1) to the lowest value of the three, and to match all three values for the White point (Color Sample Target no. 2) to the highest value of the three.

Although relatively involved, the Curves method provides by far the most accurate means of color compensation.

The Curves method

❶ The first step is to map the Shadow and Highlight points. Select the Color Sampler tool from the Tools menu. For a more accurate result, set the Sample Size (in the Options bar) to 3 by 3 Average.

❷ Using the Color Sampler tool, select first the optimum black point by scrolling and positioning the crosshair target (set the Caps Lock to on if the crosshairs don't show) over the point in the image that you want to make true black. Once you've identified the black point, click with the mouse to add your first Color Sample Target.

❸ Still using the Color Sampler tool, select next the optimum white point by scrolling and positioning the crosshair target over the point in the image that you want to make true white. Once you've identified the white point, click with the mouse to add your second Color Sample Target.

❹ Again using the Color Sampler tool, select finally the optimum midtone point by scrolling and positioning the crosshair target over the point in the image that is closest to middle tone. Once you've identified the midtone point, click with the mouse to add your third Color Sample Target.

#1 R:	23	#2 R:	211
G:	21	G:	200
B:	24	B:	196

#3 R:	122		
G:	82		
B:	58		

❺ The next step is to perform the actual remapping using the values in the Info palette (*Window > Info*, if it isn't already showing).

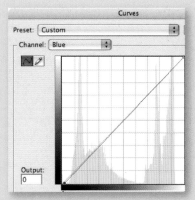

❻ Open a Curves Adjustment Layer *(Layer > New Adjustment Layer > Curves)*. Press [Ctrl]+Tab to select the Black point anchor. Open the Channel drop down menu in the Curves dialogue box and select one of the two channels where the Input color value is higher than the lowest Black Point value (in this example, I want to change the [color] channel, which has a 'before' value of x to an 'after' value of y - the lowest of the three values). With the relevant channel selected, click in the Input Value box and use the up and down arrow keys to change the 'after' figure to match the lowest of the three figures. Repeat this with the second non-matching color channel.

❼ In the same Curves Adjustment Layer; press [Ctrl]+Tab to select the White point anchor. Then, select one of the two channels which Input color value is lower than the highest value (in this example, the [color] channel. With the relevant channel selected, click in the Input Value box and use the up and down arrow keys to change the 'after' figure to match the highest of the three figures. Repeat this with the second non-matching color channel.

❽ If a color cast persists after adjusting the Black and White points then you can make a precise adjustment to the mid-tone point. Open a second Curves Adjustment Layer.

❾ I'm going to set an anchor point on the Curves line of each of the individual color channels. Scroll the cursor until it is directly over Color Sampler Target no. 3 (the mid-tone target). Then [Ctrl]+[Shift] click. A circle will flash on the RGB composite Curve line. However, when you open each of the three color channels individually, you'll notice that an anchor point has been added.

❿ To adjust the color balance, select the color channel that matches the unwanted color cast (in this example the blue channel) and use the up and down arrows on the keyboard to drag the Curve line up or down. As you do, assess the color in the image and set the adjustment when you achieve the preferred color.

Color correction for publication

It can be very frustrating for photographers who've labored over an image for hours or even days to find that the colors look completely different in print. Avoid this by fine-tuning your images for CMYK output.

One of the difficulties when working on an image for publication in RGB mode is that you are processing an image in one color space when the image will be printed using another (CMYK). And, because the gamut of the respective color spaces differ, it is possible that color clipping will occur.

To minimize the occurrence of clipping when making color enhancements, from the View menu option select the gamut warning (*View > Gamut Warning*). When the gamut warning is active Photoshop will display a gray mask over those RGB colors that fall outside the CMYK gamut, and therefore be difficult to match in print. Once

the gamut warning is displayed you can use the Hue/Saturation tool to reduce color saturation to bring all the RGB colors to within gamut.

Whether you choose to do this is another matter, as it can reasonably be argued that the responsibility lies with the publishers. If that isn't you then the chances are that you will be absolved from having to make such corrections. At the very least, make sure you clear this matter up with your clients or printers. Generally these people are specialists and by making adjustments yourself you are reducing the amount of information available to them when they prepare the document to print. It'd be a terrible

The gamut warning mode highlights areas that fall outside the CMYK gamut.

Relative and absolute methodology

When adjusting color using the Selective Color tool you can choose to add or subtract color percentages in relative or absolute terms (by clicking on the relevant button at the base of the dialog box). When Relative changes are made, calculations are made proportionally. For example, if you have a yellow with a starting value of 30% and then add a Relative 10%, the increase will equal 33%. Adding an Absolute 10%, however, would change the current value from 30% to 40%.

shame to lose the richness of the reds because Photoshop's defaults are needlessly pessimistic about the quality of your printing service's inks, for example. Don't say you haven't been warned!

Selective color

Using the Selective Color tool (*Image > Adjustments > Selective Color*) you can make precise and subtle corrections to both the RGB and CMYK primary colors, as well as black, white, and neutral gray tones. This can be a useful tool when you need to fine-tune CMYK files for print output, and this is really the only reason to use the Selective Color tool. Otherwise I recommend you perform color enhancements using the Hue/Saturation tool when editing in RGB color mode.

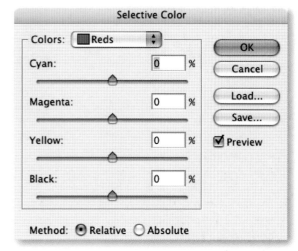

Adjusting the Red shades using the Selective Color dialog box.

CMYK files

If you work in an exclusively print-based workflow you might consider working with CMYK files. There are many reasons not to convert to CMYK until the last minute—certainly not until you're happy with all the adjustment and manipluations you have made to the image as a whole—but nevertheless there are benefits if you want to tweak the individual channels.

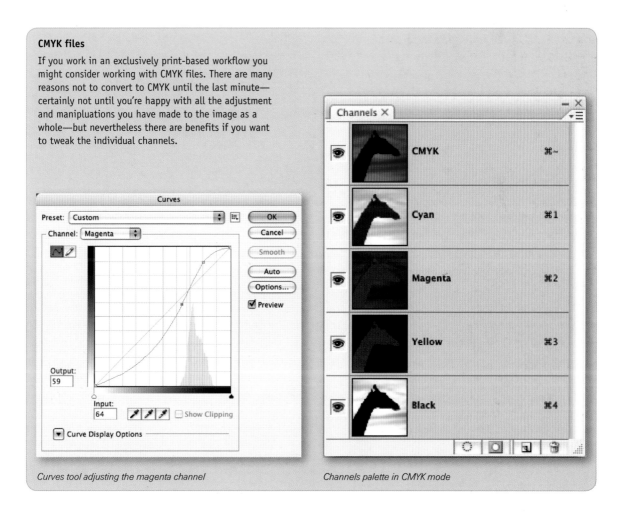

Curves tool adjusting the magenta channel

Channels palette in CMYK mode

Digital noise

Digital noise is in many ways more insidious than the film grain that preceded it. There are a variety of ways to get rid of it, notably Photoshop's Reduce Noise filter.

The phenomenon of digital noise is mentioned in several sections of this book. Although it is unrelated to film grain, the two things are often compared. This is because they both have the same general effect of degrading image quality. On the page opposite you will find a step-by-step guide to minimizing the occurrence of digital noise using Photoshop's Reduce Noise Filter.

The advantage of this Photoshop filter is that it marries noise reduction with maintaining edge detail. It also enables managing noise in the independent color channels, which further improves the overall performance of noise reduction.

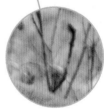

If you have several images that all require the same Reduce Noise filter settings, you can save custom settings by clicking the Save Settings icon to the right of the Settings drop-down menu.

Noise Reduction plug-ins

There are several independent software plug-ins that offer noise reduction. These include Dfine by Nik Multimedia, Noise Reduction by Neat Image, Noise Ninja by Picture Code, and Noiseware 4 by Imagenomic. I haven't had the need to use any of these products but have heard much positive feedback on Dfine (in particular) and Noise Reduction.

Noise reduction with ACR

There is a noise reduction function within ACR found under the Details menu tab. The advantage of this option is that you are working on the RAW data and so any adjustments you make are non-destructive. The disadvantage is that, compared to the Reduce Noise filter in Photoshop, the options are somewhat limited.

To apply color noise reduction in ACR, first magnify the Preview image to 100% and scroll to an area where noise is prevalent. First, apply a small amount of Luminance Smoothing, which will remove some of the noise. Be careful not to apply too much, as smoothing tends to reduce sharpness. A value between 5 and 10 should be sufficient. Then, depending on the level of noise, set the Color Noise Reduction to a value of between 50-80%. Finally, apply a small amount of Sharpness (between 10-20%).

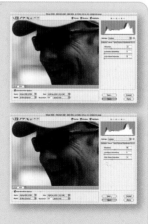

Removing JPEG artifacts

JPEG compression introduces artifacts to an image, particularly at high compression ratios. Try applying the Remove JPEG Artifacts option by checking the option box at the bottom of the Reduce Noise dialog box. This is also a useful option for rescuing GIF images that have lost significant color levels information, for example during a color mode conversion.

Using the Reduce Noise filter

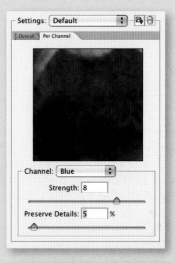

❶ Open the Reduce Noise filter dialog box *(Filters > Noise > Reduce Noise)*. You will see that it has two working modes, Basic and Advanced. Click on the Advanced button. This will add a second menu tab titled Per Channel.

❷ Using the Preview, display the image at 100% and scroll to a part of the image that contains a high level of noise, for example an area of shadow.

❸ In the Overall menu tab, set Strength, Reduce Color Noise and Sharpen Details to zero. Now click on the Per Channel menu tab.

❹ In turn, open each of the color channels and review the Preview image for the appearance of noise, which is revealed by the patches of black. Where noise occurs, increase the Strength setting. Set a low value where noise occurrence is minimal, increasing the value where noise is prevalent. In this example, there is little to no noise in the red channel and so I've left the Strength value set to zero. There is a small amount of noise in the green channel and here I set the Strength value to 1. Most of the noise is occurring in the blue channel, so I set a high Strength value of 8. So that the maximum amount of correction is applied, I set the Preserve Details value to a relatively low figure, in this case 5%.

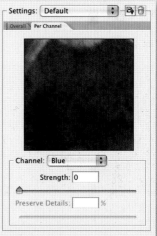

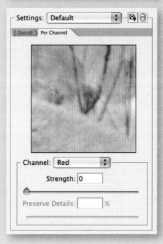

❻ You will notice that levels of noise are reduced significantly but that noise is still present. This is color noise and can be dealt with back in the Overall settings menu. Click on the Overall menu tab.

❼ Increase the Reduce Color Noise setting to a relatively high value, somewhere between 50-75%, depending on the level of noise present. Again use the Preview image to assess the adjustment.

❽ Finally, I apply an amount of Sharpen Details (between 10-20%) to recapture some of the edge definition that is lost during the noise reduction process.

Lens effects

Photoshop is equally well equipped to simulate desirable lens effects as it is to correct the problematic ones. Depth of field, focus vignettes and more are all easier to apply digitally than you might imagine.

Depth of field

Depth of field refers to the area of the picture space that appears in sharp focus. It is controlled in-camera by the lens aperture, focal length of the lens and camera-to-subject distance. A narrow depth of field means that objects in front of and behind the focus point appear blurred, while a wide depth of field means that more of the foreground and background appears sharp. Compositionally, depth of field is used to determine emphasis.

Depth of field is managed best in-camera, particularly where wide depth of field (i.e. foreground to background

sharpness) is required. This is simply because an out of focus subject will always be out of focus, irrespective of any sharpening techniques you may later apply in Photoshop. However, when the need arises, there are some Photoshop options still available to you.

Reducing apparent depth of field

Let's start with the easier of the two—reducing apparent depth of field to make sharp objects appear unsharp. You may want to do this to hide a distracting or cluttered background, for example.

The edges of the selection need to be softened, so press the Refine Edges button in the Tool Options bar and increase the feather to 20–30 pixels.

The original image has strong focus in the foreground, detracting from the real subject.

The first step in any depth of field correction is to mark out the unnecessarily sharp area. Do so roughly with the Lasso tool.

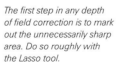

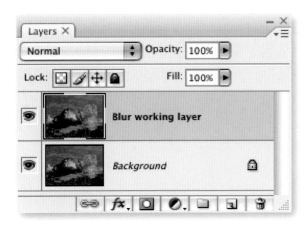

Before applying the Blur tool, at which point you'll be changing pixels, it's a good idea to duplicate the layer and work on the copy.

Select the Blur tool from the Toolbar and choose a soft-edged brush for a smooth effect. The Strength value will alter the extent of the blur from a single brush stroke. For a more accurate result, many slight strokes work better than a few heavy ones. Apply the Blur tool until you have created the required level of blur.

Using Gaussian Blur to mimic depth of field

Another method of reducing apparent depth of field is to use the Gaussian Blur filter (*Filter > Blur > Gaussian Blur*). This technique uses a minimal amount of Gaussian Blur applied in successive layers, increasing the effects of the blur as distance from the focus point increases.

As with many Photoshop techniques, reducing apparent depth of field takes a little practice so that the enhanced image appears realistic. As a rule of thumb, it is better to under-do an adjustment such as this and add to it subsequently with additional layers, than to overdo it and create an unrealistic image. With this technique there is the added danger of halos caused by the blur extending some of the sharp subject into the "out of focus" area, so make sure any sharp edges are only near light applications of the Blur filter.

The original image with a long depth of field.

Depth of field manipulations with Gaussian Blur

❶ Create a Duplicate Layer (*Layer > Duplicate Layer*) and name it Gaussian Blur 1. Turn the duplicate into a Smart Object using the flyout menu button beneath the Layer palette's close icon.

❷ Make a selection around the most distant part of the image, in this case the area behind the wooden huts in the background.

❸ Using the Refine Selection tool, apply a Feather of about 10 pixels.

❹ Apply a Gaussian Blur of between 3 and 5 pixels (*Filter > Blur > Gaussian Blur*). You will need to use trial and error to gauge the right amount, as the overall effect is dependent on the file size, but remember that we'll be adding more blur in later steps and we want to avoid the halo effect mentioned above. Click OK to apply the adjustment to the selected area (a layer mask is drawn automatically).

❺ Duplicate the layer by dragging it to the New Layer icon at the bottom of the layers palette, then click *Layer > Rasterize > Layer* to merge the blur in the duplicate layer. Turn off the visibility of the old layer and leave this in case you need to go back to it.

❻ Now select the foreground elements that you want to preserve perfectly and turn the new layer into a Smart Object too. Invert the selection (*Select > Inverse*) and apply a soft Gaussian Blur filter of only a few pixels.

❼ To further refine the effect, alter the Filter layer mask with a gradient (see Using gradients for softer blurring, opposite).

The selected area for the distant layer (non-selected area shown in red).

The selected area for the foreground layer (non-selected area shown in red).

Using gradients for softer blurring

❶ Click on the Smart Filters mask in a layer where only the subjects are highlighted, and switch to the Gradient tool.

❷ Select a White to Black gradient from the drop-down in the Tool Options bar and make sure the gradient is Linear (the leftmost of the five style buttons).

❸ Set the Mode to Multiply so that you will only add to the Black (non-effective) area of the mask.

❹ Now draw a line (holding shift if your image is perfectly horizontal) from a point at which your subjects would certainly be in depth of field (like the feet) to the point at which you want the blur to be fully effective. Alt/⌥-click the layer mask to see it in the main document window.

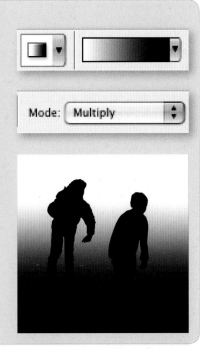

The final image has a gently increasing blur in the background, with a stronger one in the area defined first. The layers palette has a seemingly redundant first blur layer switched off, but it is a useful stage for reworking if necessary.

Applying a focus vignette

Remember having a brochure for Cokin filters? If you do, you'll recall that tucked away somewhere in the middle of the 200 or so pages was a filter that created a blur around a central clear point. Well, now you can do the same thing with Photoshop using Gaussian Blur. Just follow the instructions in the box below.

❶ Turn the Background layer into a Smart Object.

❷ From the Toolbar, select the Elliptical Marquee and draw a selection around the area you want to remain in sharp focus.

❸ Apply a Feather with a Radius of between 50 and 80 pixels—the best way to judge this is by using the overlay options at the bottom of the Refine Edge dialog.

❹ Invert the Selection *(Select > Inverse)*. This will apply the Gaussian Blur only to the area outside the original ellipse.

❺ Apply Gaussian Blur (Filters > Blur > Gaussian Blur) with a Radius of between 15-30 pixels. Use the Preview

138

Soft focus techniques

A variation on the focus vignette is to apply Gaussian Blur across the whole image to create a soft-focus effect, mimicking the effects of a soft-focus filter used in front of the camera lens. This is a technique often employed in portrait photography.

TIP

Selective soft focus
By applying a Layer Mask to a duplicate layer you can apply soft focus effects selectively. See Layer Mask—page 64.

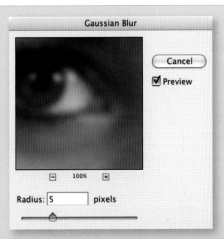

❶ Create a duplicate background Layer *(Layers > Duplicate > Layer)* and set the Blend mode to Lighten to replicate a lens effect.

❷ Apply Gaussian Blur *(Filters > Blur > Gaussian Blur)* with a Radius of between 1 and 10 pixels, depending on the subject (for portraits use a lower Radius). Use the Preview option to assess the correct level of blur. Click OK to accept the adjustment. If necessary, after applying Gaussian Blur you can restore some of the original image sharpness by reducing the layer opacity.

Sharpening

If you thought getting sharpness right finished with the focus wheel, you're in for a shock. Different media all require different looks and, if you want your work to look its best, you need to know how to achieve them.

Loss of sharpness is a photographic problem not limited to digital photography. During practically every stage of the photographic process, from image capture to output, there is potential for sharpness to be degraded. Sometimes the loss is slight, sometimes it can be significant, and if you want to minimize the effects of sharpness degradation then always use the finest lenses you can afford and a high-resolution camera.

The inevitable loss of image sharpness is, however, not the end of the world. In the days of darkroom printing, masters of the art used a technique called Unsharp Masking to improve sharpness. And, if you look in the Filters sub-menu in the main menu bar, you will find, under Sharpen, a function with the same name. In fact, there are several solutions to the problem of pixel softening, from in-camera sharpening to Camera Raw tools, and several options in Photoshop itself. Indeed, part of the problem is understanding which of the many and varied solutions available would help you most. At the end of the day the aim is always an image that is sharp in the appropriate areas and devoid of noise and artifacts.

In camera and scanner sharpening

Most digital cameras (and scanners, for that matter) have a form of built-in image sharpening, referred to as capture sharpening. In JPEG mode, this sharpening is applied during in-camera processing depending on the camera menu setting (determined by the user). In RAW mode, the Sharpen menu setting is recorded in the instruction set. The question, then, is should you use capture sharpening at all?

My answer is that it depends on certain factors. Prior to ACR, when I used Nikon Capture for my RAW conversions, I always set some level of in-camera sharpening. However, since switching to using ACR for my RAW conversion, I now switch off the in-camera sharpening and use the Sharpening function in ACR, simply because it creates a more straightforward workflow.

Then again, I always shoot in RAW mode. If I were shooting in JPEG mode and wanted to reduce the level of post-camera processing I needed to undertake, I might switch back to applying a small level of sharpening in-camera.

No Sharpening

Some Sharpening

Maximum sharpening

Sharpening in Adobe Camera Raw

ACR provides a Sharpening tool under the Detail menu tab in the Settings area of the workspace. This setting effectively replicates sharpening in-camera, but is more sophisticated and can be used with the complimentary Luminance Smoothing and Color Noise Reduction controls.

The first sample image is shown with no sharpening applied. It is a good example of a challenging image in terms of sharpening because there are areas of fine detail (the bird's feathers) that I want to appear well defined, but also there is a large area of even tone (the sky) in which I want to avoid introducing artifacts and emphasizing colored noise (often a result of oversharpening).

My first step is to set the correct exposure level and white balance setting (if appropriate). This makes judging detail easier and more accurate. Next, I enlarge the image to about 100% using the Magnification tool. I then use the Hand tool to scroll the image until I can see areas of both detail and continuous tone simultaneously.

I start the sharpening process by dragging the Sharpness slider to the right. I do this first in large adjustments so that I can gauge my "sharpness range" (i.e. knowing when enough is enough, and when some is too little). Once I have this range I then make smaller adjustments, fine-tuning the sharpening in smaller increments.

As I make these small adjustments I will begin to apply Luminance Smoothing, which removes artifacts from the area of continuous tone. This is a balancing act with the Sharpness setting, as one of the negative effects of Luminance Smoothing is a softening of edge detail (which in effect cancels out the sharpening process).

When I have the Sharpness and Luminance Smoothing settings well balanced and at the right levels, I then apply Color Noise Reduction to remove noise that has been emphasized by the sharpening process.

Going back to the sample image, compare the picture underneath with the original version at the top. Which do you prefer?

Okay, that's the ideal world, where I have all the time in the world to spend in front of my computer processing RAW files until they're perfect. Of course, this is rarely (if ever) the case. When you have a significant number of images to process, you have the option of selecting a "catch all" Sharpness (and Luminance Smoothing and Color Noise Reduction) setting, or none at all.

In its default mode, ACR is set to a Sharpness value of 25, with Luminance Smoothness and Color Noise Reduction set to 0. As a wildlife photographer I find the default value a little on the light side for drawing out detail in animals' fur and birds' feathers (for example). Therefore, I tend to tweak this value up to around 40-45. The other two I leave at zero and will deal with in other ways. For soft skin tones, however, I might be inclined to leave the default setting as a personal default as well, and deal with sharpening on a more selective basis in Photoshop itself.

Enhancement sharpening

Photoshop provides a number of alternatives in the *Filters > Sharpen* menu but for basic sharpening there are really only two options.

Unsharp Mask

Unsharp Mask, or USM, has been around since Photoshop 1 and its methodology is based on the reprographic film process of sandwiching during exposure an unsharp negative version of an image with its original positive. The purpose of this was to increase the edge sharpness on the resulting printing plate. In Photoshop, USM does pretty much the same thing, with similar results.

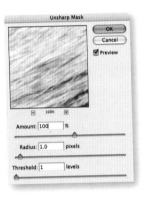

The Unsharp Mask filter requires the balancing of three criteria: the Amount of change applied, the distance or Radius around each pixel that the filter works from, and the extent of change it detects (Threshold) within that radius.

The downside of the unsharp masking process is the likely introduction of artifacts (pixel faults) that permanently degrade image quality and make digital noise more prominent. When sharpening is performed prior to retouching, and performing color adjustments in particular, these artifacts may become even more pronounced. Worse still, if any form of interpolation (resizing) is carried out prior to applying a USM filter, any artifacts will be included in the interpolation process, further degrading image quality. Therefore, sharpening is a process that should be carried out only after all other image processing has been completed.

Sharpening and Picture Agencies

If you plan to supply your images to a picture agency or photographic library then you may be aware that many such organizations request unsharpened images. The reason, as discussed above, is that sharpening will produce artifacts, which will be exaggerated if an image is interpolated (resized). Because the agencies don't know how their clients intend to use the image, and whether it will require interpolation, it is safer for them to apply sharpening once any interpolation is complete.

Unsharp Mask controls

AMOUNT
As its name suggests, the Amount control determines how much sharpening is applied (up to 500%). The higher the percentage, the more sharpening is applied. With the Preview box checked you can see the result of varying Amounts both in the USM dialog box (which shows a magnified section of the image) and in the main image. For the sake of experiment it's worth opening a test image and changing the amount value just to see the effects. After a while you'll get a feel for how much is too much. Typically, a value of between 50% and 100% (combined with a minimal Radius and low Threshold) is sufficient for replicating capture sharpening. But you may want to increase the figure to between 125% and 200% for output sharpening. However, that's a very simplified view of things and the settings you should use will depend largely on the type of pictures you take and how they will be used.

RADIUS
Together with the Threshold setting, the Radius setting controls the extent of the sharpening effect. Individually, the Radius control defines the number of pixels from the edge pixel, to which sharpening is applied. Increasing the Radius value enhances the emphasis around edges but also increases the likelihood of introducing damaging artifacts. Be wary of setting too wide a radius. Typically, a setting of between 0.5 and 1 pixel is sufficient, increasing to between 1.5 and 2 pixels for output sharpening.

THRESHOLD
While the Radius setting controls the number of pixels affected by the USM filter, the Threshold setting controls which pixels are affected. The Threshold control uses pixel brightness values to determine which pixels are sharpened and which are left alone. A low Threshold value means that more of the image pixels are sharpened, while a higher value reduces the number of pixels affected.

The advantages of the Unsharp Mask filter over two of the alternatives (Sharpen and Sharpen More) are a greater level of control and increased flexibility provided by the three filter controls.

For example, a Threshold setting of 3 levels means that any pixel more than 3 tones brighter than its neighbor will be sharpened. This is okay for mimicking capture sharpening but is less effective for improving edge sharpness, any may have a detrimental affect on areas of continuous tone, such as clear blue skies, by introducing sharpening and its associated artifacts to areas that gain no benefit from the enhancement.

A high Threshold value reduces the number of pixels to which the sharpen filter is applied and avoids areas of continuous tone from being affected, making a high value Threshold more suited to edge sharpening. For example, setting a Threshold value of 10 levels will cause only those pixels that differ to their neighbors in brightness by 10 or more tones to be affected. By definition, therefore, areas of continuous tone will be unchanged but clearly defined edges will benefit from the sharpening process.

Setting a Threshold value of zero determines that all image pixels are sharpened. The Threshold control is particularly important when using Photoshop to sharpen film scans, where scanner noise and film grain are present. With small-format film (such as 35mm) a higher Threshold value will reduce the likelihood of grain and scanner artifacts becoming sharpened. For medium and large format film (e.g. 6×6 and 4×5) the Threshold level can be set lower because grain is less apparent.

Sharpening by color channel

In its default setting, sharpening is applied to the composite RGB channel and affects all color channels equally. However, the individual red, green, and blue color channels are selectable via the Channels menu tab in the USM dialog box. See below for an example of how you can use this to perform a level of selective sharpening.

The sample image shows areas of detail (the buildings) and a large area of continuous tone in the blue sky. I want to increase contrast in the green leaves and the branches of the trees but minimise any sharpening in the sky. By opening the Channels menu tab and selecting the green channel (by hiding the red and blue channels using the Eye in the far left column) I can apply sharpening to this channel only. This minimizes the level of sharpening applied to the area of (blue) sky.

Swtching off the Blue layer allows you to apply sharpening to just the other layers, preserving sky softness.

Here the Unsharp Mask has been applied only to a single color channel.

A similar technique can be used for portraiture, where you may want to sharpen features such as the eyes and hair but not affect the soft skin tones. In this example, applying sharpening only to the blue and green channels will limit the affect of sharpening on the skin, which has a large portion of red. This is a pretty simple technique for which there is a better but more complicated solution, more of which opposite).

Let us, then, look at a working example using two different combinations of USM filter settings with an image that includes a mix of continuous tones and fine detail (below). If I set the Radius value to between 1-2 pixels and a Threshold value of zero, then apply an average amount of 100%, practically everything in the image is sharpened, without overcooking the areas of detail. However, artifacts have been introduced into the area of continuous tone.

Therefore, I adjust the Threshold setting and set a value of 10 levels. This reduces the effects of sharpening in the area of continuous tone, removing many of the previously introduced artifacts, and without adversely affecting the effects of sharpening in the areas of detail.

Edge sharpening

So far I have talked mostly about sharpening in terms of the whole image, but what happens when you want to selectively sharpen edge detail?

Edge sharpening is a technique that can be used when you want to sharpen detail but leave areas of flat tone unaffected. For example, in fashion photography, areas of fine detail such as hair, eyes, lips, and clothing need to appear sharp but skin tones benefit from a softer quality. The box opposite shows how the technique works.

Fading luminance

It is sometimes possible to limit the effects of chromatic artefacts caused by sharpening using the Fade tool. Once you have applied USM, select Fade Filter from the Edit menu. In the dialog box, change the Mode to Luminosity and use the Opacity slider to reduce the effects of the previously applied USM.

Make sure the Preview box is checked and review the effects of Opacity adjustments with the main image magnified to around 100%. Make fine adjustments until you're happy with the result. This technique produces a result similar to that previously accomplished by converting the image to Lab color mode, an old and somewhat outdated technique that degrades image quality unnecessarily.

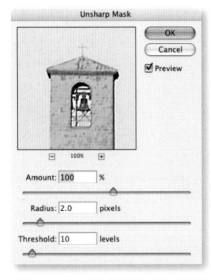

Here a standard adjustment is made to sharpen the image before the Fade tool is applied to perfect the effect (see box, left).

Edge Sharpening

❶ From the main menu, choose Select > All.

❷ Copy the Selection *(Edit > Copy)*.

❸ Open the Channels palette and make a new Channel by clicking the Make New Channel icon (second right) along the bottom of the palette.

❹ Paste the copied selection to this new channel (which by default is called Alpha 1, assuming you've created no previous new selections) by selecting *Edit > Paste* from the main menu bar. This fills the Alpha 1 channel with a grayscale version of your image.

❺ In the Channels palette, select the Alpha 1 channel to make it the active channel. Simply clicking on it will select it.

❻ From the Filter menu, select *Stylize > Find Edges*. This turns the grayscale image into something akin to a pencil drawing, emphasizing the edges in black.

❼ Make a Levels adjustment (see Levels, page 108) to increase contrast. You could try using the Auto Levels option *(Image > Adjustments > Auto Levels)* but if the auto adjustment is minimal then make a manual adjustment. What you are aiming to achieve is a very dark outline against a light background.

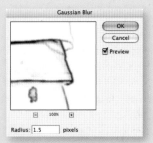

❽ Apply Gaussian Blur *(Filter > Blur > Gaussian Blur)* with a small pixel radius (around 2 pixels should do it, and no more than 5 pixels) to soften the edges of the Alpha Channel mask.

❾ We now need to turn the Alpha Channel into a selection. From the main menu, choose *Select > Load Selection*. In the dialog box, make sure that the Source Channel says Alpha 1 and then check the Invert box, to select only the black areas.

❿ In the Channels palette, reveal the RGB composite by clicking on the eye icon (which was automatically unchecked when the New Channel was created in Step 3).

⓫ Apply sharpening using either the Unsharp Mask or Smart Sharpen filters.

⓬ Once you have completed sharpening, deselect the selection *(Select > Deselect)*. If you like, at this point you can delete the Alpha 1 channel, although it isn't necessary to do so.

Using the Smart Sharpen filter

With CS2 Adobe introduced a completely new sharpening filter called Smart Sharpen. And, for most image sharpening applications I recommend that Smart Sharpen becomes your default sharpening filter. The real beauty of Smart Sharpen from a photographer's perspective is that it enables you to identify the root cause of any blurring and perform sharpening to reverse the specific effects.

Let me explain further. Image blurring is caused by one of three things. At the point of capture, blurring is caused either by inaccurate focusing, or camera/subject movement combined with too slow a shutter speed. The other type of blurring is computer-generated blurring, such as Gaussian blurring applied by the camera's processor when it assembles a RAW image file (the reason digitally originated RAW files always look soft compared to film).

In the past all Photoshop sharpening filters have worked by effectively creating a Gaussian Blur mask to define edge detail, mimicking sharpening techniques used by reprographic printers before computers came along. The Smart Sharpen filter, however, has taken things a step farther.

With Smart Sharpen it's possible to select the type of blur you want to remove with three options: Lens Blur (inaccurate focus), Motion Blur (camera shake, etc.) or Gaussian Blur (computer generated blur). Fantastic!

TIP

High Pass sharpening can be used in conjunction with Layer Masks (see Layer Masks, page 64) for selective application.

TIP

The values applied in the Smart Sharpen dialog box are sticky. That is they remain in place until they are manually changed. If you adjust the Shadows and/or Highlights settings, remember to reset them before working on a new image.

Saving Smart Sharpen settings

Clicking the Save a copy of the current settings icon, to the right of the Settings drop-down menu, saves the current settings. Saved settings can then be applied to subsequent images by selecting them from the Settings drop-down menu. To delete a custom setting, select it in the Settings drop-down menu and click the Trashcan icon.

High Pass sharpening

Most of the sharpening techniques I've described are particularly suited to capture and enhancement sharpening. High Pass sharpening produces a strong sharpening effect and is therefore particularly suited to sharpening photographs for output to a printer.

❶ Make a duplicate of the background layer *(Layer > Duplicate > Layer)*.

❷ Set the Blend mode of the duplicate layer to Hard Light. This will alter the appearance of contrast dramatically, but don't worry, it's only temporary.

❸ Select the High Pass filter from the Filters menu *(Filter > Other > High Pass)*. The original contrast levels will return.

❹ Use the Radius slider to adjust the Radius setting, assessing the effects in the Preview window (make sure the Preview box is checked). In this example, I set a Radius value of 13%.

Smart Sharpen options

Open the Smart Sharpen filter dialog box *(Filter > Sharpen > Smart Sharpen)*. In the dialog box you are presented initially with two options, Basic or Advanced. Click the Advanced option (we're going straight in at the deep end).

In the Sharpen menu tab, if you're used to the USM filter, you will notice some familiar settings, specifically Amount and Radius. These work in exactly the same way as they do in USM (see Amount and Radius, page 142).

Underneath is the Remove option, enabling the selection of the type of blur to be removed.

The Angle option is only relevant to Motion Blur. Use this option to define the direction of the motion blur. For example, vertical motion blur is a typical consequence of camera shake.

The More Accurate option is an interesting one. You'd expect to want to use the most accurate sharpening process at all times. But bear in mind that More Accurate applies to artifacts and noise just as much as it applies to detail, so this option needs to be selected with caution, and if there is a significant amount of noise or a high level of artifacts present, then I advise that you switch off this option.

In the Advanced mode are two more menu tabs: Shadows and Highlights. These settings enable you to fine-tune sharpening at the extremes of the tonal range, in effect giving you a more advanced Threshold control (see Threshold, page 142), which you may have noticed is missing from the Sharpen menu settings.

Using Smart Sharpen

The sample image shown below suffers from slight blurring caused by the animal's movement. I am going to sharpen it using the technique described in the box.

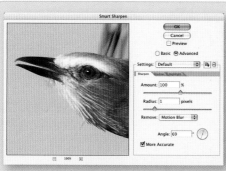

❶ Open the Smart Sharpen filter *(Filter > Sharpening > Smart Sharpen)*.

❷ As I want to sharpen the blurring caused by motion, I set Remove to Motion Blur.

❸ My main aim is to improve edge sharpness, so in the Amount box I set an initial value of 100% and a Radius of 1 pixel (an average setting).

❹ Because of the large area of continuous tone and, therefore, the increased possibility of visible artifacts and noise, I turn off the More Accurate option.

❺ I set the appropriate angle (based on the direction of movement) and I use the adjustment sliders to fine-tune the sharpening filter, concluding with settings of 150% (Amount) and 1.5 pixels (Radius).

❻ Checking the fine detail I notice that the sharpening filter has introduced some artifacts in the feathers. To remove these artifacts, I select the Shadow menu tab and apply Fade, setting the Amount to 40%, with a Tonal Width of 35%, and a Radius of 10 pixels.

Retouching an image

The word "Photoshopped" didn't find its way into our vocabulary because the program could adjust curves, useful though that is. Retouching is the ability to dramatically alter and improve upon the original image.

So far I have covered mainly those Photoshop techniques that enable you to enhance an image—taking what's there and making it better. However, there are occasions when you may want to go one step further and not just improve on image data but actually change it into something else. This is referred to as retouching, or repairing an image. For example, there may be dust spots from the digital sensor that need to be removed,

or blemishes on a model's skin that detract from the composition. This section covers some of the more simple techniques for image retouching.

The examples on these pages show how the Clone tool can be used in different circumstances. In the sky example below, I have used the Clone tool simply to remove dust marks from the image, which were caused by dust adhering to the photo sensor in the camera when

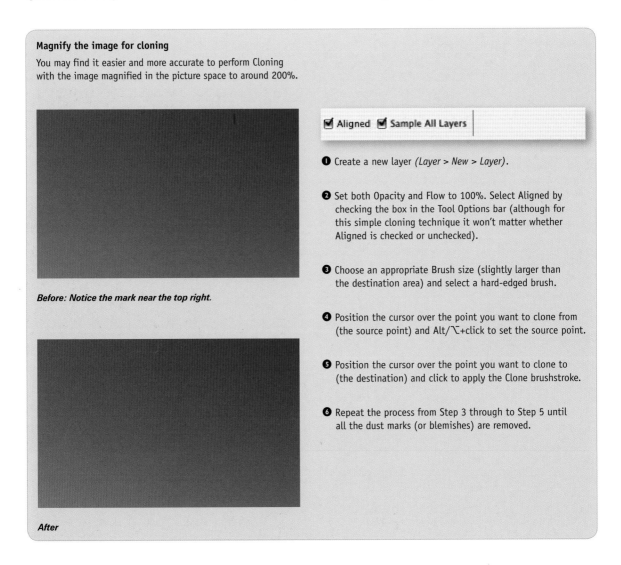

Magnify the image for cloning
You may find it easier and more accurate to perform Cloning with the image magnified in the picture space to around 200%.

Before: Notice the mark near the top right.

After

☑ Aligned ☑ Sample All Layers

❶ Create a new layer *(Layer > New > Layer)*.

❷ Set both Opacity and Flow to 100%. Select Aligned by checking the box in the Tool Options bar (although for this simple cloning technique it won't matter whether Aligned is checked or unchecked).

❸ Choose an appropriate Brush size (slightly larger than the destination area) and select a hard-edged brush.

❹ Position the cursor over the point you want to clone from (the source point) and Alt/⌥+click to set the source point.

❺ Position the cursor over the point you want to clone to (the destination) and click to apply the Clone brushstroke.

❻ Repeat the process from Step 3 through to Step 5 until all the dust marks (or blemishes) are removed.

the picture was taken. The second example is slightly more complex, as the Clone tool is used to remove a visually distracting branch from in front of the subject.

When using the Clone tool it is important to set an appropriate Brush size and hardness, and to set Opacity and Flow to their optimum level. When performing small repairs such as dust marks I always use a Brush size that is only slightly larger than the actual blemish. In areas of continuous tone, which is where you are most likely to notice dust spots and blemishes, I'll use a hard-edged Brush. I will also set Opacity and Flow to 100%. Because I want to clone from pixel data adjacent to the dust spots I want to remove, I check the Align option in the Options bar. This establishes a fixed relationship between the source point (the data to be cloned) and the destination (the area where the cloning will apply). I will then set a new source point before each stroke of the Clone tool.

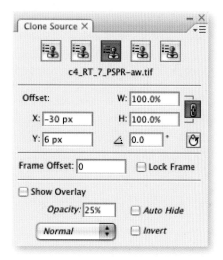

The Clone Source palette allows you to store additional source angles to copy from (see page 176).

Retouching textured areas

Repairing areas of texture requires a little more skill. I am going to remove a compositionally distracting branch from in front of my subject and retain the texture of the fur of the animal to produce a realistic result.

❶ Create a new Layer *(Layer > New > Layer)*.

❷ Set Opacity to 100% and Flow to between 10% and 20%. Deselect Aligned by unchecking the box in the Tool Options bar.

❸ Choose an appropriate Brush size (slightly larger than the destination area) and select a soft-edged brush.

❹ Position the cursor over the point you want to Clone from (the source point) and Alt/⌥+click to set the source point. For this type of cloning you need to select a source point that will accurately match the texture of pixels surrounding the destination point.

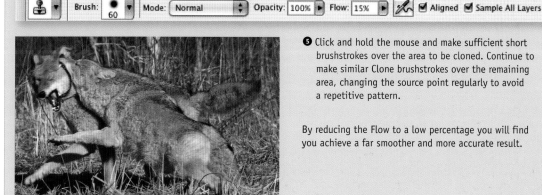

❺ Click and hold the mouse and make sufficient short brushstrokes over the area to be cloned. Continue to make similar Clone brushstrokes over the remaining area, changing the source point regularly to avoid a repetitive pattern.

By reducing the Flow to a low percentage you will find you achieve a far smoother and more accurate result.

The Healing brushes

The Healing brush's basic operation is very similar to the Clone tool, in that you select a source point and brush over the destination. However, the action that the Healing brush performs differs to that of the Clone tool. Rather than sampling pure pixel data, the Healing brush samples texture at the source point and then blends that with with the color and luminosity of the pixels adjacent to the destination point, using a feathered radius of up to 10% beyond the diameter of the brush.

This is likely to result in a smoother transition of both color and luminosity between the "healed" pixels and the "unhealed" pixels surrounding the destination. That's a useful technique when healing small areas. However, when healing larger areas of skin tone, for example eye wrinkles, changing the brush settings in the drop-down menu in the Options bar will produce more realistic results.

There is an even simpler way of healing small blemishes, though—the Spot Healing brush. In the Options bar choose a hard-edged brush of a size slightly larger than the destination area. Select Proximity Match for the Brush Type, and on the majority of occasions, blemishes (at least those surrounded by an unblemished area) will simply disappear when clicked on or brushed over.

Adjusting the brush shape

To handle wrinkles, reshape the brush from a round brush to a thin oval which matches the angle of the wrinkle. Alter the Angle to between –45 and –50, and set the Roundness to about 15%. With these settings you will produce a more random texture that looks more realistic on close inspection.

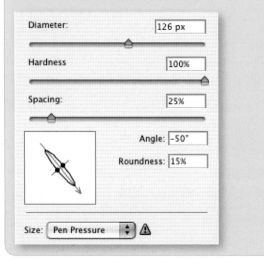

Healing and Spot Healing brushes

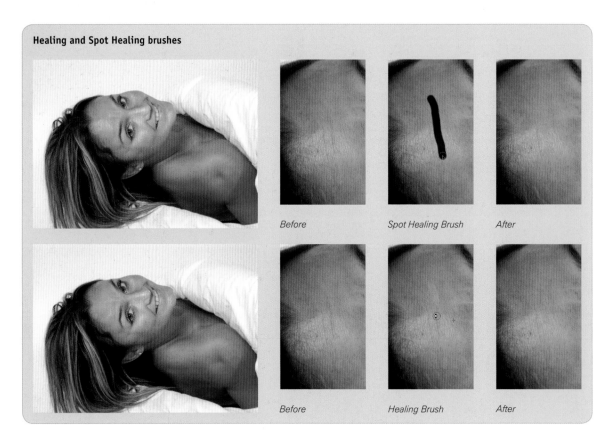

Before   *Spot Healing Brush*   *After*

Before   *Healing Brush*   *After*

Healing Brush small areas workflow

❶ Create a new layer in the Layers palette, select the Healing Brush tool from the Toolbox, and set the Sample drop-down to All Layers (so pixels from the original base layer can become the source texture, rather than the blank new layer.

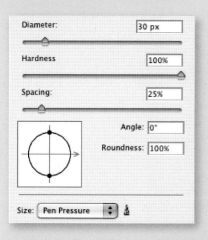

❷ Using "aligned" pixels is not as important as with the Clone tool, since the textures are blended automatically. Deselect Aligned by unchecking the box in the Tool Options bar. This fixes the sample point to a single source.

❸ Choose an appropriate Brush size (slightly larger than the destination area) and select a hard-edged brush.

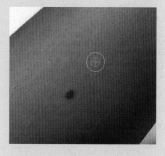

❹ Position the cursor over the point you want to use as the source and Alt/⌥+click to set the source point. It's important to select an appropriate source point. For example, if healing skin blemishes, select an area of smooth skin as your source point.

❺ Click or drag and hold the mouse to apply the Healing brush.

Using the Patch tool

Like the Healing brush, the Patch tool uses complex mathematics to blend the texture of the source point with the color and luminosity of the destination area. The difference is that it uses a selection rather than a brush. Admittedly selecting areas doesn't come up until page 154, but since this is an especially simple use for the method there is no reason to keep the Patch tool away from its natural bedfellows.

> ### Red Eye tool
>
> Worthy of an honorable mention here is the Red Eye tool. Although red eye is something you should seek to avoid at the lighting stage, this is nevertheless a retouching tool. Its use is incredibly simple—simply select the tool and click on the problem eye. You can also use the tool to change other colors by changing the appropriate setting in the Tool Options bar.

With just a few Patch alterations this model's face is made to look younger and fresher.

Patch (source) workflow

❶ Use the Patch tool to draw around the area to be patched over. In fact, you can use any of the selection tools (see Making a Selection, page 154) to make the selection, so long as you switch back to the Patch tool for the subsequent steps.

❷ Ensure that the Patch setting is set to Source in the Options bar.

❸ Drag the selection to an area of texture to sample from.

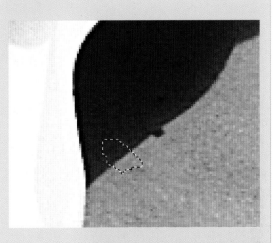

❹ When you release the mouse Photoshop will calculate a healing blend that accurately merges the texture from the source pixels with the color and luminosity of the destination area.

Using the Patch tool will generally give good results, although you may need a couple of attempts to get the source point right. This is particularly true when sampling larger areas. Try to avoid using areas of repeating patterns as the source and use the Healing brush (see page 150) to fix any slight inaccuracies.

The above example shows how to use the Patch tool to heal areas of an image. By selecting Destination as the Patch option in the Options bar, the Patch tool can be used to effectively copy and paste objects within the picture space.

Patch (destination) workflow

The destination workflow is much the same as the source method (see left) but rather than using the selection to identify a "bad" area for improvement, you use it to identify one you want to make use of.

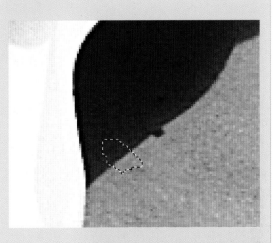

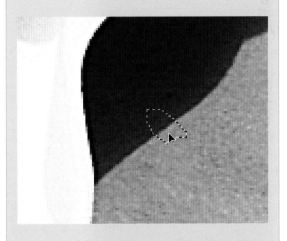

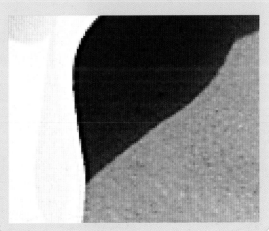

Selective editing

The first step toward making changes to specific areas of a photograph is being able to confine your work to those areas. The selection tools provide a variety of methods for marking them out.

A selection works in a way not unlike a mask—an area of the image which is "active" while you are applying other alterations. Although generally you'll want to avoid editing any of the pixels in the image's original layer—called Background in Photoshop's layers palette—there will undoubtedly be occasions when you want to work on specific regions of the photos. If you're using the Brush or Clone tools a selection is a simple way to keep you within the bounds of the area you want to change. Alternatively it is the first step towards making a layer mask (to restrict a filter or adjustment layer). In short, they're vital. In many ways they're the difference between Photoshop, a true image editor, and a catalog program like Lightroom.

Of course working within a selection is all very well, but how do you get there in the first place? Sadly it isn't (always) a matter of point and click, since the computer cannot automatically tell the difference between what is your subject and what is background. To it, all the pixels are simply numerical values. That's where the selection tools come in, with a variety of different methods to make selections, each appropriate to a different situation. The traditional Lasso, for example, simply lets you draw a shape of your choice with the pointer, while the more sophisticated Quick Selection Tool is a brush you paint roughly over your target. The computer finds everything that seems to be part of the object beneath the brush and adds it to the selection, stopping where the contrast or color implies the edge of that object.

Selections can be disabled by pressing Ctrl+D (*Select > Deselect*) as soon as you're done with them, or saved for future use via *Selection > Save Selection…*, the latter being useful if you think you might need to revisit that area of the image after you receive your client's comments.

Marquee tools

The Marquee tool provides options for making selections by predefined shapes, either rectangular, elliptical, or single row or column. To draw a marquee just click and drag to form an appropriately sized box or ellipse. To move the marquee, place the cursor inside the marquee's borders and move it with the mouse. The behavior of

A selection made with the Elliptical Lasso tool, with the Shift key held down to ensure a perfect circle.

Marquee tools can be modified with the modifier keys (see box, opposite), not least of which is holding down Shift to enforce square or circular dimensions.

Lasso tools

The Lasso tools allow a more flexible selection to be made. There are three Lasso tools: freehand, polygonal, and magnetic. To draw a freehand Lasso, simply click and hold with the mouse and draw around the relevant area. To complete the freehand Lasso, release the mouse. Photoshop will automatically join unconnected ends with a straight line to make a compete selection.

The Polygonal Lasso enables you to draw your own polygonal shapes, such as pentagons, hexagons, and octagons, of either regular or irregular design. Click and drag the mouse to draw a single line, repeating the process until you have the desired polygon. It is possible to revert to freehand mode when drawing a polygonal lasso by holding down the Alt/⌥ key while dragging the mouse. Releasing the Alt/⌥ key will take you back to polygonal mode. To complete the Polygonal Lasso, position the cursor directly over the origination point and click. Double-clicking the mouse at any point will cause Photoshop to automatically complete the lasso.

One of the more powerful Photoshop features is the Magnetic Lasso tool. The Magnetic Lasso uses edge contrast to determine where the outline should be drawn. As you drag along an edge, Photoshop continues to draw the selection outline, adding holding points where necessary, until the selection is complete (by clicking the mouse with the cursor above the origination point, or by double-clicking the mouse). To help Photoshop make an accurate selection you can manually add holding points by clicking the mouse.

If Photoshop draws an inaccurate outline you can erase the most recently drawn outline by reverse drawing over it to the holding point and pressing the Delete key. By repeating this process you can erase each outline between holding points in turn.

Improving the accuracy of the Magnetic Lasso

Because Photoshop uses edge contrast to determine the position of the selection outline, the level of image contrast affects the accuracy of the Magnetic Lasso. If the level of contrast is minimal you can add a temporary Brightness/Contrast adjustment layer, increase contrast and then apply the Magnetic Lasso. Once the lasso is complete, delete the adjustment layer. The lasso remains in place over the original image layer.

The accuracy of the Magnetic Lasso can be managed via the tool options bar by setting the amount of feathering (see Applying Feather, page 158), the brush width, and edge contrast. Typically, the smaller the brush and the greater the contrast, the more accurate the selection will be.

While using the Magnetic Lasso you can revert to freehand drawing by holding down Alt/⌥ while dragging the mouse. If you hold the Alt/⌥ key and click the mouse once, Photoshop will revert to the Polygonal tool.

Modifier buttons and keys

New selection. In its default state a Selection tool adds to the selected area.

Add to selection (hold Shift as you start to draw the selection) adds pixels to the selected area.

Subtract (hold Alt/⌥) removes pixels from the selection.

Intersect (Alt/⌥+Shift): only pixels from inside the selected area and the new selection will remain selected.

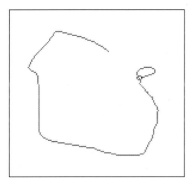

Drawing a selection with the Lasso tool is simply a matter of clicking and keeping the mouse moving in the right direction. Double-click to finish (or get back to the start point and click once).

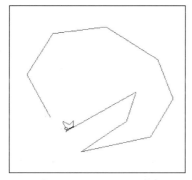

The Polygonal Lasso tool draws lines between each single click on the mouse. If you hold Shift as you work, lines are constrained to the nearest 45° angle.

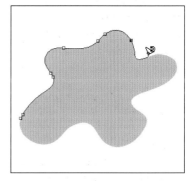

The Magnetic Lasso tool follows an edge by identifying the pixels between which there is contrast.

Quick Selection Tool

When you want to highlight an object of one or many colors, the quickest way to identify it is using the Quick Selection tool. Simply select a Brush Size from the Tool Options bar and paint over those parts of the object you want to select.

Just like the other selection tools you can subtract from the area as well as add to it, but by default the tool is usefully set to Add mode even when other selection tools aren't. This is much more natural when you're "painting" the selection on, but it would render the intersect mode useless (instead it is simply not available when this tool is selected).

Magic Wand

When making a selection of pixels of a similar tone, such as a clear blue sky, the Magic Wand tool is a relatively effective and simple tool to use. The Magic Wand selects pixels based on their luminosity within individual channels. When you click on one pixel Photoshop selects other pixels having the same luminosity value within a preset parameter, known as Tolerance.

The Tolerance setting can be adjusted in the Magic Wand's Options bar. For example, the default value is 32, which means any pixel with a value ±32 from the selected pixel will be included in the Magic Wand selection. You can also improve the accuracy of the Magic Wand selection after the event via the smoothing option (*Select > Modify > Smooth*), effectively increasing or decreasing the tolerance value to include or exclude pixels missed or picked up by the original selection.

The Magic Wand tool selects pixels the same or a similar color to the one you click on.

The Tool Options bar can be used to decide how similar in shade pixels must be to be selected (Tolerance); whether they must adjoin (the Contiguous option); and more. The higher the Tolerance, the more pixels are selected.

Using the Quick Selection tool

❶ With a good-sized, hard-edged brush, begin to paint over the area you want to select—in this case the headlamp made up of many different colors and shapes.

❸ You can switch to a slightly smaller brush to include details near the edge.

❷ Continue to brush, staying within the bounds of your object. Ocasionally stop to allow the computer to catch up as it performs additional processing as you work.

❹ With all of the headlamp selected, the selection was inverted *(Select > Inverse)* so that the yellow color could be lightened without affecting the headlamp itself.

Refining selections

Once you've made a selection it is often necessary to fine-tune it, which is what the Refine Edge tool is for. This dialog is the home of all the different methods for softening or otherwise altering a selection globally.

Each selection tool features a Refine Edge button in its Tool Options bar, or alternatively the window can be accessed via the Select menu. Despite appearing like any other dialog box, this window is somewhat deceptive, and can be kept onscreen in much the same way as a palette. Regardless of its place in the interface, this is a revolutionary addition to CS3, making the process of tuning selections infinitely faster and more pleasurable than it has been in the past. Perhaps the most useful of the five sliders (see box opposite for more information) is Feather, which allows you to soften the edge of your selection. Making it slightly fuzzy might seem silly, but in a digital photograph edges are never 100% sharp. A small feather will make a selection look much more natural on a new background, for example.

The tools and views in this box combine to make some tasks much more straightforward than they might otherwise be. When drawing a selection for a focus vignette, for example, all one needs to do is choose one of the colored backgrounds while adjusting the slider and there is live visual feedback as to how much effect this will have. Similarly, if you're trying to select an object to cut out, you can use these views to see exactly what you'll get. Oh, and if you don't like your changes, Alt/⌥-click the Cancel button to Reset.

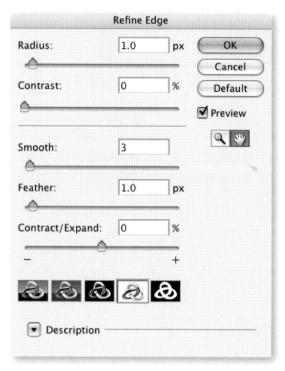

The Refine Edge dialog box. The description tab provides a handy reminder of the tools' functionality.

View options

Standard
The standard mode shows the selection in the traditional "marching ants" format.

Quick Mask
This switches to the red view available from the Quick Mask tool.

On Black
The selected area is shown on a black background.

On White
The selected area is shown on a white background.

Mask
The selection is shown as a mask, selected area as white on black.

Refine tools

Radius (low)

Contrast (low)

Smooth (low)

Feather (low)

Expand (100%)

Radius (high)

Contrast (high)

Smooth (high)

Feather (high)

Contract (-100%)

A higher Radius value catches more detail but has a tendency to leave artifacts, here shown as white fog because the On White mode is being used.

The Contrast slider can be used to eliminate the problems of the Radius slider by following the line of high contrast around the subject.

A high smooth value loses details especially in the more angular seaweed in the bird's mouth.

It is often desirable to soften the edges of a selection to make any adjustments less obvious. Applying Feather with a radius of 1 to 3 pixels is typically enough to smooth the transition between pixels.

After making a Selection you can modify its area by expanding and contracting the borders by ±100 pixels via the main menu bar *(Select > Modify > Expand/ Contract)*.

Radius and Contract

These sliders are perhaps the most difficult to predict in their operation. However, judicious use of On Black or On White can be very helpful when refining a selection on a sharp edge (for example one which, thanks to depth of field, is on an out-of-focus background). Increasing the radius will make the edge of the selection stick to shapes within that radius. Increasing the contrast will sharpen the selection along the edges.

Smooth

Perhaps unsurprisingly given its name, this option eliminates jagged edges in the selection line by softening them out. The higher the Smooth value, the less any corners remain. The practical upshot of this is that you can correct for any slight camera-shake with the Lasso tool or eliminate the telltale corner points created with the Polygonal Lasso.

Feather

As I've already noted, this mainstay of photographic selection is the simplest to grasp of the options here. It simply blurs the edge of your selection by the number of pixels indicated. A similar result could be achieved by applying a Gaussian Blur to a mask, for example.

Contract and Expand

This slider adds to or reduces the size of the overall shape of the selection. So, for example, contracting the selection by a small amount will eliminate anything near the edge which might not be part of the object you wanted to select anyway. As an alternative to the percentage-based slider, you can enter Pixel values via *Select > Modify > Expand* or *Select > Modify > Contract*. These might seem more natural measurements but the slider has the advantage of instant visual feedback.

> **TIP**
> **Quick Mask mode**
> *Another way to refine a selection is to use the Quick Mask mode (button near the bottom of the Toolbox). This allows you to paint a selection with the Brush tool (pressing X swaps between adding and subtracting from the selection).*

5 manipulation

The previous chapter covered techniques to enhance an image, overcoming the limitations of cameras, film and digital photo sensors, and physical and environmental circumstances. In this chapter I'm going to take things into a different realm by examining some of the more advanced Photoshop techniques for manipulating photographs and applying enhancements of a more obvious and dramatic nature.

Now, this section isn't for everyone. Some photographers—for example natural history photographers such as myself, and news and reportage photographers—would rarely, if ever, use many of the techniques I describe in the following pages. However, that isn't to say they have no legitimate part to play in other fields of photography, such as advertising, and there is no doubt that digital imaging has created brand new avenues for using photography in a commercially artistic way.

Clipping paths

Attaching a clipping path to a file is the best way to make sure designers include everything you want, and leave out everything else, when using irregularly shaped crops of your images.

One of the first things you'll need when performing advanced enhancements and manipulations is the ability to more precisely define areas of the image space using selections, masks, and extractions. The following section looks at drawing Paths with the Pen tool, as well as making extractions and masking subjects that are difficult to define, such as hair.

The basic concept of Paths was discussed in Chapter 2 (see Paths, page 70). In the following section I'm going to demonstrate how to use the Pen tool to draw a Path and convert the Path into a selection. For many photographers, drawing with the Pen tool may at first be a bit of a challenge. However, for outlining complex shapes, it is the ideal Photoshop tool to use. That said, it is a skill and will take some time and practice before you become efficient in its use. It has the further advantage—or necessity, from some clients' perspectives—of being saved as a clipping path in the industry-standard TIFF file. That clipping path can then be used by a layout program to create a cutout more accurate than would be possible with pixel data alone.

Editing a Pen Path

The speed at which you can draw a Pen Path, particularly in the early stages, may depend on how quickly you can edit your Path drawing. The Ctrl/⌘ key temporarily converts the Pen tool into a pointer that you can use to reposition anchor points. The Alt/⌥ key changes an anchor point into a corner point, and vice versa. Press the Alt/⌥ key and mouse down and drag to turn a corner point into a curve. You can change the direction of an individual handle by Alt/⌥+dragging on the handle. Finally, to add an anchor point to an active path, simply click on the position along the Path where you want the anchor added. To remove an anchor, just click on it.

The Paths palette allows for storage of more than one group of paths, and each can be saved as another clipping path.

Create New Path

Delete Path

Principal drawing tools

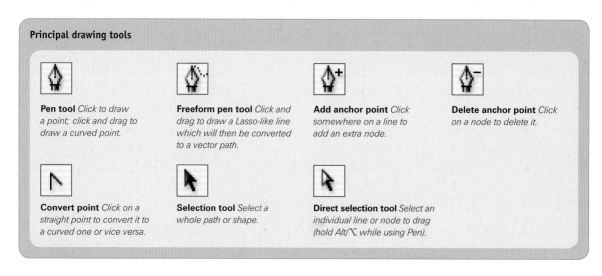

Pen tool *Click to draw a point; click and drag to draw a curved point.*

Freeform pen tool *Click and drag to draw a Lasso-like line which will then be converted to a vector path.*

Add anchor point *Click somewhere on a line to add an extra node.*

Delete anchor point *Click on a node to delete it.*

Convert point *Click on a straight point to convert it to a curved one or vice versa.*

Selection tool *Select a whole path or shape.*

Direct selection tool *Select an individual line or node to drag (hold Alt/⌥ while using Pen).*

Drawing Pen Paths

More straightforward outlines are relatively easy to follow. For this example, I'm going to draw around a straight-edged object.

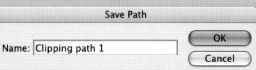

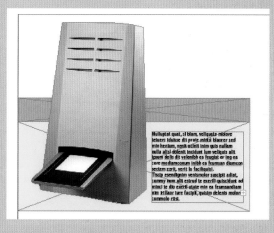

Here, the cutout image—saved as a TIFF—is placed in layout program InDesign and the clipping path can be selected from the program's menus.

❶ From the Toolbar, select the Pen tool. Then, select the Path icon in the Pen Tool Options bar.

❷ Define your starting point by clicking on the relevant point in the image. Then scroll the Pen tool to the next point in the Path, and click to add an anchor point.

❸ Repeat Step 2 until you have completed the Path and you are back at the starting point. When you mouse over the starting point anchor, a small circle will appear next to the cursor. Double-click to complete the Path.

❹ Drawing a regular-shaped Path like this is very similar to using the Polygonal Lasso tool. However, using Paths has the advantage that you can magnify the image and tweak the positioning of the Path to create a more precise outline. With the Pen tool selected, hold the Ctrl/⌘ key to turn the Pen temporarily into a pointer. Use the pointer to click and drag relevant anchor points to a new position.

❺ To convert the Path to a Selection, open the Paths palette *(Window > Paths)* and drag the Work Path icon to the Load Path as a Selection icon (third icon from left) at the bottom of the palette.

Sounds easy enough. But Paths come into their own when outlining complex shapes, including curved shapes. Unfortunately, this is also where it gets trickier.

Before embarking on drawing curved Paths I suggest you turn on the Rubber Band option by selecting it from the drop-down menu in the Pen Tool Options bar. With the Rubber Band selected, the segments you draw appear on the image as you create them, making it easier to assess what you're doing.

Extraction

The Extract filter is used to isolate pixel data from its background—whether for effect or as the first step in preparing a composite image.

If you want to isolate an object from, say, a distracting background, you can use the Extract tool from the Filter menu (*Filter > Extract*). The Extract command is like an automatic masking tool and, with some limitations (see Masking hair, page 166), it can be surprisingly effective. Its operation is much like a more methodical version of the Quick Selection tool.

> **TIP**
>
> *The Extract filter only works with 8-bits/channel files. Make sure the selected image is in 8-bits/channel mode via the Image > Mode menu option.*

Using the Extract tool

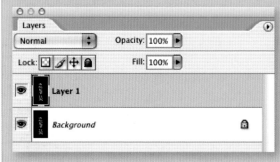

❶ Create a duplicate Layer *(Layer > Duplicate Layer)* and make it the active Layer, then select *Filter > Extract* from the main menu bar. This will open the Extract filter dialog box.

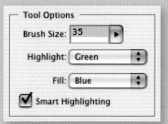

❷ Choose an appropriate brush size. For objects with relatively smooth edges, set a small brush size of about 20–30. Rougher or more detailed edges will require a larger brush size. You may also choose the colors for the Outline Highlight and the Fill. Color choice is a personal preference, but try to choose colors that are easily distinguishable from the image colors. While you're making adjustments, choose Smart Highlighting by checking the option box. This forces the Extract brush to closely follow the outline of the object, in much the same way as the Magnetic Lasso tool.

❸ Select the Edge Highlighter Tool (top icon in the Extract filter Toolbar) and draw a neat outline around the object to be extracted. If you make a mistake while tracing the outline, press the Alt/⌥ key to switch to Erase mode. You can then trace over the outline highlight to erase it.

❹ Trace a complete outline of the object.

Extraction modifier tools

Textured Image
Textured Image uses texture information to help define the outline.

Smoothness
The Smooth control is used to drag into the Extraction pixels that were excluded by the outline highlight. A value between 0 and 100 can be set. The higher the value, the more "missing" pixels are dragged in.

Force Foreground
Use the Force Foreground option when it is difficult to distinguish the object's interior edge. Select the Eyedropper tool (fourth icon from top in the Extract toolbar) and sample an interior color to set the foreground color. Then check the Force Foreground option box.

Edge Touch-up Tool
The Edge Touch-up Tool adds definition to less well-defined edges by adding or removing opacity.

Clean-up Tool
Use the Clean-up Tool to make pixels transparent. This is useful for fine-tuning the extraction during Preview. By pressing the Alt/⌥ key in the Clean-up Tool mode, you can reveal transparent pixels.

❺ Then select the Fill icon (second icon from top in the Extract filter Toolbar) and click on the area inside the outline highlight. This will fill the area with a color overlay.

❻ Click the Preview button to see a Preview of your extraction. You can now modify and clean the extraction using one or more of three tools (see box above). After applying any of these modifications, click the Preview button again to see their affect on the extraction.

❼ To apply the Extract, click on OK.

Masking hair

Hair is one of the most difficult things to select or mask, even using dedicated tools like the Extract function. This is an alternative method for generating masks that can handle the finer details.

The Paths tool and Extract filter are excellent at making selections of objects with relatively smooth edges. However, they perform less well when making a selection of a subject with a more random edge, such as a model's hair or an animal's fur. In these instances, there is a more accurate technique for making a selection that uses not only Paths, but also the information contained in the color channels to create an effective mask.

When you've isolated an image from its background using a mask, it can easily be applied to a new background.

TIP

When photographing a subject with the intention of extracting it from its background, I advise using a white or light colored continuous tone background. This will make creating an accurate mask easier to achieve.

Masking hair using Channels

❶ Open the Channels palette *(Window > Channels)* and analyze each color channel in turn before selecting the one with the greatest level of contrast between the background and the subject's hair. Create a duplicate of the selected channel by dragging it over the Create New Channel icon (second from right) in the bottom of the Channels palette. Select the duplicate channel to make it the active channel.

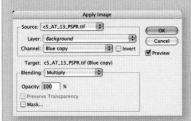

❷ Open the Apply Image dialog box *(Image > Apply Image)*. What we need to do now is increase the visual density of the hair to exaggerate the contrast. We can achieve this by selecting a Blend mode that will darken the image. Here I have chosen Multiply. You may need to tweak the effectiveness of the blend by reducing the Opacity. Click OK to apply the blend.

❸ Next we want to increase the contrast between the hair and the background. Open the Apply Image dialog box a second time. This time, set the Blend mode to Overlay and set an Opacity of 100%. Click the OK button to apply the blend.

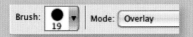

❹ The next step is to fine-tune the mask. Select the Paintbrush tool from the Tools menu, set Black as the foreground color and set the brush Blend mode to Overlay in the Brush options bar. The Overlay blend mode is ideal for tidying the edges of masks, which is what we're going to do next.

❺ With the Paintbrush tool, fill in the inner areas of the hair, then switch the foreground color to white and use the Paintbrush to clean background areas around the model, as necessary.

❻ Select the composite channel in the Channels palette. Draw a selection around the outline of the model, leaving the hair outside.

❼ In the Channels palette, select the duplicate channel created at the beginning of this process. Select Black as the foreground color and Fill the selection using the *Edit > Fill* menu option (set Use to Foreground Color, set Mode to Normal and set Opacity to 100%). Click the OK button to apply the Fill.

❽ Deselect the selection *(Select > Deselect)* then Use *Image > Threshold* to make the mask pure black and white, then select the black area with the Magic Wand tool and Contiguous switched off.

❾ With the selection active, switch to the composite image and apply the selection as a mask. You can now use the image over any background.

Retouching portraits

Building on the techniques of healing, patching, and cloning, it is possible to retouch away a wide range of blemishes and marks while still preserving the character of the original subject.

I have already covered some of the main techniques for retouching your pictures, such as the Healing brush and the Patch tool (see Retouching an image, pages 148–153). Here are some more techniques used specifically for retouching portraits.

Depending on your ambitions for your work, you could find yourself using some or all of the tricks here, but bear in mind that some are quite dependent on the others. For example, if you're making an alteration to hair color, it's a good idea to make sure you make similar adjustments to the eyelashes.

Before and after removing facial blemishes

Removing facial blemishes

This is a technique that quickly diminishes the appearance of facial blemishes such as freckles or acne.

❶ Open the Gaussian Blur filter *(Filter > Blur > Gaussian Blur)* and set the Radius to an amount where the blemishes are no longer distinguishable.

❷ Open the History palette *(Window > History)*. Select the history state called Open.

❸ In the History palette click on the empty box next to the history state titled Gaussian Blur. This will add a History brush icon in the box.

❹ Select the History Brush from the Toolbar and in the History brush Options bar change the Blend mode to Lighten. Use the History brush to paint the area of the face. Because the Blend mode is set to lighten, the painting will affect only those pixels darker than the Gaussian blur state.

Before and after the advanced wrinkle technique (see box). Some wrinkles are preserved to prevent the image looking unnatural.

TIP

You can reduce the effect of the History brush to reveal more detail by reducing the Opacity in the History Brush options bar.

Advanced wrinkle removal

It's not always appropriate to remove every wrinkle as the results can be less than convincing. Here's a technique to lessen the appearance of wrinkles without removing them altogether.

❶ Create a duplicate background layer *(Layer > Duplicate)* and select it as the active layer.

❷ Use the Healing brush to remove the wrinkles (see Patching and Healing, page 150-155).

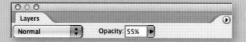

❸ Reduce the Opacity of the duplicate background layer. This will allow some of the original detail (wrinkles) in the main background layer to show through. You'll need to tweak the Opacity level and visually assess the optimum value.

Enhancing eyes

Eyes are often a subject's most important feature. There are a couple of factors that help make the eyes stand out, and perhaps the most obvious (but still highly effective) trick is to simply whiten them. The next is to perform a localized sharpening. This will create a sharpened eye without affecting the skin tones or producing artifacts in other areas of the image. Finally, no book on Photoshop is complete without its section on removing red-eye, though to be honest this is something that shouldn't happen to anyone using decent equipment. Red eye is the result of using flash lighting perpendicular to the eye when the pupils are dilated. It can be avoided quite easily by angling the flash or by using a diffuser to scatter the light from the flash. However, in case neither option has been possible, there is a simple solution. Just click inside the affected eye with the Red-eye Removal tool.

The simple act of whitening the eyes has improved this picture dramatically.

Whitening eyes

❶ Create a Curves adjustment layer *(Layer > New Adjustment Layer > Curves)*. When the Curves dialog is displayed, click OK without making any adjustments. In the Layers palette make the Curves adjustment layer the active layer and set the Blend mode to Screen.

❷ Set the background color to black (press D on the keyboard) and then select the Curves adjustment Layer Mask. Press Ctrl/⌘+Delete/⌫ on the keyboard. This will Fill the Mask with Black and the image will revert to its normal state.

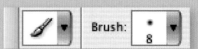

❸ Make sure the foreground color is set to white (it should be, as pressing D reverts this to its default white). Select the Brush tool from the Toolbar. Select a soft-edged brush and set a very small brush Size.

❹ Carefully paint over the whites of the eyes. You may find it easier to make a feathered selection. As you paint, the Screen effect of the Curves Adjustment Layer will show. If the new white looks too bright, reduce the Opacity of the layer in the Layers palette. Tweak the adjustments until you get a natural-looking effect.

Mixing techniques

Although they are presented separately on this page, there is no reason not to combine the two methods. If you are doing so, be sure that your Curves adjustment ends up above the Sharpening Pupils technique in the layers stack or it will not work.

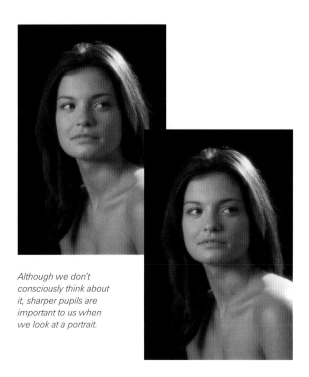

Although we don't consciously think about it, sharper pupils are important to us when we look at a portrait.

Sharpening pupils

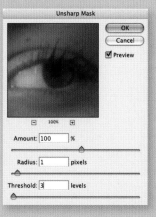

❶ Open the Unsharp Mask filter *(Filter > Sharpen > Unsharp Mask)* and set an Amount of 100%, a Radius of 1 pixel, and a Threshold of 3 levels. Click OK to apply the filter.

❷ Repeat Step 1 twice more. In all you should sharpen the image three times. At this point the image will look pretty awful.

❸ Open the History palette. There should be four History States, starting with Open followed by three Unsharp Mask states.

❹ Select the Open history state by clicking on it.

❺ Click on the empty box adjacent to the last Unsharp Mask history state. A History Brush icon will appear in the box.

❻ Select the History Brush from the Toolbar. Select a soft-edged brush and set the size to match the size of the iris. Click once over the iris with the History Brush.

To remove red eye, select the Red Eye tool from the Toolbar. The default options will work in most cases and it's best to try it and make any necessary adjustments if necessary, after performing an Undo (Edit > Undo). Then center the crosshairs in the section of the eye that is red and click. Photoshop does the rest. Remember to do both eyes!

171

Recoloring hair

In an age when hair stylists can achieve international fame, Photoshop has found a role not only in altering fashion photography but in simulating possible hair changes in high-class hair salons. Inevitably that means that rather than simply selecting the hair area (for which you can try variants of the technique on page 166) and applying a Hue/Saturation adjustment, it is also sometimes necessary to simulate highlights and other "regional" applications of dye. The technique shown here is a good solution, however you'll inevitably find yourself needing to rely on artistry as much as technique since you'll need to follow the lines of the hair by hand.

The hair in this image is the result of a masked color change. To try the effect for yourself, see the box.

Changing the color of hair

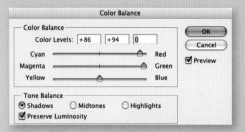

❶ Create a Color Balance adjustment layer *(Layer > New Adjustment Layer > Color Balance)* and make this the active layer. Use it to adjust the color settings to produce the new hair color. I've opted for a strawberry blonde effect. At this point the whole image will be affected by the Color Balance adjustment, but that doesn't matter.

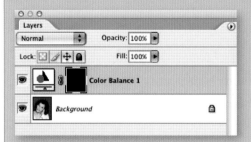

❷ Set the background color to black (press D on the keyboard). In the Layers palette, select the Color Balance mask and press Alt/⌥+Delete/⌫ on the keyboard. This will fill the Color Balance Mask with black and the image will revert to its uncolored state.

❸ Draw a selection around the hair. Select the Brush tool from the Toolbar. Select a soft-edged brush and set the Opacity to around 20-25%. Use the Brush to paint over the hair. As you paint on the Mask, the new color shows through. To increase the color effect, increase the Opacity of the brush.

Hotspots

Uneven lighting or light reflecting off shiny surfaces can cause hotspots on any surface, and skin is especially vulnerable, not least because the irregular shape of a face or body means at least one side is likely to be facing a light source. This is what you labor to avoid when placing lights in the studio, but there is little you can do when working outside in the sunshine, especially when taking candid shots. Hotspots can ruin a good portrait photograph. Mercifully they can be easily removed using the Clone Stamp tool and the right combination of settings (see box below).

The bright hotspot where this fisherman's hair parts detracts from his concentrated expression. A minor reduction in this has great effect.

Removing hotspots

❶ Create a new layer *(Layer > New > Layer)* and set this as the active layer.

Mode:	Darken	⬍

❷ Select the Clone tool from the Toolbar and in the Clone tool Options bar select a medium-sized, soft-edged brush. Set the Blend mode to Darken and then reduce Opacity to between 40 and 50%. This means that any adjustments we make affect only the pixels that are lighter than the surrounding area, i.e. the hotspots. Make sure the Sample all Layers option is checked.

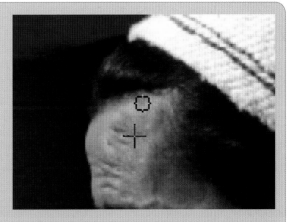

❸ Select a source point (Alt/⌥+click) from an area of skin unaffected by hotspots (or other blemishes) but that is of a similar tone to the skin surrounding the area you want to fix.

❹ Paint the areas where the hotspots occur, remembering to regularly resample nearby areas of skin as you paint on different areas.

Softening skin

Fashion photographers are probably very familiar with the Hasselblad Softar No. 2 filter. This technique mimics this filter's effects, softening skin tones, lowering contrast, and adding a touch of soft flare.

Softening an image with the Gaussian Blur filter and painting some details back gives finer control than is possible with a camera-mounted filter.

Softening skin

❶ Create two duplicate background layers *(Layer > Duplicate Layer)*. In the Layers palette, hide Layer 1 copy (click on the eye icon to the left) and make Layer 1 the active layer.

❷ Still in the Layers palette, set the Blend mode of Layer 1 to Darken.

❸ Open the Gaussian Blur filter *(Filter > Blur > Gaussian Blur)* and set a Radius of between 35 and 45 pixels. Click the OK button to apply the filter.

❹ Open the Layers palette and hide Layer 1. Then reveal the top layer (Layer 1 copy) by clicking the empty box on the left. The Eye icon will reappear. Make Layer 1 copy the active layer and set the Blend mode to Lighten.

❺ Open the Gaussian Blur filter and set a Radius of between 55 and 65 pixels. Click the OK button to apply the filter.

❻ Make Layer 1 the active layer and reduce Opacity to 40%.

❼ Hide the background layer, then create a new layer *(Layer > New)* and move it to the top of the layer stack in the Layers palette.

❽ Hold the Alt/⌥ key and select Merge Visible from the Layers palette flyout menu. This creates a flattened version of the visible layers in the new layer.

❾ In the Layers palette, reveal the background layer and hide Layer 1 and Layer 1 copy. Layer 2 should remain visible.

❿ Make Layer 2 the active layer and set Opacity to around 40%. This creates a softening effect over the entire image.

⓫ Because we don't want the entire image to be soft (we want the eyes, hair and lips to appear sharp) we're going to paint on a Layer Mask. With Layer 2 still the active layer, create a Layer Mask (click the New Layer Mask icon).

⓬ Set the foreground color to black. Select the Brush tool and select a small, soft-edged brush in the Options bar.

⓭ Carefully paint over the areas you want to show full detail.

Remodeling the mouth

The Liquify tool is one of the most useful in Photoshop, although it does require working in a seperate sub-program. It works by allowing you to edit a mesh which starts out as a square grid. You can push it this way and that and the image is warped to fit the new mesh. The result of this is that you can reposition features and—if you don't go over the top—convincingly alter someone's look or their expression.

The digital equivalent of your mother's favorite request: "Turn that frown upside down."

The Liquify tool

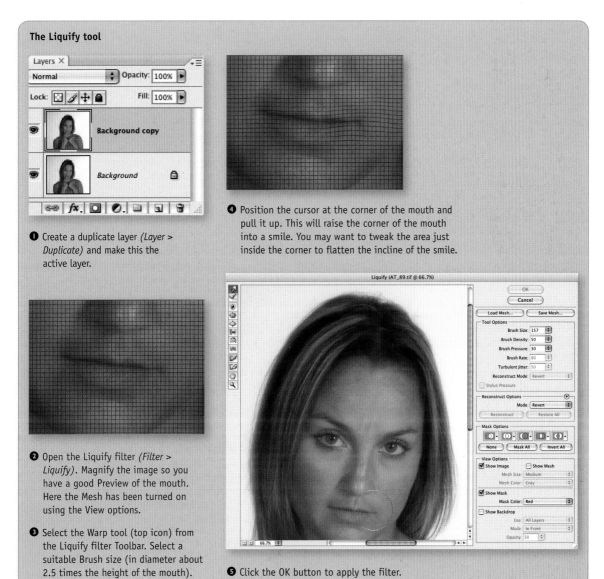

❶ Create a duplicate layer *(Layer > Duplicate)* and make this the active layer.

❷ Open the Liquify filter *(Filter > Liquify)*. Magnify the image so you have a good Preview of the mouth. Here the Mesh has been turned on using the View options.

❸ Select the Warp tool (top icon) from the Liquify filter Toolbar. Select a suitable Brush size (in diameter about 2.5 times the height of the mouth).

❹ Position the cursor at the corner of the mouth and pull it up. This will raise the corner of the mouth into a smile. You may want to tweak the area just inside the corner to flatten the incline of the smile.

❺ Click the OK button to apply the filter.

Cloning across multiple images

Cloning using the Clone Source palette means you're not restricted to taking data from pixels in the same image. You can build up an image with textures from anywhere you choose.

The Clone Stamp tool can acomplish a lot simply by duplicating pixels from one area to another, but when accompanied by its Tool Options bar variations and the Clone Source palette it's possible to achieve even more without changing tools. Perhaps the single biggest difference when using the Clone Source palette is that you can make your Alt-click to choose a source in another, wholly different image. It doesn't even have to have the same resolution as you can scale it as you apply it (though obviously scaling up would harm the crispness).

Combine this with the Show Overlay option, which can show you a representation of the whole source image, and you have a very powerful tool for applying elements from one image to another using a fluid and natural brush-based tool. Because you can see what you'll be applying you can decide where to begin painting perfectly, or even revisit the relative positioning of the source without having to return to it. In many ways this palette merely shows you the processing behind the Clone Stamp, but that's no bad thing.

When cloning it can be useful to copy information from one layer and put the new pixels onto another. In order to do this, choose Sample: All Layers using the drop-down menu at the right of the Clone Stamp's Tool Options bar. Indeed if the tool is not behaving as expected, check this setting first. You might also want to ignore the effects of adjustment layers, which can be achieved by clicking the icon next to this option (this applies equally to cloning within one image).

A word of advice. Many will tell you to choose a lower opacity and then slowly build up the cloned area using a low-opacity brush. This might be good advice for removing facial blemishes, but if you're placing a large area of another image then repeatedly stopping will only slow you down. Far better to get the texture across the image where you want it and, if necessary, make corrections later with a layer mask or the Eraser tool.

As with many of Photoshop's features, it takes time to master and varies from image to image, but eventually you'll find the technique that works for you.

Using graphics from outside the image

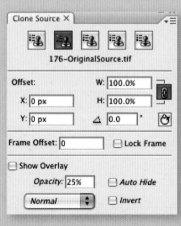

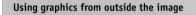

The original image needs some more detail in the empty sky, and that detail is found, although the wrong way up, in this spare horizontal frame.

Selecting Clone Source 2 (it's useful to leave 1 for the current or target image), Alt/⌥click on the cloud in the source image.

Switch back to the target image and check the Show Overlay button in the Clone source. The overlay follows the pointer.

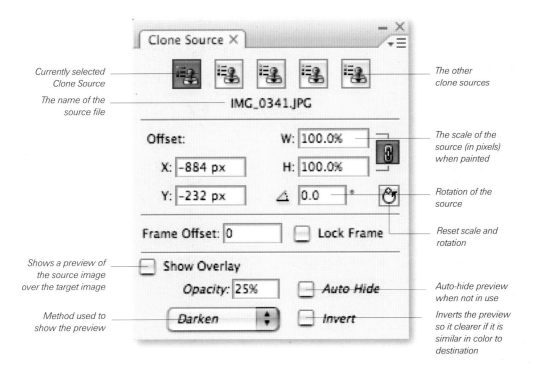

Currently selected Clone Source — *(icon)*

The name of the source file — **IMG_0341.JPG**

The other clone sources —

The scale of the source (in pixels) when painted —

Rotation of the source —

Reset scale and rotation —

Offset:
X: -884 px
Y: -232 px
W: 100.0%
H: 100.0%
△ 0.0°

Frame Offset: 0   Lock Frame

Shows a preview of the source image over the target image — Show Overlay

Opacity: 25%   Auto Hide — Auto-hide preview when not in use

Method used to show the preview — Darken   Invert — Inverts the preview so it clearer if it is similar in color to destination

---

TIP

Layers
It is not necessary to use the Aligned mode in cloning at all—uncheck the option to paint with the pattern beneath the original sample

---

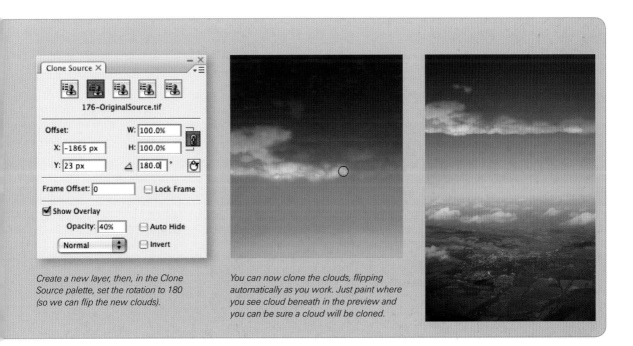

Clone Source ✕
176-OriginalSource.tif
Offset: W: 100.0%
X: -1865 px   H: 100.0%
Y: 23 px   △ 180.0°
Frame Offset: 0   Lock Frame
☑ Show Overlay
Opacity: 40%   Auto Hide
Normal   Invert

Create a new layer, then, in the Clone Source palette, set the rotation to 180 (so we can flip the new clouds).

You can now clone the clouds, flipping automatically as you work. Just paint where you see cloud beneath in the preview and you can be sure a cloud will be cloned.

Lighting techniques

One of the more interesting filters is the Lighting Effects tool. This feature, almost a program in its own right, allows you to alter the mood and atmosphere of a shot surprisingly effectively.

The Lighting Effects filter (*Filter > Render > Lighting Effects*) enables you to add a multitude of different lighting effects to an image. At first glance the Lighting Effects dialog box looks complex, and indeed you could spend hours perfecting your lighting techniques. However, it's also possible to add some simple lighting effects when you know what all the controls are for.

The Style setting provides several predefined lighting styles selectable from the drop-down menu. Underneath the Style setting are the Light Type settings, which enable you to control the type of light source (Spotlight, Omni, or Directional), its Intensity, and the Focus.

You can also change the color of the lighting effect. In default mode color is set to white light. But this can be changed by clicking on the color swatch next to the Intensity adjustment slider. This brings up the Color Picker dialog box, from which you can choose any color for the lighting effect. The Properties adjustments enable you to alter other light attributes defined by external factors, such as reflective surface and climate.

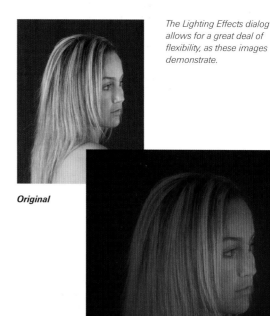

The Lighting Effects dialog allows for a great deal of flexibility, as these images demonstrate.

Original

A single red light applied

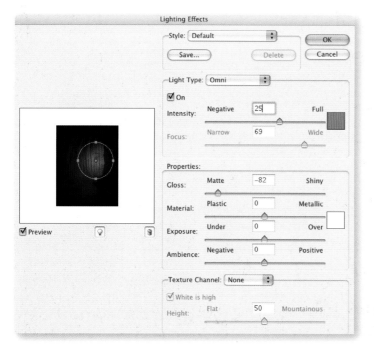

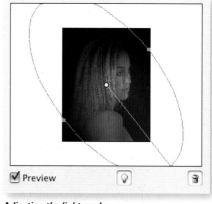

Adjusting the light angle

Lighting Effects properties

GLOSS

The Gloss control defines the surface of your subject, switching between Matte and Shiny. Toward Matte the lighting effect will appear partially absorbed. As you increase the value towards Shiny, a more reflective effect is achieved.

MATERIAL

The Material slider produces a similar effect to the Gloss slider. Dragging the slider towards the Plastic setting reduces the light's spectral characteristics. Shifting the slider towards the Metallic setting focuses the effect and adds more highlight.

EXPOSURE

As the name suggests, the Exposure slider control lightens and darkens the entire image. Dragging towards the Underexpose setting darkens the image, while dragging towards the Overexpose setting lightens it.

AMBIENCE

The Ambience slider defines how much ambient light is applied to the effect. The higher the value, the more ambient light is introduced and the lighter the overall picture. As the Ambient value is decreased, the effects of the filter become more apparent.

ADDING TEXTURE

The Texture Channel settings enable you to add three-dimensional relief to the filter effect. The application is based on the grayscale values of a specific color channel, where white or black becomes the highest relief area. The Texture Channel drop-down menu lets you select the RGB (in RGB color mode) color channel on which the effect will be based. Selecting None turns off any texture styles. Once you've set the source color channel, adjust the Height slider to vary the amount of the relief. Dragging the slider to the right increases the appearance of texture. Conversely, dragging the slider to the right will reduce texture effects. Click the White is High option box to set white tone as the high relief spot. Alternatively, leave it unchecked to set black tone as the highest area.

To add multiple light effects, drag the light bulb icon under the Preview image on the left side of the dialog box into the thumbnail Preview area. You can then reposition the light and change its type and color using the method described above. However, because Properties and Texture Effects apply to the image and not to individual lights, any Properties and Texture settings will affect all lights in a multiple lighting filter effect.

SAVING LIGHTING EFFECTS

Once you have created a specific Lighting Effect you can save it using the Save button under Style. Give the effect a meaningful name. When you want to reuse the effect, open it from the Style drop-down menu.

SPOTLIGHT

Spotlight recreates the type of light produced by a point light source, with a hotspot that fades as it dissipates. It has a center point with an oval that defines the spread of light. Drag the handles to increase or decrease the spread. The intensity of the effect is greater when the oval is smaller, in the same way as a spotlight is more intense the closer it is to the subject.

OMNI

The Omni light type recreates light from a diffused source, such as sunlight on an overcast day or bounced flash lighting. As with the Spotlight, the spread of lighting from the Omni light type can be spread using the handles of the control area. The wider the spread, the less intense the light.

DIRECTIONAL

The Directional light floods the surface with even light. Adjusting the directional control makes the entire effect brighter or darker, without changing the direction of the light source. The hardness of the light can be increased by moving the directional line closer to the center point. Shifting it farther from the center softens it.

INTENSITY AND FOCUS

The Intensity slider controls the brightness of the light in the same way that altering the size of the oval or circle. But this slider enables you to compose the correct spread, while modifying the intensity to suit. The zero setting effectively switches off the effect, creating a flat result. At its highest setting, 100, the effect is at its most intense. Setting a negative intensity value casts a black smudge across the image.

The Focus control further defines the spread between pinpoint and omni-directional. Widening the focus creates a more diffused lighting effect, while narrowing the focus gives an effect more like a spotlight.

Adding an additional lighting effect from the opposite side completely transforms the image.

Vanishing Point corrections

Cloning only works well on a flat plane, but real life tends to involve perspective. The Vanishing Point filter can often provide the solution in these situations.

The Vanishing Point filter enables you to copy details from one perspective plane to another, while matching the perspective of the image. Incredibly useful in itself, and with some of the bells and whistles that this tool has gained it can be even more effective. For example, if you're working on an image of a building with two planes it is even possible to Clone around the side of it.

Once again this tool takes you out of the standard Photoshop interface into a specialized window, so perform all your work on a duplicate flattened layer to be sure all the pixel data you need is available to you. The interface consists of a main viewer with all the usual controls (Hand and Zoom) as well as a set of Clone-like tools and two less familiar icons which allow you to define and edit perspective planes. What this means is that you draw a four-sided shape over a surface which would be a perfect rectangle if viewed straight-on. The Vanishing Point tool can use this to determine the perspective and adapt the clone so that—rather than copying pixels exactly—they are realistically scaled to fit.

This tool is well designed and incorporates a few neat touches, such as color-coding grids based on the extent to which they'll trouble the perspective engine (blue is good, yellow or red less so). The Healing option helps ensure a smooth blend between the healed areas and others but there are some things you'll still need to look out for yourself. In the example images, the cloned tiles had slightly different reflections because they come from farther down the wall. This is something that could perhaps be addressed with Dodge and Burn if necessary.

> **TIP**
>
> **Shift-click**
> *When painting with the Vanishing Point filter's Clone tool, you can click once at the beginning of an area to paint over, then Shift-click at the end and the brush will paint a stroke directly between the two points.*

The Vanishing Point filter's tools

TOOL	EFFECT
Edit Plane tool	Use this tool to move the corner points of a plane to adjust the perspective and better match your image. Only available after a plane is created.
Create Plane tool	This is where you'll start out. Once the tool is selected click in sequence to place the first, second, and third points to draw a plane. Once one plane is drawn you can tear off secondary planes (for example the other side of a building) by dragging the center points of the lines. You can also draw additional planes without reference to those already there by starting away from the first.
Marquee	Works just like its main-program counterpart, but the rectangles selected are affected by perspective and it is possible to use them like the Patch tool via the options.
Clone tool	Alt/⌥-click to choose a source point, then click to paint. By default it shows a preview before you begin to copy the source (the shape of the brush will be affected by perspective). This tool has a healing option which will soften the blend between old and new data.
Brush	A standard (or healing, depending on options) brush which alters shape dependent on perspective. Use this for touching up small areas for which you would like to use a solid color rather than a cloned source.
Transform	Scale a selected area by dragging corner handles.

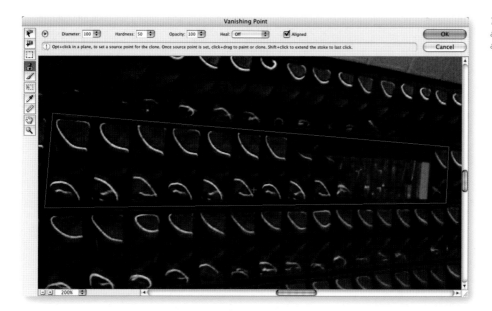

The Vanishing Point tool in action, as the perspective-altered clone is made.

Using the Vanishing Point tool

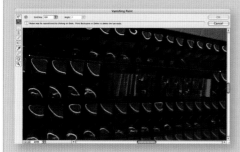

1 Open the Vanishing Point filter dialog box (*Filter > Vanishing Point*). The Create Plane tool should be selected automatically. Click in a corner of a plane in which you want to draw (make sure you include source and target pixels).

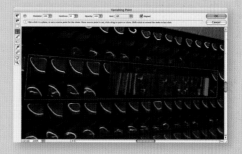

3 Select the Clone tool and adjust the brush size as you see fit. Alt/⌥-click in your target area then move the preview to your target area until it lines up the way you would like.

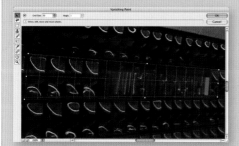

2 Click to set the second point and then draw a line parallel to the vertical perspective. Click to set the third point. Now draw a horizontal line in the opposite direction to complete the grid. Once you have completed the grid it will appear colored red, yellow, or blue (see main text).

4 Begin cloning as you would with the standard Clone Stamp tool. If you defined a secondary plane then you can clone into that plane too. When you're done, click OK.

Filters

Filters have surprisingly little in common with their analog counterparts, allowing far more flexibility. Whether the effects are gaudy or stylish is a decision for you (or your clients), but there is certainly a good selection.

Up until this point the tools encountered from the Filter menu have generally taken the form of seperate tools. These features—Liquify, the Extract tool, and Vanishing Point—might more accurately be thought of as plug-ins to Photoshop's otherwise orderly interface. They appear on the Filter menu for want of a better location in the menu structure.

What, then, are the bulk of the Filters, the "real ones," if you will? They are routines that can alter the state of a pixel either directly or based on those that neighbor it. For example the Gaussian Blur (introduced on page 136) makes a pixel closer in shade to those around it, softening the overall image, while the Sharpen filter (see pages 140–147) exaggerates pixels' shades where neighboring pixels are of a contrasting shade. The process is mathematical, so it's possible to adjust the criteria (for example the distance from which the Gaussian Blur filter examines pixels).

Given that mathematics is where computers truly excel, a range of alternative routines have been developed

Using Masks

An advantage of the Smart Filters approach—which is new to Photoshop CS3—is the ability to use masks. You can apply a filter to a specific area of an image simply by making a selection then applying the filter to the Smart Object layer. A mask to match the selection will automatically be created.

that create a quite staggering range of effects. There is a whole selection of pencil effects, for example. Obviously each is reasonably limited in its use, but since Smart Objects prevent you harming the original pixels there is little cause for alarm. What is worth remembering, however, is that because filters are pixel-based their results will vary depending on the image resolution. Look for adjustments like Radius to balance the effect to your picture's resolution.

The Dry Brush filter, one of the Artistic suite of filters.

Applying a filter

Before applying a filter, make the layer into a Smart Layer so that you can remove the filter again later if necessary. Simply click *Layer > Smart Objects > Convert to smart objects*. Filters can now be added via masked sub-layers.

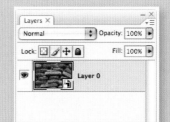

Artistic filters

Colored Pencil

Cut Out

Dry Brush

Film Grain

Fresco

Neon Glow

Paint Daubs

Palette Knife

Plastic Wrap

Poster Edges

Rough Pastels

Smudge Stick

Sponge

Underpainting

Watercolor

Artistic

Converts the image into an artistic interpretation based on the chosen option. For example an image filtered using Watercolor will be recreated to mimic a watercolor painting.

Distort

Used for creating pixel distortions, and for correcting optical distortions.

Blur

Creates artificial image blur of various types. Particularly useful are the Gaussian Blur and Lens Blur filters.

Noise

Filters for reducing or adding digital noise.

Brush Strokes

Used for creating artistic effects. Several different style options are available.

Pixelate

Rearranges an image into clumps of solid color.

Render

Provides specialized lighting filters and other options that require the computer to render (draw) pixels—adding clouds, for example.

Sharpen

Filters for managing image sharpening.

Sketch

Filters based on simulating sketch effects.

Stylize

Enhances the edges of an image, with several effects options.

Texture

Produces a texture effect to an image. There are several style options available.

Video

Manages color for transfer to videotape.

Photomerge and Align

Digital cropping is one way to create alternative-format images, but it has one principal disadvantage—the loss of data. Merging files, on the other hand, creates much more detail.

Photoshop's Photomerge tool (*File > Automate > Photomerge*) can be used to stitch two or more images to create a panoramic or otherwise merged shot. It is also surprisingly simple to use, although following the hints in the next paragraph will help you achieve the best results. Even with less than perfect shots, however, the software is well able to take a scattering of images from across a wide area and join them into a single image.

Where possible select a standard lens or focal length (e.g. 50mm or 50mm digital equivalent). If you are using a zoom lens keep the set focal length constant for each picture in the series. Camera exposure settings should be set manually to avoid automatic adjustments during exposures. If you must use an auto-exposure mode then choose aperture-priority so that any shift is made to shutter speed and not lens aperture (which controls depth of field). Similarly set the white balance manually, or use a custom preset, so that any color cast caused by light temperature is consistent.

When making the exposures, overlap each image in the series by at least 10%, preferably more (a maximum of 20% is sufficient). This makes the stitching process easier for the computer, since it has more to work with,

A slightly more unusual merge—two frames were fired to fit the whole building in, one above the other—but the processing engine has handled it admirably. All that remains is to crop it.

and it also makes any corrections easier on you since you can alter the masks once the merge is completed. The process will be quicker if you use fewer images, and if you use 8-bit rather than RAW files.

Photomerge dialog options

OPTION	EFFECT
Auto	The computer will select automatically the best way to handle perspective, and it usually seems to choose Perspective.
Perspective	The computer will simulate perspective around a center frame (an odd number is not required) and stretch the other frames to keep verticals consistent. Best for panoramas.
Cylindrical	Maps the images so they remain the same height at each end—good for QuickTime VR cips.
Reposition Only	Rather than scaling any of the images, the pixel information will be left the same and they will simply be lined up as closely as possible. This option works well with images shot at high zoom lengths.
Interactive layout	The computer will first attempt to automatically align your images, but then let you into its thinking via a separate dialog which allows you to drag and reposition images and choose a different frame to be the center of the perspective.

The final cropped panorama created from the three separate files shown beneath.

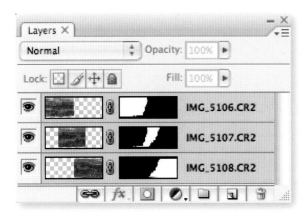

The results of the merge are returned as masked layers.

Creating the merged file

❶ Click *File* > *Automate* > *Photomerge* to open the Photomerge utility.

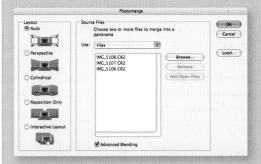

❷ Use the menu to add the images you want to merge and choose the method. There is rarely any call for switching from Auto (see box), so when you're ready, click OK.

❸ After quite some time processing, Photomerge will present you with a new layered Photoshop file, including masks over each aligned image.

Aligning with Auto-Align

The photographer's solution to almost any problem is to take more and more frames until the result is perfect. That's fine in theory, but in reality it's more likely than not that there will be perfect elements in more than one of your shots. Merging them together isn't always an easy process, but the Auto-Align Layers tool—essentially an offshoot of the processing in the Photomerge utility—is also available directly from the File menu. One use of this is in group poses where, even if there is a lot of movement in the foreground, a static background will be enough. You can then preserve elements from the "perfect" shots while masking away the rest. The same technique can be used, as in the example, to remove tourists from a popular scene. Obviously it helps to shoot with a tripod, but thanks to Auto-Align this is not as essential as it would have been in the past.

Auto-Blend

In a similar vein is the *Edit > Auto-Blend Layers* function (indeed the two are next to each other in the menu). It attempts to use blending modes and automatically generated masks to create an evenly-toned merged image, mimicking Photomerge. This is especially useful where there has been some shift of camera settings or conditions between shooting your originals.

This series of three images was aligned using Auto-Align. This enabled the tourists to be removed using masking.

Using Auto-Align

❶ Open each of the separate frames into Photoshop and decide which you'd like to be your front frame. This is the image from which you will retain as many pixels as possible. Put this image to one side, then select any of the others so that it becomes the active window.

❷ Drag the thumbnail from the Layers palette for this image's background layer to any of the other document windows (except the final top file). That second destination document window will be where you start to build up the layers. Close the picture once you've copied it into the stack.

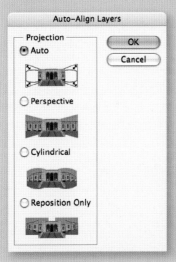

❸ Repeat the process until the only remaining image is your choice of top image. Drag this onto the other document and close it. You should now have a full set of layers.

❹ Select all the layers in the Layers palette by clicking on the top one then Shift+clicking on the bottom one. Now choose *Edit > Auto-Align Layers* from the main menu. This brings up a dialog similar to the one from Photomerge (see page 186). Choose a method (Auto or Reposition Only are sensible choices here, the latter if all you're trying to correct is minor knocks to a tripod).

❺ Create a new layer mask set to reveal all on the top layer (*Layer > Layer Mask > Reveal All*).

❻ Select Black (Press D then X) as the foreground color and begin to paint over any passersby you want to remove from the shot. The mask will reveal the perfectly lined-up layer beneath.

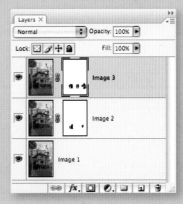

❼ Continue until you have removed all the extraneous elements of the top layer. If there are still some people you don't want visible through the mask, create a similar mask on the layer beneath and mask them out. Continue in that fashion until you've removed all the unwanted elements.

Black and white

Black and white photography remains popular, and is considered by many to have great artistic merit. That art once came from manipulating light with filters, but now it can be done with Photoshop.

Black and white photography still holds a fascination for many photographers and has a steady following of dedicated enthusiasts. And there is little doubt that a well-executed black and white image has a certain power and majesty about it.

As you read the last paragraph, the name Ansel Adams was perhaps already in your mind and, although he shot on film through filters, his techniques have more in common than you might imagine with Photoshop's process. That's because the quality of a black and white conversion is based on the balance of the image's color channels and they, in turn, reflect the real makeup of visible light (red, green, and blue). The filters were just another way to influence the color channels, though admittedly one without an Undo option. To see the practical effect of these channels, look at the examples opposite.

The reason I mention this right away is that it is an issue in all of Photoshop's conversion methods, even the simplest, which is to convert the image to grayscale. Admittedly this sidesteps the thought process for the users, but the computer is still using information from each channel according to a preset balance (using a ration of approximately 30% red, 60% green, and 10% blue). While this conversion formula produces an acceptable result, it's certainly not ideal in all circumstances. It is better suited to faces than skies, for example.

That's where Photoshop's Black and White and Channel Mixer tools step in. The former, though newer, is unquestionably the best option here, since it works naturally. Looking at channels is, after all, a very scientific approach, leaving you to deal with the less than natural idea that yellow is composed of red and blue before you can get involved. The Black and White adjustment, which can be applied as a non-destructive adjustment layer, does away with that, providing sliders for six points on the color wheel which you might want to boost of knock back.

The Channel Mixer is a longstanding feature of Photoshop, and by checking the Monochrome box in the lower corner can become a powerful conversion tool.

The Black and White tool, introduced in CS3, has revolutionized the conversion process, switching it from cumbersome to elegant at a stroke.

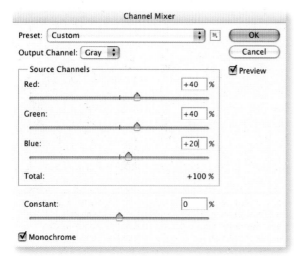

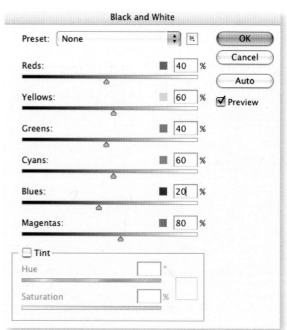

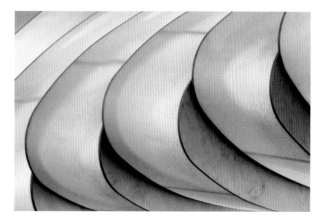

An original color image.

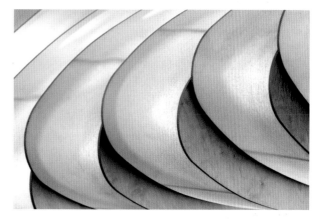

The original image desaturated using the Image > Adjustments > Desaturate *command. The result is similar to that of the green channel, which is not a surprise since it draws relatively more data from it, but the influence of red can still be seen in the buoys.*

Converted using the Channel Mixer with 50% Red, 50% Green, and 0% Blue.

The original color image, which is formed of all three channels, red, green, and blue. 100% of any of these colors is shown as white in the Channels palette, and 100% of all three mix to form white (see Color theory, page 26).

The red channel is quite strong in all the buildings, which all have at least a hint of pink or yellow (red and yellow mix to make green). The buoys are also picked out strongly against the dark water since these are very red.

The green channel is slightly stronger than the others in the trees, though since they're still dark they are still only dark gray here. Green also shows strongly in the buildings, especially the more yellow ones, and their reflections.

The blue channel is predictably strong in the sky, and relatively weak in the buildings. As a result, looking at only this channel tends to emphasize the contrast of white (which still includes blue) against the yellow/red paintwork.

Darkroom effects

The many changes in technology over the years have brought with them a variety of different styles, and all have earned a place in some hearts. At some point you'll find yourself needing to simulate one.

Using Photoshop it's possible to recreate many of the artistic effects that were first conceived in the traditional darkroom, or mastered using special film stock. What follows are some Photoshop techniques that will recreate artistic effects, such as cross processing, infrared, and toning.

Cross processing

Cross processing is a darkroom technique typically involving processing E-6 type film using C-41 type chemicals or C-41 type film using E-6 type chemicals. The result is an image with unusually vibrant colors. As with most things in Photoshop there is more than one technique for achieving a cross processed effect. The following example is effective and simple to apply. What's more, you can adjust the Opacity levels to increase the vividness of the effect.

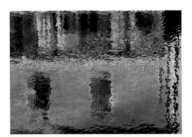

The cross processing effect, before (top) and after.

> **TIP**
>
> **Plug-in filters**
> *Darkroom effects like cross processing can also be achieved with plug-in filters such as Exposure by Alien Skin Software. These plug-ins create special effects using presets, and can be applied at the touch of a button.*

Cross processing

❶ Create a duplicate of the source image (*Image > Duplicate*).

❷ Change the color mode of the duplicate image to Lab Color (*Image > Mode > Lab Color*). Then open the Channels palette. You will see that in Lab Color mode the duplicate image has "a" and "b" channels. Select the "a" channel.

❸ To stretch the channel contrast, select *Image > Adjustments > Equalize* from the main menu.

❹ Reselect the Lab composite channel in the Channels palette.

❺ Copy the duplicate image to the original source image by selecting the Move tool and dragging the duplicate onto the original. Hold down the Shift key while dragging the image to align the two images. Keep the duplicate image available, as you'll need it again in a moment.

❻ Make the original image the active image and select the new layer in the Layers palette of the original image. Set the Blend mode to Color and set Opacity to between 25-35%.

❼ With the new Layer still active, apply a Gaussian blur of around 2-3 pixels (*Filter > Blur > Gaussian Blur*).

❽ Go back to the duplicate image and select the "b" channel in the Channels palette. Then repeat Steps 5 through 7.

Sepia toning

Sepia toning recreates the brownish tint associated with "antique" photography. The term sepia derives from the Greek word for cuttlefish, sepia being the reddish brown pigment of the ink sac. You didn't really need to know that but I found it interesting.

The following example shows how to take a color image and create a sepia tone effect. You could of course just apply the Sepia photo filter (*Image > Adjustments > Photo Filter > Sepia*), which is a quick and easy way of achieving a sepia tone, but without the level of control the following procedure provides.

The Duotone conversion tool is useful not just for effects like this, but for creating images that use the same mixture of spot color that a job you're working on might do. Many commercial jobs use only two or three inks rather than full color, and you can take advantage of this using the conversion shown. If you double-click on the box to the left of each ink's shade you'll be able to edit the curve too. You might, for example, want to reduce the black in the lighter tones and increase the spot color. You can also add additional inks into the mix (though in a commercial job it'll be unlikely you'll use four inks that aren't CMYK).

Sepia toning

❶ Convert the source image to grayscale (*Image > Mode > Grayscale*). Click OK to Discard Color Information.

❷ For the next conversion the image needs to be in 8-bits/channel mode (*Image > Mode > 8-bits/channel*).

❸ To apply a duotone select *Image > Mode > Duotone* from the main menu. This opens the Duotone dialog box. Set Type to Duotone using the drop-down menu. Keep the dialog box open.

❹ Click on the color patch for Ink 1 and enter the number EB8B23 in the number box at the bottom of the Color Picker dialog box. You need to give this color a name ("Sepia" should do the trick).

❺ Click on the color patch for Ink 2. You'll notice that a different dialog box appears called Color Libraries. Click on the Picker button to bring up the Colur Picker dialog box. Enter the number 000000 in the numbers box. This gives you black.

❻ Convert the image to RGB mode (*Image > Mode > RGB*).

❼ To modify the intensity of the toning effect you can adjust the level of Saturation (*Layer > New Adjustment Layer > Hue/Saturation*). Move the saturation slider right to increase the effect, or left to decrease the effect. This is really a matter of personal taste but I have found that around −10 to −15% Saturation gives a nice balance.

Simulating infrared film

Infrared film is most sensitive to infrared light waves—light that human eyesight can't detect but that is everywhere around us. The step-by-step technique below mimics the effect of using infrared film, which makes infrared radiation glow, but it is far from the only technique for achieving this look. If you don't mind sacrificing the many opportunities that this method affords you for altering values, then why not use the preset built into the Black and White adjustment layer dialog? There are several options, including Infrared, available instantly and non-destructively.

❶ If possible, open the source image *(File > Open)* as a 16-bits/channel image *(Image > Mode > 16-bits/channel)*. This will improve the smoothness of the adjustments you perform later. If the file type of the source image doesn't support 16-bits/channel (e.g. JPEG files) then continue with the file in 8-bits/channel mode.

❷ Create a duplicate background Layer *(Layer > Duplicate Layer)*.

❸ Create a Levels adjustment layer *(Layer > New Adjustment Layer > Levels)*. In the Levels dialog box, click on Options and select Enhance Per Channel Contrast. Click OK. You'll notice a slight change in the color balance but it's nothing to be concerned about, as we're going to convert the image to monochrome.

❹ Create a Channel Mixer adjustment layer *(Layer > New Adjustment Layer > Channel Mixer)* at the top of the layer stack. In the Channel Mixer dialog box, check the Monochrome option box at the bottom. Leave the dialog box open.

❺ We can use the RGB color channels to affect how the image appears in monotone (see Black & White, page 190). In this example, I want to significantly lighten the foliage and so I'll increase the level of the green color channel. To get the Infrared effect I'm after, I'm going to increase it to 200%.

❻ To balance this increase in the green channel, I'm going to adjust the red and blue channels to –80% and –20% respectively. This gets me back to the 100% ideal mix discussed earlier (see Black & White, page 190). Click on OK to apply the channel mix.

❼ Make the Background Copy layer the active layer by clicking on it in the Layers palette.

❽ Open the Channels palette *(Window > Channels)* and select the green color channel.

❾ We're going to apply Gaussian blur filter to the green channel to create a diffused effect. Open the Gaussian blur filter *(Filter > Blur > Gaussian Blur)* and set a radius of between 4 and 7 pixels. In this example, I set the blur to 5 pixels.

❿ I'm now going to fade the effect of the Gaussian Blur filter. Select *Edit > Fade Gaussian Blur* from the main menu. Set Opacity to a value between 20 and 30% (in this example I used a value of 22%) and set Mode to Screen. This has the effect of brightening the whole image. Don't worry if the highlights appear overly bright.

⓫ Open the Histogram *(Window > Histogram)*. Then, reopen the Levels dialog box from the Levels adjustment layer (double-click the Levels icon).

⓬ We're going to drag back some of the lost highlights. Using the Output Levels adjustment sliders (at the bottom of the Levels dialog box) drag the white arrow slider and set an Output Level of between 230 and 245. Use the Histogram window to assess the exact value.

Film effects plugins

One of the aspects of photography that we have lost with digital capture is the ability to select and use a preferred film. Yes, we can change the color space settings to refine the balance of RGB colors, but it's not as easy to predict in advance as the defined choices we enjoyed when shooting film. Because of the inherent differences between the two media it would be impractical to use Photoshop's normal tools to try and replicate exactly the tones and grain of a film like Velvia Kodachrome.

The good thing is we don't have to (assuming, that is, you're willing to fork out for a plugin that provides this functionality at the click of a mouse). One of the better solutions is a product called Exposure, developed by a company called Alien Skin Software. Using this software it is possible to digitally simulate a close match with the vivid colors of Fuji Velvia, so beloved of landscape photographers; the rich blacks of Kodak Kodachrome; and the sensitivity of Kodak Ektachrome, as well as the characteristics of around 30 other film stocks.

*AlienWare Exposure adds istelf to the bottom of the Filters menu (*Filters > Alien Skin Exposure*) and has separate dialogs for color and black and white. The default settings are just the beginning.*

> **TIP**
>
> **PhotoKit Color 2**
> *Another plugin option for recreating traditional film effects is PhotoKit Color 2 by PixelGenius.*

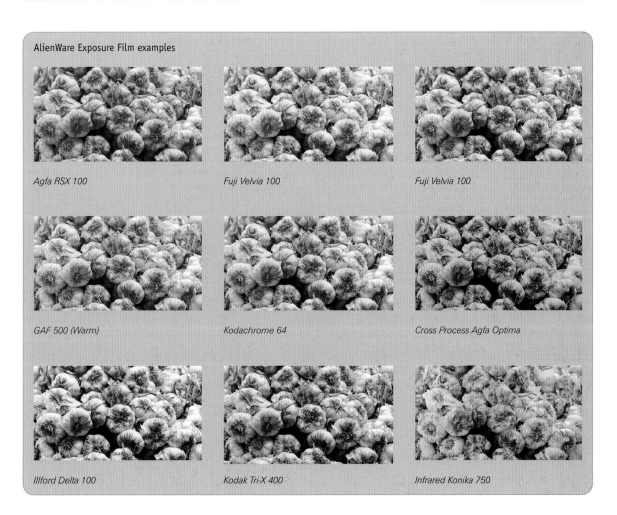

AlienWare Exposure Film examples

Agfa RSX 100

Fuji Velvia 100

Fuji Velvia 100

GAF 500 (Warm)

Kodachrome 64

Cross Process Agfa Optima

Illford Delta 100

Kodak Tri-X 400

Infrared Konika 750

Photo composites

Whatever your purpose, using more than one image to create a final result is something you'll find yourself needing to do. Getting the job right requires many of the tools we examined earlier in the book.

Taking image elements from one or more pictures and combining them (compositing) is an area of Photoshop where the artistically minded can let their imagination run riot. In certain photographic fields—not least that which presents itself as factual or for record—there is debate on the ethics of using compositing techniques. In other fields, however, such as commercial advertising photography, it is an intricate and essential aspect of the work (in any case, any debate on ethics, let alone the ethics of advertising, is well beyond the scope of this book).

Compositing draws mainly on skills that you'll have already encountered if you've been working through this book in order. Two other features you'll come across are Alpha Channels and Quick Masks, which are described below. In this section I'll also cover the Transform commands, as well as adding text.

Quick Masks

The Quick Mask tool (selected from toward the bottom of the Toolbar) converts a selection into a mask, making it editable using the Fill or any of the painting tools. Effects filters, including plugins, can be applied, as well as edge distortions. Once adjustments and enhancements have been made, the mask can be converted back into a selection.

To apply a Quick Mask, first make a selection. Then, select Quick Mask from the Toolbar. A semi-transparent, colored mask (red by default, although the color can be changed by double-clicking the Quick Mask icon and selecting a new color from the color picker) will overlay unselected areas.

With the Quick Mask selected it can be painted with any of the painting tools, and the standard rules apply: set the foreground color to black to add to the mask and set it to white to subtract from the mask. When edits and adjustments are completed, reverting to Standard display mode (via the appropriate icon in the Toolbar) converts the mask back to a selection.

Selections can be saved and reused by selecting *Select > Save Selection* from the main menu. Selections are saved as Alpha Channels, which can then be loaded as a selection at a later time, and can be viewed and edited in the Channels palette. Alpha channels can also be read by other applications in a similar way to clipping paths, though because they are bitmapped they won't keep their shape when scaled.

Transform tools

The Free Transform tool is easily accessed by pressing Ctrl/⌘+T but sometimes it is better to constrain the behavior of the corner points. Right-click for the options.

OPTION	EFFECT
Scale	The simplest of the effects. Simply drag a side or corner point to stretch in that direction. Hold Shift as you do so to force Photoshop to scale proportionally (usually wise).
Skew	Clicking and dragging on one of the corner points will allow you to move it along the plane of either of the lines it is on.
Distort	Dragging a corner point will allow you to move that point freely.
Perspective	Dragging a corner point along one of the planes will cause the opposite point to be moved in order to maintain the perspective effect of the shape.
Warp	Adds handles to each of the corner points which can be pulled in order to apply a non-geometrical map onto the area being transformed.

Adding a more interesting sky to this image is simple with Photoshop.

There is no reason why images should have the same number of pixels—a potential problem when compositing that is solved by the Transform options.

Creating a composite

❶ Make a selection of the sky in the main image. You can use any of the selection tools to make the selection. In this instance the Magic Wand tool is appropriate given the uninterrupted color of the sky.

❷ Click *Select* > *Inverse* to make the foreground the selection.

❸ Create a new layer by cut (*Layer* > *New Layer via Cut*).

❹ Choose the source image from which to select a new sky. If necessary, make a selection of the area of the source image you want to use.

❺ To copy the source image or source image selection to the main image, use the Move tool to drag the sky and drop it onto the main image. This will create a new layer in the main image.

❻ If the sky covers the foreground area, in the Layers palette bring Layer 2 to the front by dragging it between Layer 1 and the Background layer.

❼ Position the sky so that it covers the old sky.

❽ If necessary, use the Transform tools to create a convincing match between the two image parts.

❾ If the sky appears too bright, reduce the opacity of the layer containing the new sky in the Layers palette.

TIP

Repeating transforms
Transforms can be replicated across layers using the Edit > Transform > Again *menu option*

TIP

Select before masking
There's no imperative to make a selection before applying a Quick Mask. However, a selection limits the area to which an adjustment is applied, making for a more precise edit.

Filter menu tools

The Filter menu is often home to features that don't quite belong anywhere else, as well as being where plugins frequently install themselves. Pattern Maker and Liquify both qualify on these grounds.

The Filter menu will always be home to features that push the description filter to the limits, and most of them have already been discussed. For the sake of completeness, here is another look at two more of the menu's valuable tools. That they have little in common is a testament to my point about the Filters menu, but they both serve their purpose well. And remember to look out for plugins in the Filter menu too.

Pattern making

The Pattern Maker filter is used to create randomly generated abstract patterns from a source sample image. Patterns created this way can be saved as custom pattern presets for future application via, for example, the Fill tool (which allows you to choose Pattern rather than Fill from the leftmost option).

Using Pattern Maker

❶ Select a source image and open the Pattern Maker filter *(Filter > Pattern Maker)*. This opens the Pattern Maker dialog box.

❷ Using the Marquee tool in the Pattern Maker toolbar, draw a marquee around the area to be used as the pattern.

❸ Set the width and height of the pattern tile (I chose the sample dimensions shown along the bottom of the dialog box), and then set the Smoothness and Sample Detail values. Increasing smoothness will produce more accurate results. Increasing Sample Detail value produces a more lifelike effect. Conversely, a low value creates a more abstract effect. In this example, I chose a Smoothness value of 2 and a Sample Detail value of 7.

❹ Click the Generate button.

❺ If you're happy with the result, click the Save Pattern as Preset icon (left icon under the pattern preview in the Tile History box.) and give the pattern a meaningful name. This saves the pattern as a custom pattern preset.

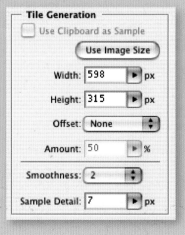

Liquify

Opening Liquify presents you with a sizable toolbox on the left and a complex-looking set of options on the right. A second glance, however, will reveal that this is broken down into sections. The first section contains the Tool Options, enabling you to select Brush Size, Density, Pressure, and Rate. The Reconstruction Options provide two options for undoing distortions. The Reconstruct button undoes distortions a step at a time. To restore the entire image, canceling out all distortions, press the Restore All button. There are several Mask Options available, which can be used to freeze and constrain the effects of any Liquify distortions.

Finally, the View Options enable you to define what appears on screen. The Liquify filter can be used to produce all kinds of artistic distortions but I'm now going to show how this filter can be put to a more practical photographic use. When I showed the model the image shown on the right, she was unhappy with the line of her stomach. So here's how we flattened it for her.

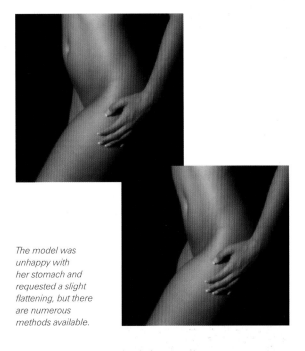

The model was unhappy with her stomach and requested a slight flattening, but there are numerous methods available.

Liquify tool summary

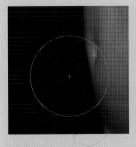

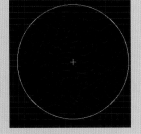

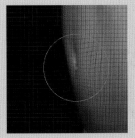

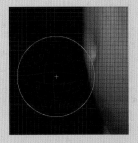

Forward Warp
Pushes the grid in the same direction as the mouse is stroked (conversely, Reconstruct pushes the grid back toward its original shape).

Swirl
Drags the grid around inside the brush area. The longer the brush is held, the more pronounced the effect.

Pucker
Sucks the grid in towards the click point. To use on the stomach it must be placed a little way over the body rather than on the background.

Bloat
This tool pushes the grid outwards from the center, so it can be used to expand the non-stomach area and gently push into the "problem" area.

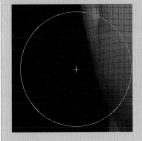

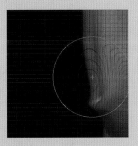

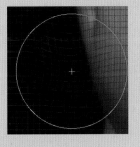

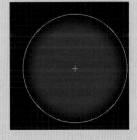

Push left
Moves pixels to the left or right as you drag the pointer up and down.

Mirror
With all the predictability of a funfair sideshow, this tries to move the grid over the page.

Turbulence
Adds a random effect, and works similarly to Forward Warp when dragged.

Masks
Brush on, brush off masks stop the grid being moved in selected areas.

printing and beyond

So far this book has been focused on getting the capture and processing stage of the photographic process to a point where you feel comfortable in producing high-quality digital images. Once you have reached that stage, the next question is how to reproduce in print the image you see on screen. And, beyond printing, you may want to use your images for other applications, such as the web.

Everything discussed up to this point has had in mind the complete input to output process. So, for example, the sections on Getting set up (pages 12–33) and Enhancement tools (pages 106-159) have as much bearing on how your images appear in print or on the web as anything taken in isolation from this section.

The purpose of this chapter, then, is to add the finishing touches and look more closely at the various options available for outputting and displaying your work.

Printing

It's not just a question of how big and how many—Photoshop comes with a daunting array of output and color management options. You'll need to identify which ones are appropriate for your individual workflow.

Printing in Photoshop CS3 has been given a gentle but welcome overhaul, discarding the unnecessary choice between printing with and without a preview. Now the *File > Print* dialog includes a page preview by default which should clarify the proportions of your printout as against the page you're printing to. The settings—now almost exclusively on the right save for the Portrait/Landscape button—have changed little, with the self-explanatory Copies, Position, and Scale options first and a larger box which can either show Output settings or Color Management options. This doesn't make them mutually exclusive; you just have to make decisions about them one at a time.

In addition to the generous array of options in this dialog, there is the sticky issue of the Page Setup options. This is not strictly a Photoshop issue, but it will have just as big an impact on your printout if set wrong, so in practice this is the first place you should go unless you're confident that the settings are correct, and you can only be sure if the last print was OK. The Page Setup dialog (and any sub-menus) is an operating system level set of options that, in effect, tells programs like Photoshop how your printer should be spoken to. Specifically, what sort of assumptions to make about the printer, like the size of paper you're using, and whether it is loaded portrait or landscape. If your printer has any special features, like borderless printing, they'll be handled here too.

Only after your Page Setup is correct (you can reach this directly from Photoshop's File menu, or from the button in the Print dialog) should you proceed to the other options. Most of them only work properly once the computer knows what size paper you're printing to.

Main options

Perhaps the most obvious difference you can achieve in a printout is whether you print landscape or portrait. The button beneath the Preview window allows you to make the choice; this is a shortcut to the option in the Print Setup dialog, but you do not need to load your paper into the printer a different way.

I shall not insult your intelligence by discussing the Copies option, and the Position one is also quite straightforward. If you choose to uncheck the default centering, then you can enter the distance, in the units of your choice, from the top left corner of the page that you'd like the top left of the image to appear.

Similarly intuitive is the Scaled Print Size subset, which allows you adjust the size while maintaining the proportions of the image (as indicated by the link icon to the right of the three fields). The resulting resolution on the page is shown, in pixels per inch. This is a good guide to quality, since anything below about 200 will look poor, and professional repro generally aims for a 300ppi minimum. If you prefer not to type your adjustments,

In the Page Setup dialog, choose your printer from the Format for drop-down menu and the Paper Size list will be adjusted to reflect the paper sizes that your printer can handle. This is the Mac version, but Windows is similar.

TIP

If you want to mask off a portion of your image when printing, use the selection tools to highlight the portion you would like to print, then check the Print Selected Area option in the Print dialog. This may not appear in the preview, but will have an effect on the printout.

The Print dialog's options are split over two columns to the right side of a preview which shows what proportion of the page your image will print on (here it will print right to the edge).

checking the Show Bounding Box option box will add a box line around the image in the Preview screen. If the Scale to Fit Media option box is deselected, you can resize and rescale the image using the corner handles. If the Center Image option box in the Position panel is also unchecked, you can move the position of the image by dragging it with the mouse.

Output options

The Output options menu has several options that you can use to define what is printed along with your image. Of the available settings the ones shown in the box opposite are those you are most likely to use. It'd be fair to say of all of these options that they're only worth using if you know what they are. There's no shame in never having had any need to make an Emulsion Down print, but for other users it might be their bread and butter.

Beneath the printer's marks checkboxes are a group of buttons for other occasionally useful additions. The Background option allows you to change the background color for the whole page—I'll leave you to come up with a good reason to do so—and the Border button allows you to add a black keyline around the edge of the image. Bleed simply moves the crop marks in by a specified amount so that when the image is trimmed a small amount is lost. Screen and Transfer are best left in the hands of the printers.

Output Options

BACKGROUND—lets you print with a colored border, with colors selected from the Color Picker or Color Libraries.

BORDER—prints with a black border of a user-determined size (designated in inches, mm, or points).

BLEED—lets you determine indentation of crop marks.

CALIBRATION BARS—prints an 11-step grayscale on the left and a smooth gray ramp on the right of the image.

REGISTRATION MARKS—help to align separate plates during printing.

CORNER CROP MARKS—indicate trim lines.

CENTER CROP MARKS—indicate trim lines.

DESCRIPTION—prints text entered in the Description field *(File > File Info)*.

LABELS—prints the filename below the image.

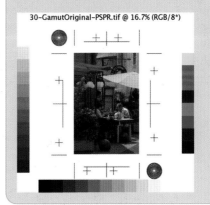

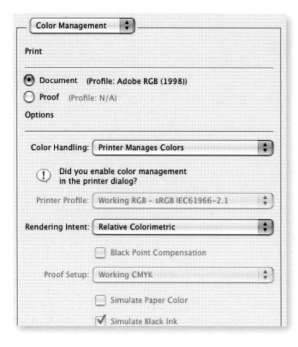

Color management set to Document mode but leaving the printer software in charge of color management. It is still possible to select the rendering intent of your choice.

TIP

Simulated CMYK proofs often produce white colors that appear too dull. This is usually a trick of the eye and should not be seen as inferior.

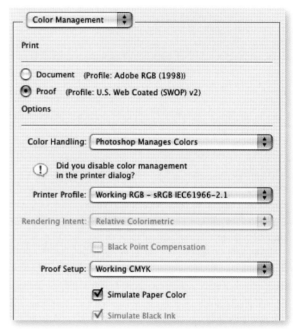

TIP

If you hold Alt/⌥ as you click the Print button, you will only print only one copy, however many you have chosen in the Copies box.

Color management set to Document mode, with Photoshop put in charge of things. This requires a Printer profile—Working RGB is unlikely to do the job.

Color management set to Proof mode, in which the final result on a different device (presumably one with a smaller gamut) is simulated with either Photoshop or the Printer handling the color management.

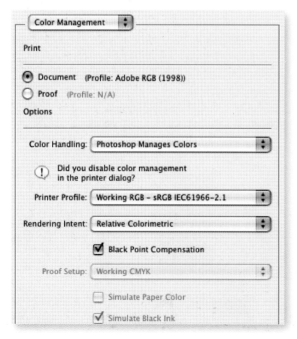

Rendering intent summary

PERCEPTUAL: The color space is shrunk to fit. Good for images with a lot of color detail near the edges of gamut, like a closeup of vivid flower petals.

SATURATION: Good for tables and charts, not photography.

RELATIVE COLORIMETRIC: Adjusts only the colors that are out of gamut, generally the norm for photography.

ABSOLUTE COLORIMETRIC: No adjustment to white point, so a potential color shift.

Color Management

When Color Management is selected in the drop-down menu, the Output options panel is replaced by the Color Management panel. The first set of options covers Print space. Leave this set to Document. Underneath is the Options panel.

If you know the profile of your printer then set Color Handling to Let Photoshop Determine Colors via the drop-down menu. Then select the appropriate profile in the Printer Profile drop-down menu. Otherwise, select Let Printer Determine Colors in the Color Handling option and turn on ColorSync in the Print dialog box.

The Rendering Intent option determines how out of CMYK gamut colors are handled. I recommend selecting Relative Colorimetric and selecting the Black Point Compensation option by checking the option box. There is more on this and the reasons behind this in the first chapter, but check the box for a quick summary of the four Rendering Intent options.

Proofing for press output

In the "old days" of supplying transparencies to printers, the printer had a visual reference from which he could determine the accuracy of printed colors. If you only supply a digital file, however, there is no visual reference. Unless, that is, you create one.

Providing a targeted CMYK print proof is standard practice for professional photographers. Initially you will need to gather information from the printer, including either a suitable proofing standard ICC profile, or information pertaining to the printing inks and other specifications used for the print press.

With this information, you can create a custom CMYK dialog via the Colour Settings menu *(Edit > Colour Settings)*, selecting Custom CMYK in the CMYK options drop-down menu in the Working Space panel. With this information saved as a custom CMYK setting, you can accurately convert an RGB image into a CMYK, TIFF, or EPS file.

Once you have a working CMYK image file, you will need to produce a print proof. You could go so far as to provide a contract proof, which is produced using an approved proofing device, such as the Epson 5000 inkjet (with RIP). Alternatively you could take your CMYK image file to a prepress bureau. That might all become expensive, however.

Another option is to produce a CMYK proof on a desktop inkjet printer using the Print With Preview dialog box. Check the Simulate Paper Color option box. This sends an instruction to Photoshop to calculate how the data should be converted and sent to the printer to achieve an accurate simulation.

And finally...

Once you've set everything up, whether you're printing a document or a proof, the final step is to click Print. This returns you to a Print dialog generated by the operating system rather than Photoshop. This is an area where generally you'll need to refer to your printer manual, since the driver software is created by them and varies from machine to machine, but there are some key features across systems, not least the necessity of telling the software what paper you are using.

If the printer is managing the colors, then it will have a specific filetype for each of the paper varieties listed by the Print dialog. Make sure you choose this from the menu.

The Print dialog on a Mac always takes a form similar to this. The printer's individual settings, accessed via the third drop-down menu, vary from machine to machine, but look for Quality and Media, Paper Type, or similar options and be sure the settings are correct.

Electronic display and the web

New in Creative Suite 3, the Save for Web and Devices function allows you to optimize your file sizes for use on cellphones and other electronic gadgets as well as the Internet.

Formerly known as the Save For Web commend, Adobe have acknowledged the burgeoning supply of digital displays in the world with a slight rebranding exercise, though tacking on the words "and devices" hasn't affected the core functioning of the tool—to optimize file sizes. As we've seen, there are various kinds of compression, with the principal battle on the web being between JPEG and GIF. The former is undoubtedly the best suited for photography, since GIFs must work from a defined color palette of perhaps just 8, 16, or 32 shades, but never more than 256.

Files saved from the Save for Web and Devices window also have the advantage that all extraneous information is stripped from them, like the previews that Photoshop generally adds to a File.

Extra fine-tuning

JPEG's compression algorithm is "lossy," meaning that it discards detail to reduce file size. It follows that detailed areas of the image are a sticking point for it, so you'll find a Blur option in the dialog box. Use this if the image is especially sharp and can stand not to be and the compression might seem easier on the eye (and easier for the computer).

The Progressive option affects how the image's information is arranged in the file. Unchecked, the data is sent arranged normally (which is most space-efficient), but if it is checked, it is arranged so that web browsers can build up the image's detail as the file is downloaded; in other words there is something to put on the screen much sooner, but it takes longer for the whole file to arrive.

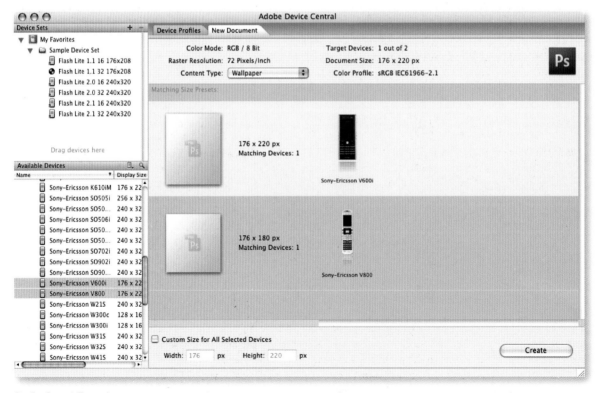

Device Central: Turns pictures into cellphone wallpaper.

Using Save for Web and Devices

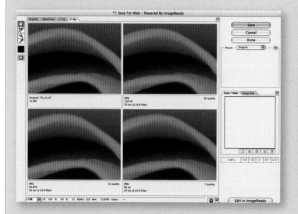

❶ Open the Save for Web dialog box *(File > Save for Web and Devices)* and click the 4-Up screen view tab at the top of the Preview screen. This will show the original image along with three optimized Previews.

❸ You may now click on other previews and repeat Step 2, selecting a different compression level and even file type for the alternative previews.

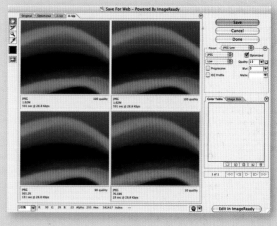

❷ In the Preset panel on the right of the dialog box, select JPEG (it doesn't matter at this stage whether you choose High, Medium, or Low). Check that the Optimized option box is selected. Select the first optimized preview by clicking on it and set a compression level via the drop-down menu (you'll find it to the left of the Quality drop-down menu). Choose a level of compression (typically I set this to maximum).

❹ Compare the three optimized preview images against the original file. What you are looking for is a balance between image quality and file size. You may find this easier if you increase the preview magnification to around 200%, but remember the appearance at 100% is the most important.

Device Central

If you're saving your image for display on a particular kind of mobile phone, Creative Suite 3 has introduced another new tool worth adding to the workflow; a catalog of devices with templates for their individual screens and features. In general this is a specialized tool for commercial designers, but if you want to offer images

perfectly prepared as cellphone wallpaper, it's perfect. Simply open the tool by clicking *File > Device Central*. Select the kind of phone you're targeting (or even more than one), and the type of file you'll be creating (wallpaper, user ID photo, etc.). Photoshop can then generate one or more blank documents for you to fill with a suitably cropped image.

Galleries

Photoshop can automatically generate galleries of your images to place on the web. Clients can append their feedback instantly, so you can avoid unnecessary post-production work.

Using the Web Photo Gallery option in the Automate menu *(File > Automate > Web Photo Gallery)* enables you to create a fully formed gallery of images ready for the web. This is because, when constructing the gallery, Photoshop generates all the HTML code needed, including producing thumbnail images, gallery pages, and navigation buttons.

Better still, this option has a distinctly commercial use beyond making it relatively easy to show off images on the web. For example, I sell my images via a photo library and I'm constantly providing them with new material. As part of their process they will review my submissions and select the images that are suitable for their needs. The Web Photo Gallery speeds this process and, in so doing, also makes my own workflow more efficient.

Using Web Photo Gallery

❶ Open the Web Photo Gallery dialog box *(File > Automate > Web Photo Gallery)*.

❷ I use a style from the Photoshop templates and, since I need to gather feedback on the images, I choose the Horizontal—Feedback template.

❸ Enter the e-mail address to which the agency can send the Acceptance list.

❹ Select the folder that Photoshop uses to generate the Gallery. As this folder has no sub-folders I leave the Include All Subfolders option box unchecked. Then also select a Destination folder.

❺ In the Options panel I select Banner from the Options drop-down menu. This enables me to give the site a bespoke name, and add my own name and details.

❻ Click OK to generate the Gallery.

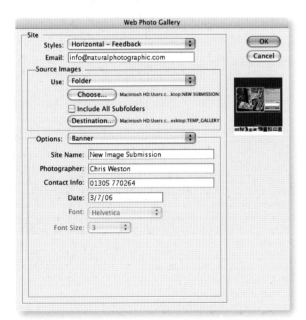

Once you've chosen your Site style at the top, you need to fill in all your details in the large Options pane at the bottom of the window. Don't forget to browse through the Options using the drop-down menu.

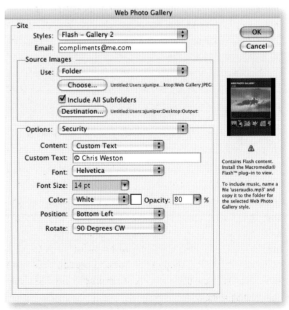

The Security option in the Web Photo Gallery dialog is useful for adding a watermark to all images you'll be putting on the web.

A page created using Adobe Web Photo Gallery.

Options panel settings

The Options panel drop-down menu has options that enable you to dictate the display size of large images and thumbnail images, as well as customizing background colors and security options. In the General menu options I select always the Add Width and Height Attributes for Images, and the Preserve All Metadata options.

After I have completed my initial edit I am left with a folder of RAW images that I want to keep. I then sort the images I intend to submit to my agency (using the Star Rating system in Bridge, see page 38) and transfer these to an empty folder on my desktop that I've named New Submissions.

Usually the RAW images number in the hundreds, and I don't want to waste time completing a full Photoshop processing cycle on images that are then rejected by the agency as unsuitable. So, I create a Web Photo Gallery using my New Submissions Folder and upload this Gallery to a web server.

I then pass the URL for the Web Photo Gallery to the picture editor at my agency. By using one of the Feedback templates that Photoshop provides, the agency can simply mark those images they want to accept (and, if they have the time and inclination, add notes against any they reject) and email this information back to me.

Once I have the complete list of accepted images I can then process them, without spending valuable time processing rejects.

One of the Flash-based galleries which features a scroll bar and buttons at the bottom right.

Creating custom Galleries

Instead of using a Photoshop template you can design your own Gallery style.

Watermarking for the web

Copyright violation is all too common in the digital age. Adding a personal watermark is a quick and easy way to make life difficult for those who'd like to take advantage of your hard work.

For anyone serious about photography it is important to assert and maintain copyright, and one of the concerns about digital imaging, particularly with regard to the Internet, is the security of digital files. Photoshop has the tools to add watermarks and append copyright data to images prior to outputting them to the web or via any other media. Perhaps even more usefully, Photoshop also has the power to apply these marks to a whole batch of images, a valuable workflow step to consider before creating a web gallery.

A great way to add a watermark to your images is to start by creating a custom preset Brush tool, which can then be applied easily to any and all images. You can do this to a single image using the Brush tool in the Tools palette. You will find the design you created in the custom brush flyout. Your custom brush will have been added after the previous last brush and the symbol may appear squashed. You can change the size of the brush and, therefore, the size of the watermark by adjusting Master Diameter in the Brush Presets library dialog box.

Watermarks such as this make it much more difficult for people to make usable copies of your work from digital files.

TIP

When adding personal website details type in the full URL of your website, including the http:// prefix into the Copyright Info URL: field.

TIP

To add text to a watermark, select the Type tool from the Toolbar and enter the text onto your document under the copyright symbol (or other position as you prefer). To style the text to match the copyright symbol you first have to rasterize the text layer *(Layer > Rasterize > Layer)*. Then follow the styling instructions given in the box opposite for the copyright symbol.

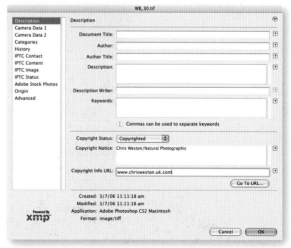

Creating a copyright watermark

❶ To create a preset Brush tool, first create a new document *(File > New)* with a size of 11 x 8 inches at 300 dpi with a white background.

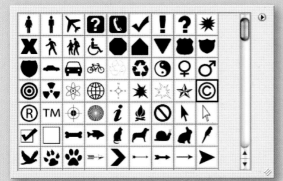

❷ From the Tools palette, select the Custom Shape tool from the Shape Tools box. In the Options bar, click on the arrow next to Shape to open the Custom Shape Picker box and select the copyright symbol (©) from the default library.

❸ Click on the Create New Layer icon (second right, at the bottom) in the Layers palette *(Window > Layers)* and set the background color to black (shortcut D on the keyboard). You can choose any background color but black is the best option.

❹ Make sure that the Fill Pixels icon is selected in the Options Bar (third icon in the first group of three icons). The cursor is currently the shape of a cross. In the new layer, draw the copyright symbol over the image by clicking and dragging to your preferred dimensions.

❺ Optionally, Select *Filter > Stylize > Emboss*. Use the default settings (angle: 135°, height: 3 pixels, and amount: 100%). Click on OK to apply.

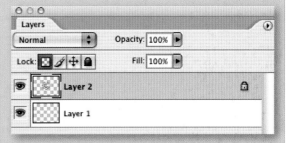

❻ Turn on Lock Transparent Pixels (first icon on the left next to Lock in the Layers palette) and add Gaussian Blur to a radius of about 3 pixels *(Filter > Blur > Gaussian Blur)*. This gives the watermark a smooth finish.

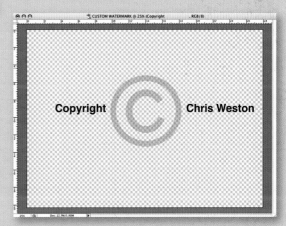

❼ Finally change the Blend Mode (in the Layers palette) from Normal to Hard Light and set opacity to around 50%, then click on the Rectangular Marquee tool in the Tools palette and drag a marquee selection around the watermark. Select *Edit > Define Brush Preset* from the main menu bar and enter a name for your brush, such as Copyright Watermark. Then click on OK to add your new brush to the Brush Presets library.

Using the Image Processor script

The scripting tool has a few tricks up its sleeve that Actions cannot cope with. Specifically it can apply logic, though admittedly only with regard to the file size. It's possible to create an action to scale images on either their horizontal or vertical axis, but it cannot compare them and choose the optimum. The Image Processor script, however, can. To access it, click *File > Scripts > Image Processor*.

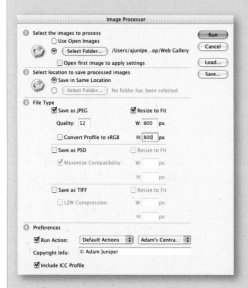

❶ Specify the folder with all your high resolution images in—no matter what file format—with the Select Folder button.

❷ There is no need to specify a destination folder. The processor will automatically create a new folder inside the original one and add all the processed files there, leaving the originals untouched.

❸ Choose your final file type and maximum dimensions. The image will be resized to fit these (with proportions preserved) if you check the box.

❹ You can also choose to run an action, such as the one in the Watermark box opposite, and add your name to the Copyright Info metadata of all expoted files.

Adding embedded data

Information such as your name, image title, keywords, and copyright status can and should be embedded with an image, a topic touched on earlier in the book. To see the metadata from within Photoshop select *File > File Info* from the main menu bar, which opens the File Info dialog box, and enter any information you deem appropriate in the relevant fields.

The Batch Processor

An alternative to the Image Processor script is the Batch tool, which applies an action to a series of images, as well as allowing you to rename files with a convenient automated numbering system. Just choose Serial Number from the drop-down menu in the File Naming pane and (if you don't want to start at 1, alter the start number too). Photoshop will then do two chores in one: file renaming and whatever your specified action does.

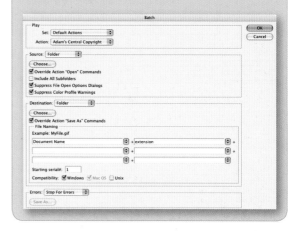

To add copyright data open the pop-down menu next to Copyright Status and select Copyrighted (this will cause Photoshop to automatically add a © symbol next to the file name in the Title Bar and before the document size in the Info Bar whenever the file is opened in Photoshop). Then, add your personal copyright details into the Copyright Notice field.

Batch copyrighting

It's one thing being able to apply a watermark to one image, but what if you're about to put hundreds onto the internet? You don't want to open each one, add the watermark, resave each one (with a different name of course) and then send them to a web application (which might include the Create Web Gallery tool). It would be far better to automate the process.

Photoshop provides two different tools that might be of use here, though neither are entirely intuitive. The first is Actions, the second is Scripts. The latter is very useful for resizing images so that they do not exceed a certain width or height, while Actions are all about applying individual steps—like adding a watermark. Since scripts can include a basic action, it is probably better to create an action to apply the watermark before moving on to the Scripting to prepare a folder full of images that fit your other requirements.

Now you'd be forgiven for reading the word "scripting" and slamming the book shut, but there is no cause for alarm. While you can create your own scripts, scaling images and applying copyright (or an Action) can be achieved automatically via the options in the *File > Scripts > Image Processor* window. Just follow its numbered options panes.

Recording a watermark action

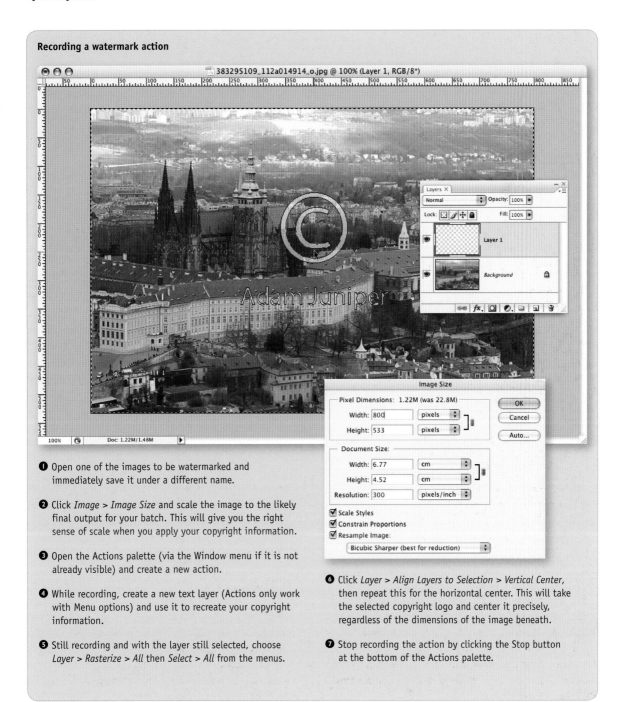

❶ Open one of the images to be watermarked and immediately save it under a different name.

❷ Click *Image > Image Size* and scale the image to the likely final output for your batch. This will give you the right sense of scale when you apply your copyright information.

❸ Open the Actions palette (via the Window menu if it is not already visible) and create a new action.

❹ While recording, create a new text layer (Actions only work with Menu options) and use it to recreate your copyright information.

❺ Still recording and with the layer still selected, choose *Layer > Rasterize > All* then *Select > All* from the menus.

❻ Click *Layer > Align Layers to Selection > Vertical Center*, then repeat this for the horizontal center. This will take the selected copyright logo and center it precisely, regardless of the dimensions of the image beneath.

❼ Stop recording the action by clicking the Stop button at the bottom of the Actions palette.

Glossary

A thorough guide to the jargon and terminology of digital photography.

Aberration The flaws in a lens that distort, however slightly, the image.

Aperture The opening behind the camera lens through which light passes on its way to the CCD.

Artifact A flaw in a digital image, especially those caused by compression techniques like JPEG.

Backlighting The result of shooting with a light source, natural or artificial, behind the subject to create a silhouette or rim-lighting effect.

Banding An artifact of color graduation in computer imaging, when graduated colors break into larger blocks of a single color, reducing the "smooth" look of a proper graduation.

Bit (binary digit) The smallest data unit of binary computing, being a single 1 or 0. Eight bits make up one byte.

Bit-depth The number of bits of color data for each pixel in a digital image. A photographic-quality image needs eight bits for each of the red, green, and blue RGB color channels, making an overall bit-depth of 24.

Bracketing A method of ensuring a correctly exposed photograph by taking three shots: one with the supposed correct exposure, one slightly underexposed, and one slightly overexposed.

Brightness The level of light intensity. One of the three dimensions of color in the HSB color system. *See also Hue and Saturation.*

Buffer Temporary storage space in a digital camera where a sequence of shots, taken in rapid succession, can be held before transfer to the memory card.

Calibration The process of adjusting a device, such as a monitor, so that it works consistently with others, such as a scanner or printer.

CCD (Charge Coupled Device) A tiny photocell used to convert light into an electronic signal. Used in densely packed arrays, CCDs are the recording medium in most digital cameras.

Channel Part of an image as stored in the computer; similar to a layer. Commonly, a color image will have a channel allocated to each primary color (e.g. RGB) and sometimes one or more for a mask or other effects.

Clipping The effect of losing detail in the lighter areas of your image because the exposure was long enough for the photosites to fill (and record maximum values).

Clipping path The line used by desktop publishing software to cut an image from its background.

CMOS (Complementary Metal Oxide Semiconductor) An alternative sensor technology to the CCD, CMOS chips are used in ultra-high resolution cameras from Canon and Kodak.

Color temperature A way of describing the color differences in light, measured in Kelvins and using a scale that ranges from dull red (1,900K), through orange, to yellow, white, and blue (10,000K).

Compression Technique for reducing the amount of space that a file occupies, by removing redundant data.

Conjugate The distance between the center of the lens and either the subject or the sensor.

Contrast The range of tones across an image from bright highlights to dark shadows.

Cropping The process of removing unwanted areas of an image, leaving behind the most significant elements.

Delta E (ΔE) A value representing the amount of change or difference between two colors within the CIE LAB color space. Industry research states that a difference of 6 ΔE or less is generally acceptable.

Depth of field The distance in front of and behind the point of focus in a photograph in which the scene remains in acceptably sharp focus.

Diffusion The scattering of light by a material, resulting in a softening of the light and of any shadows cast. Diffusion occurs in nature through mist and cloud-cover, and can also be simulated using diffusion sheets and soft-boxes. *See Softbox.*

Dynamic range A measure of image density from the maximum recorded density to the minimum, so an image with a DMax (maximum density) of 3.1 and a DMin (minimum) of 0.2 would have a dynamic range of 2.9. Dynamic range is measured on a logarithmic scale: an intensity of 100:1 is 2.0, 1,000:1 is 3.0. The very best drum scanners can achieve around 4.0.

Edge lighting Light that hits the subject from behind and slightly to one side, creating flare or a bright "rim lighting" effect around the edges of the subject.

Extension rings An adapter that fits into an SLR between the sensor and the lens, allowing focusing on closer objects.

Extraction In image editing, the process of creating a cut-out selection from one image for placement in another.

Feathering In image editing, the fading of the edge of a digital image or selection.

File format The method of writing and storing information (such as an image) in digital form. Formats commonly used for photographs include TIFF, BMP, and JPEG.

Filter (1) A thin sheet of transparent material placed over a camera lens or light source to modify the quality or color of the light passing through. **(2)** A feature in an image-editing application that alters or transforms selected pixels for some kind of visual effect.

Focal length The distance between the optical center of a lens and its point of focus when the lens is focused on infinity.

Focal range The range over which a camera or lens is able to focus on a subject (for example, 0.5m to Infinity).

Focus The optical state where the light rays converge on the film or CCD to produce the sharpest image.

Fringe In image editing, an unwanted border effect to a selection, where the pixels combine some of the colors inside the selection and some from the background.

***f*-stop** Lens aperture size calibration (also used by the Exposure slider in the Camera Raw utility).

Gamma (also written "Ψ") is a fundamental property of video systems which determines the intensity of the output signal relative to the input. When calculating gamma, the maximum possible input intensity is assigned a value of one, and the minimum possible intensity (no input) is assigned a value of zero. Output is calculated by raising input to a power that is the inverse of the gamma value (output = input $(1/\Psi)$).

Graduation The smooth blending of one tone or color into another, or from transparent to colored in a tint. A graduated lens filter, for instance, might be dark on one side, fading to clear at the other.

Grayscale An image file made up of a sequential series of 256 gray tones (assuming that it is an 8-bit image), covering the entire gamut between black and white.

Halo A bright line tracing the edge of an image. This is usually an anomaly of excessive digital processing to sharpen or compress an image.

HDRI (High Dynamic Range Imaging) A method for taking images at different exposure values and combining them to see a single merged image. The practical result is that it's possible to expose for both shadows and highlights in the same frame so you can clearly see, for example, a room and the view from the window.

Histogram A map of the distribution of tones in an image, arranged as a graph. The horizontal axis goes from the darkest tones to the lightest, while the vertical axis shows the number of pixels in that range.

HMI Hydrargyrum Medium-Arc Iodide Light A recently developed and increasingly popular light source for studio photography.

Hotshoe An accessory fitting found on most digital and film SLR cameras and some high-end compact models, normally used to control an external flash unit.

HSB (Hue, Saturation, and Brightness) The three dimensions of color, and the standard color model used to adjust color in many image-editing applications. *See also Hue, Saturation, and Brightness.*

Hue The pure color defined by position on the color spectrum; what is generally meant by "color" in lay terms. *See also Saturation and Brightness.*

Inverter A device for converting direct current into alternating current.

ISO An international standard rating for film speed, with the film getting faster as the rating increases, producing a correct exposure with less light and/or a shorter exposure. However, higher speed film tends to produce more grain in the exposure.

Kelvin (K) Used to measure the color of light based on a scale created from the color changes that occur when a black object is heated to different temperatures. Normal midday sunlight is considered 5,000K. Lower temperature light (less than 5,000K) is more red or yellow, while higher temperature light is more blue.

Lasso In image editing, a tool used to draw an outline around an area of an image for the purposes of selection.

Layer In image editing, one level of an image file to which elements from the image can be transferred to allow them to be manipulated separately.

Local contrast The contrast range found in smaller areas of a scene or an image.

Luminosity The brightness of a color, independent of the hue or saturation.

Macro A mode offered by some lenses and cameras that enables the lens or camera to focus in extreme close-up, or, in computers, a user-programmed sequence of steps.

Mask In image editing, a grayscale template that hides part of an image. One of the most important tools in editing an image, it is used to limit changes to a particular area or protect part of an image from alteration.

Megapixel A rating of resolution for a digital camera, related to the number of pixels output by the CMOS or CCD sensor. The higher the megapixel rating, the higher the resolution of images created by the camera.

Midtone The parts of an image that are approximately average in tone, falling midway between the highlights and shadows.

Modeling lamp Small lamp in some flashguns that gives a lighting pattern similar to the flash.

Monobloc An all-in-one flash unit with the controls and power supply built in. Monoblocs can be synchronized to create more elaborate lighting setups.

Noise Random pattern of small spots on a digital image that are generally unwanted, caused by non-image-forming electrical signals.

Pentaprism Abbreviation for pentagonal roof prism. This prism has a pentagonal cross-section, and is an optical component used in SLR cameras. Light is fully reflected three times, so that the image displayed in the viewfinder is oriented correctly.

Photomicrography Taking photographs of microscopic objects, typically with a microscope and attachment.

Pixel (PICture ELement) The smallest unit of a digital image—the square screen dots that make up a bitmapped picture. Each pixel carries a specific tone and color.

Plug-in In image-editing, software produced by a third party and intended to supplement the features of a program.

ppi (pixels-per-inch) A measure of resolution for a bit-mapped image.

Prime lens One with a fixed focal length. *See also Zoom lens.*

Rectifier A device for converting alternating current into direct current.

Reflector An object or material used to bounce available light or studio lighting onto the subject, often softening and dispersing the light for a more attractive end result.

Resampling Changing the resolution of an image either by removing pixels (lowering resolution) or adding them by interpolation (increasing resolution).

Resolution The level of detail in a digital image, measured in pixels, lines-per-inch (on a monitor), or dots-per-inch (in a halftone image, e.g. 1,200 dpi).

RGB (Red, Green, Blue) The primary colors of the additive model, used in monitors and image-editing programs.

Saturation The purity of a color, going from the lightest tint to the deepest, most saturated tone. *See also Hue and Brightness.*

Selection In image editing, a part of an on-screen image that is chosen and defined by a border in preparation for manipulation or movement.

Sensitometer A measuring instrument for measuring the light sensitivity of film over a range of exposures.

Shutter The device inside a conventional camera that controls the length of time during which the film is exposed to light. Many digital cameras don't have a shutter, but the term is still used as shorthand to describe the electronic mechanism that controls the length of exposure for the CCD.

Shutter speed The time the shutter (or electronic switch) leaves the CCD or film open to light during an exposure.

SLR (Single Lens Reflex) A camera that transmits the same image via a mirror to the film and viewfinder, ensuring that you get exactly what you see in terms of focus and composition.

Snoot A tapered barrel attached to a lamp in order to concentrate the light emitted into a spotlight.

S/N ratio The ratio between the amplitude of the signal (S) to be received and the amplitude of the unwanted noise (N) at a given point in a receiving system.

Softbox A studio lighting accessory consisting of a flexible box that attaches to a light source at one end and has a diffusion screen at the other, softening the light and any shadows cast by the subject.

Soft proofs Refers to proofs on the monitor.

Spot meter A specialized light meter, or function of the camera light meter, that takes an exposure reading for a precise area of a scene.

TFT (Thin Film Transistor) A kind of flat-panel LCD with an active matrix for crisper, brighter color. This is now virtually the only kind of flat-panel monitor available, but if buying used, avoid passive matrix LCDs.

Tonal range The range of tonal values in an image. The histogram feature in an image-editing application displays tonal range. When an image has full tonal range, pixels will be represented across the whole of the histogram. Analyzing variation and deficiencies in the distribution represented in the histogram is the basis for making tonal corrections.

Telephoto A photographic lens with a long focal length that enables distant objects to be enlarged. The drawbacks include both a limited depth of field and angle of view.

Transformer A device that converts variations of current in a primary circuit into variations of voltage and current in a secondary circuit.

TTL (Through The Lens) Describes metering systems that use the light passing through the lens to evaluate exposure details.

Value A particular color tint. Also a numerical value assigned to a variable, parameter, or symbol that changes according to application and circumstances.

White balance A digital camera control used to balance exposure and color settings for artificial lighting types.

Zoom lens A camera lens with an adjustable focal length giving, in effect, a range of lenses in one. Drawbacks compared to a prime lens include a smaller maximum aperture and increased distortion. *See also Prime lens.*

Keyboard shortcuts

Although you can create your own shortcuts, here are some of the defaults that—unless you have a good reason—you should stick to.

MENU COMMAND	SHORTCUT
Photoshop menu	
Preferences General...	Ctrl//⌃+K
Hide Photoshop (Mac)	Control+Ctrl/⌃+H
Hide Others	Alt/⌥+Ctrl/⌃+H
Quit Photoshop	Ctrl/⌃+Q
File menu	
New...	Ctrl/⌃+N
Open...	Ctrl/⌃+O
Browse...	Alt/⌥+Ctrl/⌃+O
Close	Ctrl/⌃+W
Close All	Alt/⌥+Ctrl/⌃+W
Close and Go To Bridge...	Shift+Ctrl/⌃+W
Save	Ctrl/⌃+S
Save As...	Shift+Ctrl/⌃+S
Save for Web & Devices...	Alt/⌥+Shift+Ctrl/⌃+S
Revert	F12
File Info...	Alt/⌥+Shift+Ctrl/⌃+I
Page Setup...	Shift+Ctrl/⌃+P
Print...	Ctrl/ ⌃ +P
Print One Copy	Alt/⌥+Shift+Ctrl/⌃+P
Edit menu	
Undo/Redo	Ctrl/⌃+Z
Step Forward	Shift+Ctrl/⌃+Z
Step Backward	Alt/⌥+Ctrl/⌃+Z
Fade...	Shift+Ctrl/⌃+F
Cut	Ctrl/⌃+X
Copy	Ctrl/⌃+C
Copy Merged	Shift+Ctrl/⌃+C
Paste	Ctrl/⌃+V
Paste Into	Shift+Ctrl/⌃+V
Free Transform	Ctrl/⌃+T
Transform Again	Shift+Ctrl/⌃+T
Color Settings...	Shift+Ctrl/⌃+K
Keyboard Shortcuts...	Alt/⌥+Shift+Ctrl/⌃+K
Other menu actions	
Menus...	Alt/⌥+Shift+Ctrl/⌃+M

MENU COMMAND	SHORTCUT
Levels...	Ctrl/⌃+L
Auto Levels	Shift+Ctrl/⌃+L
Auto Contrast	Alt/⌥+Shift+Ctrl/⌃+L
Auto Color	Shift+Ctrl/⌃+B
Curves...	Ctrl/⌃+M
Color Balance...	Ctrl/⌃+B
Black & White...	Alt/⌥+Shift+Ctrl/⌃+B
Hue/Saturation...	Ctrl/⌃+U
Desaturate	Shift+Ctrl/⌃+U
Image Size...	Alt/⌥+Ctrl/⌃+I
Canvas Size...	Alt/⌥+Ctrl/⌃+C
New Layer...	Shift+Ctrl/⌃+N
Layer via Copy	Ctrl/⌃+J
Layer via Cut	Shift+Ctrl/⌃+J
Group Layers	Ctrl/⌃+G
Ungroup Layers	Shift+Ctrl/⌃+G
Bring to Front	Shift+Ctrl/⌃+]
Bring Forward	Ctrl/⌃+]
Send Backward	Ctrl/⌃+[
Send to Back	Shift+Ctrl/⌃+[
Merge Layers	Ctrl/⌃+E
Merge Visible	Shift+Ctrl/⌃+E
Select All	Ctrl/⌃+A
Deselect	Ctrl/⌃+D
Reselect	Shift+Ctrl/⌃+D
Inverse	Shift+Ctrl/⌃+I
All Layers	Alt/⌥+Ctrl/⌃+A
Refine Edge...	Alt/⌥+Ctrl/⌃+R
Feather...	Alt/⌥+Ctrl/⌃+D
Last Filter	Ctrl/⌃+F
Extract...	Alt/⌥+Ctrl/⌃+X
Liquify...	Shift+Ctrl/⌃+X
Pattern Maker...	Alt/⌥+Shift+Ctrl/⌃+X
Vanishing Point...	Alt/⌥+Ctrl/⌃+V
Proof Colors	Ctrl/⌃+Y
Gamut Warning	Shift+Ctrl/⌃+Y
Zoom In	Ctrl/⌃++ or Ctrl/⌃+=
Zoom Out	Ctrl/⌃+-
Fit on Screen	Ctrl/⌃+0

MENU COMMAND	SHORTCUT
Actual Pixels	Alt/⌥+Ctrl/⌘+0
Extras	Ctrl/⌘+H
Show Target Path	Shift+Ctrl/⌘+H
Show Grid	Ctrl/⌘+'
Show Guides	Ctrl/⌘+;
Rulers	Ctrl/⌘+R
Snap	Shift+Ctrl/⌘+;
Lock Guides	Alt/⌥+Ctrl/⌘+;
Minimize	Control+Ctrl/⌘+M
Actions	Alt/⌥+F9
Brushes	F5
Color	F6
Info	F8
Layers	F7
Create/Release Clipping Mask	Alt/⌥+Ctrl/⌘+G
Merge Layers	Ctrl/⌘+E
Merge Visible	Shift+Ctrl/⌘+E

Tools

Move Tool	V
Rectangular Marquee Tool	M
Elliptical Marquee Tool	M
Lasso Tool	L
Polygonal Lasso Tool	L
Magnetic Lasso Tool	L
Quick Selection Tool	W
Magic Wand Tool	W
Crop Tool	C
Slice Tool	K
Slice Select Tool	K
Spot Healing Brush Tool	J
Healing Brush Tool	J
Patch Tool	J
Red Eye Tool	J
Brush Tool	B
Pencil Tool	B
Color Replacement Tool	B
Clone Stamp Tool	S
Pattern Stamp Tool	S
History Brush Tool	Y
Art History Brush Tool	Y
Eraser Tool	E
Background Eraser Tool	E
Magic Eraser Tool	E
Gradient Tool	G
Paint Bucket Tool	G
Blur Tool	R
Sharpen Tool	R
Smudge Tool	R

MENU COMMAND	SHORTCUT
Dodge Tool	O
Burn Tool	O
Sponge Tool	O
Pen Tool	P
Freeform Pen Tool	P
Horizontal Type Tool	T
Vertical Type Tool	T
Horizontal Type Mask Tool	T
Vertical Type Mask Tool	T
Path Selection Tool	A
Direct Selection Tool	A
Rectangle Tool	U
Rounded Rectangle Tool	U
Ellipse Tool	U
Polygon Tool	U
Line Tool	U
Custom Shape Tool	U
Notes Tool	N
Audio Annotation Tool	N
Eyedropper Tool	I
Color Sampler Tool	I
Ruler Tool	I
Hand Tool	H
Zoom Tool	Z
Default Fore/Back Colors	D
Switch Fore/Back Colors	X
Toggle Std/Quick Mask	Q
Toggle Screen Modes	F
Toggle Preserve Transparency	/
Decrease Brush Size	[
Increase Brush Size	]
Decrease Brush Hardness	{
Increase Brush Hardness	}
Previous Brush	,
Next Brush	.
First Brush	<
Last Brush	>

TIP

Shortcut list
Photoshop can create an HTML page of your keyboard shortcuts which you can browse or print off and keep to hand. Go to Edit > Keyboard Shortcuts *and click the Summarize button and you will be asked to choose a save location. You can then open the file in Firefox, Safari, Internet Explorer or your choice of web browser.*

Index

Find tools and features by page reference.

New and enhanced features compared	Photoshop CS3	Photoshop CS3 extended
PRODUCTIVITY AND WORKFLOW		
Streamlined interface	●	●
Zoomify export	●	●
Adobe Bridge with stacks and filters	●	●
Photshop Lightroom integration	●	●
Improved print experience	●	●
Adobe Device Central	●	●
Workflow enhancements	●	●
EDITING		
Nondestructive Smart Filters	●	●
Black and white conversion	●	●
Improved Curves	●	●
Photomerge with advanced alignment and blending	●	●
Adjstable cloning and healing with overlay preview	○	●
Enhanced 32-bit HDR support	○	●
Next-generation camera raw	●	●
COMPOSITING		
Quick selection tool	●	●
Refine Edge feature	●	●
Automatic Layer alignment	●	●
Automatic layer blending	●	●
3D AND MOTION		
Vanishing point	○	●
3D visualization and texture editing		●
Motion graphics and video layers		●
Movie paint		●
Animation	○	●
IMAGE ANALYSIS		
Measurements and data		●
Ruler and count tools	○	●
DIACOM support		●
MATLAB support		●
Image Stack processing	○	●

KEY: ○ = Basic feature ● = Advanced feature